SELECTIONS

Selected short fiction, nonfiction, poetry & prose
from The Association of Rhode Island Authors

Visit our website at **www.StillwaterPress.com** for more information.

First Stillwater River Publications Edition

ISBN-10: 1-946-30080-2
ISBN-13: 978-1-946-30080-5

Library of Congress Control Number: 2018957311

1 2 3 4 5 6 7 8 9 10
A publication of the Association of Rhode Island Authors (ARIA)
Cover Design by Kody Lavature
Published by Stillwater River Publications, Pawtucket, RI, USA.

Contents

Nonfiction

Introduction

By Lamp

By lamp go I,
By fire, match, strike,
Or by a plug, chord or switch,
By make or model, aright,
Accompanies like a guided bright,
Speaking in lumens
What must now be put in words,
Truant to the steady balm of energy
That courses, ebbs, currents.
By this steadfast Emory:
The rose by any some name,
There but grace of deity goes self,
Burns but gives a lovely light,
Oh night, oh blackest loss to write,
By burning, wick, wax, watts,
By this torch I go.

~Lénore M. Rhéaume

WElcome to the new anthology, "Selections," from the Association of Rhode Island Authors, a group of varied writers who bring their expertise, experience and enthusiasm from the imagination of their inner hearts to the pages before you.

There is something enticing about anthologies; the intrigue begins in whimsy, wondering just what brought these entries together?

What is their common theme? Who collected these particular essays, stories, poems? Curiosity makes a cat out of anyone. Yet all of us have this secret guilty pleasure, considering what we would write in such an inclusion. Something makes us read through the table of contents with a hidden smile. We feel the power of what we have in hand. In one spirit, these works will live together, to represent the author's hours of effort, in research, in brainstorming, in the excitement of phrases being scratched from the pen in hand to the imprinting of pages.

Consider what made this book worth picking up. We can fancy and choose which section or genre to read first in our own solitary way. We can daydream as we sometimes do, about having an entire afternoon to browse languidly a whole section of tomes, sliding our hands across titles, picking up the brown notebook or the colorful trade. We revel in the cover, we cross our fingers across the raised text, we even check out the last few pages, somewhat cheating to figure out "who done it?" or "how did it turn out?" Our little grin becomes an auditory wow.

Just as if we peruse through the stacks, be it a library's new book section, or the new artful bookstore, and find a table to spread out across, or a comfy recliner to snuggle into, we open each bind to discover a new author, a prospective friend in words. Skimming through we discover new subjects, murmuring, "I didn't know there was material about this," or "Oh, this is my favorite type of writing!" We learn new ways, we travel new places, we find new adventures, we hide in new caves, we fly though new universes.

Presented in this anthology is the universal passion found in every author, who this year was challenged to enter their sincere path of literary skill. The theme was to submit their own chosen genre, which included a wide variety of style and tradition. Poets included metered and free verse, short story writers ranged from mysteries, comedies, action, drama, and introspective pieces. Subjects included health advice and children's themes. Some authors gave us longer glimpses into their novels by offering full chapters. In all, combined they shared a beautiful symmetry: ensconced in what they do, spending hours upon hours with their higher selves, isolated in the cortex of their possibilities, mapping out their plots and protagonists, grinning from ear to ear as they crafted their storytelling.

The Association of Rhode Island Authors, known as ARIA, is comprised of more than two hundred and fifty members who attend statewide events, sharing and selling their literary material. Many have been featured in journals, newspapers and magazines. The range of subject matter these writers create is not measurable, and none are necessarily similar. Yet, they support each other in marketing their work, and engage in workshops and expositions throughout the year, both in state and at large venues such as The Big E Exposition in Springfield, Massachusetts, the Boston Book Fair, the Rhode Island Comic Convention and their own annual event, the Rhode Island Author Expo in December at Rhodes on the Pawtuxet in Cranston, RI. These authors engage in live presentations at local libraries, at varied public and college workshops and donate their time to reading at open mikes throughout the state. Yet for all their occupations, there is a welcoming atmosphere, where all writers, beginners and established, are invited to join, and be part of the next gathering of works.

It is a privilege to be the one encouraging and accepting submissions for this book. With the assistance and dedication of volunteers from ARIA, this large edition was a joy to assemble. A jury of judges and a small staff of editors happily read material and helped writers if needed. The result is unique, because it is up to the reader just how to enjoy this sampler of so many books.

Therefore, the wonder of ARIA's anthology "Selections" is the relationship between how a reader will approach the genres and themes included. I believe no two writers, or two readers can entwine with the words in quite the same way, whether they choose to review it cover to cover, or to open the pages by types of entry, length or style. Maybe the wide choice of subjects will encourage those who read to find methods to try their own emerging voice.

Like getting together for a good ol' New England dinner, the participating authors brought their favorite dish, with a big spoon for sharing. All you have to do is dip in, like collecting what books you would scoop in your hands to bring back to your chosen table or comfortable sofa, and savor for hours.

Lénore M. Rhéaume
Poet, Anthology Chair

Poetry

My Darkness Not Seep

By Don J. Metivier

The darkness I see does not seep nor lie
In the cracks of my old wooden floor;
It surrounds me as a shadow well-nigh,
Tormenting me to my very inner core.

Oh then, I've lived days of laughter without cow;
Sunny light, and I've seen the beauty in all-
But here cold and empty comfort me now,
Like icy winds visit the dying leaves of fall.

Such a sullen state of staleness wafts in the air,
Neither sound nor conversation could deter.
I find my attention now turning to great fear;
Of which to "Death" itself, I abjectly refer.

It's followed me whither, and to where I lay,
As if there to take some form of measure.
It's then I smell my own vile human decay-
Death is there for reasons of pure displeasure.

I'm stirred by the sound of a creak of the floor;
Still in light slumber, I peer in the gray lit room.
A tall black object stands vigil at my door,
Like a soldier guarding a precious tomb.

Death hides in the light, so to this I quickly attend!
Like magic the dark figure there is gone and I see—
I see that my light is fading and I can't pretend;
I fear Death now, because it has come to take me.

Bridge Over

By Adele MacVeagh Bourne

Yesterday, her daughter called–after the storm began–
from three hundred miles away: "Come as soon as you can!"
Twice this mother failed to keep those she loved alive…
Focus on the road ahead. It's clear enough to drive.

Beyond, the highway shines with recent fleece of snow
hiding lane dividing lines. The traffic doesn't slow.
Buffeted by harsh blasts of ten-degrees wind chill,
as silver cars rush past, her old car sways uphill.

The air is crystalline, refracting brilliant light,
bare trees at left are green; red, those on the right.
No mirrored web of steel against a high cloud scud,
the river roils its bed with chunks of ice and mud.

Up the causeway's climb she's jarred by each conjunction,
short notes in two-four time—Swoosh of the main suspension
dizzies her as she passes. Arches flash against the sky.
Rays shoot behind her glasses, slice across her eyes,

reverse her cone of sight. An image in her brain
becomes a tunnel vision—The sun, a subway train,
bears down on two familiar shades crossing railroad tracks.
She does not run to give them aid, she does not call them back.

Still blinded, she begins to feel the car veer toward the
right;
her fingers twist the wheel, a band in her chest grows tight.
She senses the rail is near but she's held in a buzzing hum.
A clear voice speaks inside her ear: *What you've done, or
not, is done.*

Helpless, but present again, at least for a moment more,
Death is not her intent. *Nor had it been before*—
A hard way to learn. The knowledge lets her breathe.
A chance cloud hides the sun. The shadow gives her ease.

With brain and eyes in tandem, she finds that she can steer
toward what will happen next. Her child awaits her there.
Ahead, the road's a gleaming knife, the vanishing point's
in view,
She's released to confidence as sky resolves to blue.

A Woman's Cries

By Frances L. O'Donnell

What was left were the remains of pain.
The memory of war and illness not quieted;
A mother weeps.
The stench of death the story told.
It is the presence of black clouds seeping
through the war of illness of people hiding,
not wanting to be noticed in all the memory.

War, tampered with the sacred lives of children.
There is no singing of little angel voices
to comfort one's soul.
Everyone remains wrapped tight and
continues to hide.
The War so far away, yet the affects
so alive, so present

The fern persists on growing in the well of
sadness, despite its' lack of nourishment.
Even the air, as heavy as it is, embraces
the cool evening, while the people of
the temple liberate their illnesses by
dreaming; always abiding by the rules of
their Culture, their Universe.

All the houses are white, yet there are no signs
of pureness; for no one will refer to their
memory of the *woman's cries.*
Nor will they admit to hearing the music as once
they did; with sounds of harmony and gentle voices,
singing from the heavens of love.

But I will; I remember the angels singing and I heard
the woman's cries; I felt her pain.
And I wept for her.

She Wore Purple Velvet

By Joni Pfeiffer-Moser

My memory will treasure a beautiful gift given to me
By a special son one sunny Sunday in May.
My early mornings were enriched by multi deep purple
velvet petals
Frolicking in balmy breezes as I savored my favorite brew

Waking up.
Watching.
Waiting
for my day to unfold.

I never wanted to throw her away
I loved her from the start
My view dazzled by her sway in the breeze
Countless cascading countenances opening to the sun.

Every day I made certain she drank
And I picked her dry and brittle dead.
I fed her special food at times
Still, she left me
Still, she died.

I thought I could hold on to her longer
That everything I did would make a difference.
I shudder with the knowledge
No matter what I did
No matter my diligence
My tender loving care
Or my desire to keep her blooming
I cannot change nature.

August came—her instinctual time to leave.
She bloomed no more and closed the door.
Her time came, as does everyone's and everything's.

Red Rose

By Jessica Collette

Across the garden
Red rose climbs
Up the stonewall
Where death resides

Dotted with tombstones
The yard is full
Of weeds gone wild
With no one left to pull

From the consecrated ground
They grow thick and tall
On lives and stories
Engraved stones recall

Of time well spent
And plans cut short
And for the lucky ones
A visitor reports

On how they've been living
Since time's ticked on
They pluck the weeds
That have encroached upon

Their dear friend's plot
In the crowded yard
As red rose, too
Offers her sentimental regard

Filling the air
With the sweetest perfume
Where memories endure
As life outside the yard resumes.

That Witchy Music You Like

By D.R. Perry

The riff is itchy like a damp woolen sock
It beats me in 3/4 time, my favorite
And then the lyrics start,
Worming through my ear to my brain
Some songs are like this,
Pushing past you through the front door
Self-invited guests who just introduced themselves
On a street corner, at a mall, through a well-meaning friend's offered ear-bud
But not all of them are the kinds of guests you want to keep around.
Some overcook bacon at the stove, the grease-fire smoke setting off all your alarms until you want to flee your own house and let it burn.
Some leave a smell that sticks in your nose, the fusty odor unpleasant and indelible like the ink mark of a burst pen in a work-shirt pocket.
A chorus of friends echo "You'll get used to it" and "It'll grow on you" but why bother when the next guests sing a more welcome refrain?
Others bring fruit and wine, sustaining joy as they work their changes.
Few brew comfort, their echoes lingering in the halls like the end coda of a time signature that matches your heartbeat so exactly it could have been written for you.
The lick warms, like a Gulf Coast wave dampening your tired feet as the sun sets.
That's the kind of musical company to keep,
The aural equivalent of a lifeboat.

Weeping Willow

By Donna Lomastro

Weeping Willow, why do you weep?

You can't hold on – your roots don't go that deep.

Are you constantly struggling to reach the sky?

But your branches cannot – no matter how hard they try.

Are you struggling against the wind, desperate to hold onto anything?

Grasping and reaching
But only grabbing the air
Grasping and reaching,
but you're going nowhere.
Life is like that sometimes.
Life can bring despair.
Weeping Willow,
Your beauty resplendent
and so serene.

Your grace so comforting, your leaves so green.

Weeping Willow, why do you weep?

Hold on and stand firm, your magnificence must keep.

Dreams

By Debbie Kaiman Tillinghast

The sign was painted white on red,
Across from the rolling sea.
"Reduced for sale," is what it said,
But I heard, "Come look at me….

Walk along the clamshell beach
Breathe the tang of sweet salt spray
Return at night with sun-kissed cheeks
Whisp'ring waves will end the day."

There is a rhythm to the tides,
A compelling ebb and flow
That fosters peace in island life,
Brings balm to my aching soul.

Not all embrace the island's call,
Feel the lure of its commands.
A puppeteer it moves the strings
To guide my feet, wave my hands.

The sign was painted white on red,
Across from an ocean view.
"Reduced for sale," is what it said,
I heard, "I'm waiting here for you."

Short Fiction

Senior Science Project: Earth

By Mike Squatrito

A weathered man stood on his proverbial soapbox, clutching a Bible and preaching to anyone within earshot. "Repent, for the end of days is now at hand!" he shouted. People bustled past the poor soul, paying him no attention. Taxis whizzed by, trying in vain to get their occupants to their destinations.

The disheveled man scanned the city streets again. Horns beeped, brakes screeched, everyone oblivious to their surroundings save for their critical personal agendas. "Repent! Repent! For our time is close at hand!"

A twenty-something urbanite wearing an expensive designer suit walked past. "Get a job," he said out of the side of his mouth, eyes narrow, cellphone clutched in his hand and pressed against his ear, rushing off to an important meeting.

The July heat beat down upon the poor soul, and the city's summer stench filled the air. Something, though, tugged at the man's spirit. *It's a bit too warm*, he thought as he gazed skyward.

* * *

Johnathan B. Carson High School boasted the brightest students in the county and today three of their finest students waited impatiently for their teacher. Jimmy, Megan, and Matt alternated gazes at the clock and the window. Megan waited for the digital number to turn from 11:02 to 11:03. Jimmy felt it was time for lunch. Matt fidgeted in his chair, knowing his teacher would review his science project today.

A spunky young woman, all of 5' 2" tall, bounded into the classroom, gracing her students with a wide smile, just as the time changed to 11:03. "Sorry I'm late, kids," she said in her high, nasally voice, "but Principal Perkins's meeting ran late."

Ms. Angelina Kowalski, with her tight button-up blouse enhancing her already ample breasts, sashayed to the front of her desk, resting her hands behind her for support, crossing her legs in the process. Her green eyes gazed through a pair of black-framed glasses, and she said, "All the teachers know how much time and effort you put into your world creations and we're happy to wrap things up today."

"Why are we all here?" groaned Megan, leaning forward in her desk. Outside, she could see her friends leaving the school's grounds, their summer vacation starting early.

Ms. Kowalski furrowed her brow. "You're here to support Matt. It's his big day and he was here for yours, and for Jimmy's presentation." Megan sat up, crossed her arms across her chest, shook her head, and looked longingly into the distance. Summer vacation was still an hour away.

"Matthew," said the teacher, startling the nervous boy. Matt had taken the opportunity to gaze down the length of Ms. Kowalski's legs, right down to those black heels.

Shaking his head and pushing his glasses firmly against his nose, he muttered, "Yes, Ms. Kowalski?"

"Are you ready to present your science project?"

Sweat broke across the young man's brow and his armpits were soaked, but he was ready. Anything for Ms. Kowalski. "I believe so."

Matt's teacher beamed. "Great!" she exclaimed, her pearl white teeth gleaming. "Why don't you come up to the front of the class and get yourself started?"

Ms. Kowalski moved in her heels with the grace of a dancer, taking a seat behind one of the desks near Jimmy, allowing her pupil the head of the class. Jimmy leered at Ms. Kowalski, mesmerized by her … assets.

Matt shuffled to the front of the room, carrying with him a large open box. He positioned himself next to the gadget near his teacher's desk and, flicking a couple of switches, activated the Simulated Anti-Gravity Starlight System (SAGSS). A low hum resonated throughout the room as the simulated star shined its soft light. Using extreme caution, he gingerly removed his science project from the box.

He placed the biosphere as close to the SAGSS as possible before the anti-gravity simulator sucked the globe into place and began to rotate ever so slowly. Matt adjusted the artificial starlight to work with his designated planet's atmosphere and environment. A couple of minutes later, his world reached 100% biological optimization.

Turning to face his peers, the young man exhaled his nervous energy before beginning his speech. "As you know," he said, gazing directly at Ms. Kowalski, "you tasked us all with creating a living, breathing world and challenged us to document our findings on life." Matt pressed a finger to his glasses, pushing them higher up the bridge of his nose. "However, I chose a different path of scientific exploration."

Ms. Kowalski crinkled her brow. "Different path? What do you mean?"

The teenager knew his teacher would ask this question first and he was ready with his answer. "I granted my creations free will." He closed his eyes and then waited for the barrage.

"Free will!" exclaimed Jimmy, a wide smile stretching across his rotund face. In his southern drawl, he exclaimed, "You should've asked for an F and saved us all a lot of time!"

"Hush, Jimmy!" said Ms. Kowalski.

Megan stared at her teacher, mouth agape and a hand outstretched toward her classmate in front of her. "Ms. Kowalski," started the redhead, her green eyes round, "we discussed free will and you said it was a waste of time! Why did Matt get to study it?"

Ms. Kowalski pursed her lips before answering. "He wasn't supposed to."

Matt raised his palms to his audience. "Please, if you let me explain my findings, I think you'll change your minds."

His teacher leaned back in her chair, folding her arms across her chest. Matt's classmates did likewise, albeit with grins compared to his teacher's scowl.

"Your grade is on the line, Matt," said Ms. Kowalski. "You best do a good job."

Matt nodded repeatedly. "I will, I will!" The young man then closed his eyes and focused, regaining his composure. "Okay, the first thing I did was to create a world that could withstand multiple environments."

The student gestured toward the spinning globe. "As you can see, there are land masses and seas, deserts and ice caps, forests and jungles." Matt allowed his audience to gaze at his rotating sphere, then continued. "Once I stabilized the atmosphere and brought the habitat to an appropriate temperature, I introduced my life forms."

Ms. Kowalski, arms still folded, cocked her head and said, "How did you introduce your life forms?"

Matt's eyes widened, knowing he had the right answer. "I used the microbes that you supplied for us and added it to the biosphere. Everything worked great!"

His teacher remained skeptical. "How much microbial life did you use?"

The boy's sweat glands kicked into overdrive. "A lot." Dark patches expanded from his armpits and beads of liquid formed on his brow.

His teacher's expression did not change. Head still cocked, she pressed, "Matt, how much is a lot?"

The young man contemplated how he would answer the question and, after a few excruciating seconds of thought, thrust his arms out by his sides with his palms up and shouted, "Enough to begin the evolutionary process!"

Megan's eyes almost popped out of her skull. "What?"

Jimmy clapped his hands together and laughed, then said, "Evolutionary process! You're killing me!"

Ms. Kowalski pivoted in her seat and stared at the laughing student. Leaning forward, she shouted, "Hush, Jimmy!"

The force of her statement caused the top button of her blouse to pop off and float harmlessly through the air toward the awaiting boy's desk. As if in slow motion, the miniature projectile landed hard on the desk's resin surface, then bounced a couple of times before falling to the floor. A quiet fell over the room as the button rolled away.

"Oops," said Ms. Kowalski before returning her gaze to the already nervous boy, revealing a bit more cleavage, and a new challenge to his attention.

Without missing a beat, the teacher continued. "You were *not* supposed to commence the evolutionary process for obvious reasons."

The student took a hand to his head and closed his eyes. "I know, I know, but by the time I figured out what happened it was too late!"

Ms. Kowalski shook her head. In a forceful voice, she said, "I ought to stop your presentation right now, but I know you spent all year on this project. I'll let you continue but your grade has already taken a serious hit."

Regaining his composure, Matt said, "Thank you, Ms. Kowalski. Okay, having established an evolutionary cycle on my world, things began to evolve quickly."

"You used the life accelerator, right?" said Megan, giving Matt an incredulous stare.

"Duh, of course I did!"

"What became of your microbial life?" asked his teacher, her arms pressed against her chest, pushing her breasts up higher.

"It exploded, creating an infinite number of single cell bacteria before evolving into more complex life." Matt stopped, almost wishing that he did not have to continue.

Ms. Kowalski, recognizing the awkward pause, leaned forward and said, "And?"

Unable to hold back anymore, Matt exclaimed, "Life exploded on my world! First there was marine life that filled the seas, then they migrated to the land where they took on the form of insects and reptiles and amphibians …"

"What about plant life?" asked his teacher.

Matt pointed to the globe where dark patches of green cascaded throughout the planet. "I couldn't stop that from spreading either! It was a botanist's dream!"

Ms. Kowalski knew where Matt's evolutionary process was heading. Looking down, she exhaled and interlocked her fingers in front of her, placing them on the desk.

Slowly lifting her gaze to meet her student's, she asked, "Matt, can you explain what these creatures looked like?"

A glazed look overtook the boy's face. "They grew, and they grew, and they grew …" Matt's voice trailed off as he gazed off into a far corner of the room.

Jimmy followed Matt's line of sight before snapping his head back at his friend. "How big we talkin'?"

"Monster sized," said Matt, still in his far away land, recalling the joys and horrors of his creations. Bringing his focus back to his audience he said, "The plant-eaters ate everything. The meat-eaters ate them. I had massive creatures in the sea, on the land, in the air. It was uncontrollable!"

"But you did control it, right?" asked his teacher.

"I tried everything, but the evolutionary cycle was too strong, so I forced a cataclysmic event." Matt lowered his head.

"Matthew!" exclaimed his teacher. "You know that goes against the Prime Directive! Even for school projects!"

"You are so screwed!" said Megan with a laugh, snapping her gum.

Matt tried his best damage control. "I understand, but I did it to allow for a different evolutionary path. One that would result in a better outcome."

His teacher narrowed her eyes behind her glasses. "That is *not* a good enough reason!"

"Please, hear me out!"

"You're on thin ice, Matt," said his teacher, crossing her arms again and leaning back in her seat. "What precipitated this cataclysmic event?"

"I introduced a solid mass into the orbiting sphere," said the boy, his head hung low with his chin resting close to his chest.

"Woohoo!" howled Jimmy, slamming his palm against the desk time and time again, laughing in hysterics. "You probably killed everything in your world!" The chubby boy peeked at his teacher, hoping she would have another tantrum due to his outburst that would result in another miniscule projectile hurtling his way.

"90% of all life," answered Matt, his head still hung low.

Ms. Kowalski kept a cold demeanor. "This is atrocious, but I need to know what you did to rectify your situation." Her buttons remained intact, to Jimmy's dismay.

Matt once again composed himself, then said, "Before the event, I introduced a smaller life form, one that had a bit more intelligence."

Ms. Kowalski cocked her head as she had once before, and said, "And?"

The young man shook his head in disbelief. "These creatures exploded as well, but this time I tried to slow their advancement by moving around the tectonic plates, introducing ice ages followed by hot spells, and more."

"You didn't destroy them with another one of your *events*, did you?" asked Ms. Kowalski.

"No," said Matt. "I watched them very closely and their actions pretty much have doomed themselves."

"Elaborate on these *actions*," said his teacher.

Matt nodded as sweat continued to bead on his forehead. "Right, actions. Well first they huddled together to hunt and gather, but they didn't evolve very well. I made them small and scrawny but their brains were bigger. After some time I gave them the ability to really think and that's when things got out of control."

The teenager held his head in his hands, shaking it from side to side. "They learned how to speak and build civilizations, but they were real mean. They started fighting over food, land, females, greed, you name it! They started killing each other, over and over!"

Megan's eyes went round. "They killed each other? For their own purposes and not for survival?"

Matt nodded repeatedly. "Then I did something stupid."

"Sounds like your whole world's stupid!" exclaimed Jimmy.

"At least my creatures evolved and flourished," shot back Matt. "Your dumb water world had sea creatures that grew only fins and swam around and around and around." The teenager mocked his friend, pulling his arms close to his sides, mimicking a swimming fish.

"Enough, boys!" cried Ms. Kowalski. Shaking her head, she said, "I'm afraid to ask, but what stupid thing did you do?"

Matt sighed and hung his head low, again. "I gave them religion."

Megan's eyes widened. "Oh my God!" she exclaimed, covering her open mouth with her hand in the process.

Jimmy could barely contain himself. In between guffaws, he bellowed, "At least I wasn't dumb enough to give my creatures religion!"

Ms. Kowalski's innards simmered. Narrowing her eyes, she asked Matt, "Who was the God in your world?"

"That would be me, Ms. Kowalski," said Matt, swallowing in fear, knowing that this petite bombshell of a teacher was about to explode. "And I created them in my image."

"You!" exclaimed his teacher, practically jumping out of her seat. "Oh, I can't wait to hear how this goes!" She gestured in her student's direction. "Continue."

Matt swallowed hard again. "Okay, I chose a region in the world where there appeared to be the most suffering and injected a code of rules, commandments, so to speak. Something that would help straighten out their wicked lives."

"And what happened?" asked Ms. Kowalski.

"They fractured into hundreds of religions! No one believed one another! They all twisted their teachings to fit into what suited their personal agendas best!"

"This is so much fun!" said Megan with a wide smile, peering to Jimmy who was hunched over his desk, his shoulders heaving, unable to contain his laughter.

"It's not funny!" said Matt.

"Oh, yes it is!" said Jimmy, his head remaining down, muffling his voice.

"Stay focused, Matt!" said his teacher. She then glared at her other two students, raising her right index finger into the air. "You two are walking on thin ice!"

"Thank you, Ms. Kowalski." Matt regrouped for the umpteenth time. "With everything spiraling out of control, I decided to grant these creatures free will as well. I decided to let them evolve and see what became of them."

"Go on," said Ms. Kowalski.

"They never stopped their bloody ways. They kept killing and killing, but they got cleverer as time went on. They developed cities and empires, and expanded all over the globe. They learned technology and developed sophisticated machines and weaponry. Their population exploded and they consumed more and more natural resources. Then came the hydrocarbons." He shook his head, holding his face in his hands. "Oh, the hydrocarbons."

"This world you created is a mess, Matthew!" said Ms. Kowalski. "What's the current state of your biosphere?"

"These creatures are all over the globe, no one is getting along, and they're killing off the other species, consuming all their resources, and have no population control. They're literally killing themselves." Matt raised a finger in the air. "And did I mention their nuclear technology?"

"I have heard enough!" said Ms. Kowalski, rising from her seat and walking to the front of the class. "Your biosphere experiment was reckless and not well thought out, Matt. Allowing for free will, evolution, and religion? All in one world? I ought to give you a failing grade right now.

"However, you did go through great lengths to try and fix things, but these little creatures sound horrible." Ms. Kowalski leaned against her desk, placing her hands on it for support. She then looked up into the air, her mind racing in thought.

"Since you did well in your other courses and you need a passing grade to graduate, I'm giving you a C. A gentleman's C, so to speak." Ms. Kowalski winked at her student.

Matt sported an expression of shock before his teacher's comments sunk in. His eyes then bulged from behind his glasses. "You mean I'm getting a passing grade?" The teenager could not hide the grin from his face.

"What?" exclaimed Megan. "That world is atrocious and he still gets a C?"

Ms. Kowalski glared at the redhead. "You got an A, you little smarty pants, what's it to you?" Megan pursed her lips and crossed her arms across her chest, unamused.

"And not a peep from you," said the teacher, pointing right at Jimmy. The chubby lad feigned zippering his lips, not tempting fate.

"I hope you learned a valuable lesson, Matthew," said Ms. Kowalski, looking at the nervous teen. "You can't just go around allowing species to evolve unsupervised. Free will is a very dangerous thing." The buxom blonde gestured for her two other students to rise from their desk.

"Now we all know what we must do with our creations. It's the humane thing to do."

Megan and Jimmy went to a pressurized vault to retrieve their class projects while Matt removed his from the SAGSS machine. After the students retrieved all three biospheres, Megan went about starting up the incinerator.

"I can't believe you got a C," she lamented, waiting for the flames to get good and hot. Within a minute, the furnace's flames roared, ready to accept the students' projects.

"I guess it's better to be lucky than good," said Matt with a smile, as he watched Megan dump her sphere into the flames.

"Better to be good looking than dumb!" said Jimmy, tossing his water world into the fire, nearly extinguishing the flames.

Matt allowed the incinerator to heat up again before bringing his globe to the furnace's opening. He peered into the red-orange glow a second longer, then said, "Goodbye, you wretched souls!" A second later, his blue-green world dropped into the depths of the raging inferno.

* * *

The prognosticator pointed up into the reddening sky. “It’s too late! We’re all doomed! The hour of God is at hand!”

All those around him looked skyward as the world around them began to burn. Men, women, and children shouted and screamed, running in every direction, shocked that the crazy man’s prophecy had come true.

The wretched soul lowered his hand and maintained his gaze on the descending fireball. Then he smiled. “I’m coming home, Father. I’m coming home.”

A Most Unusual Proposal

An excerpt

By Joann Mead

Mai loved the looks of Scandinavians. The taller, the blonder, the better. By Scandinavian standards she was average in height, but Mai towered over most Chinese women. She confidently glided into the coffee bar and removed her winter coat, revealing a business professional suit that accentuated her shapely figure. More eyes than one gazed in her direction, including a middle-aged man who sat cross-legged on a leather sofa sipping black coffee from a huge ceramic mug. As she walked in, she noticed the well-dressed man and his suave veneer. He was obviously a man of means.

Like most Swedes, Lars's coffee or *fika* break was accompanied by his favorite pastry, hazelnut coffee cake. And like most Swedes, strong coffee in both the morning and afternoon is a way of life. Lars often came across beautiful women in Göteborg but none with the exotic yet elegant look of Mai. In hotel bars, attractive women often trolled for wealthy men, either for marriage or barter. He generally avoided them; he didn't need any complications. But this young woman did not fit that picture. Perhaps she was not quite what she appeared to be. He thought he detected a note of deception in her guise. What was it she was trying to hide? She glanced his way more than once. He suspected some form of entrapment.

Mai blatantly observed his reserved manner. She knew she had his attention when he momentarily held her gaze, equally curious of her. She slipped into a comfortable lounge chair at an adjacent table.

Catching Lars's eye again, she sipped her cup of unadorned green tea. Leaning in his direction, she asked. "Do you speak English?"

Surprised by her directness, he answered. "But of course. But I don't hear well, at this distance." Lars was just testing, but it worked. She picked up her tea cup and joined him on the settee.

"Do you live here? Have a family?" she asked.

Amused at her candid questions, he uncharacteristically engaged her in dialogue. "I come often to Göteborg, but my home is Stockholm." He was surprised by his own spontaneity with this stranger.

"Do you have children?' She played her sweetest game.

Lars could not resist her interest in him. "Unfortunately, no."

"But why not?" Mai was never shy about probing too deeply into the personal lives of men. She found most were willing to divulge their deepest secrets, in hope of intimacy. Seduction was a game she had perfected over time, only now she would try a different tactic. She wanted men to reveal what they really wanted, beyond any carnal desires. She was practicing her new marketing approach.

"Why no babies? You are so handsome. So tall and blonde." Mai encouraged him, feigning curiosity, as though she found him fascinating. He mentally flinched at the flattery. He knew he was no oil painting, average in looks, but handsome? No.

Lars thought her appearance was mixed, an Asian-European fusion. Her unnatural curvature, to his professional eye, was voluptuous and likely augmented. Her eyes seemed artificially round. He leaned toward her as if unable to hear, but only to get a closer look. He detected small but visible incision lines, the telltale scars of surgery to remove part of the eyelid for a rounder, more oval shape. It only heightened his curiosity; he wanted to know more about her. He knew plenty of women in his line of work. Cosmetic surgery.

Lars suspected that Mai was not the same person she once was. Augmented and altered but not obscenely so. He tried to imagine the original shape of her eyes. Her long legs appeared flawless, but not likely adulterated. He couldn't be sure if she had other procedures. Well-shaped hips, he thought, but no evidence of a Brazilian butt lift. She had no excess fat to spare.

"I'm Lars." He avoided her family questions, wondering why she persisted at prying into his personal life.

"I'm Mai." She paused only slightly. "Why no children, Lars?"

"I inherited a bad gene that I would not inflict on any child of mine." He could see no harm in divulging his secret in exchange for the attention of such a charming yet mysterious woman. Lars, by choice, never had children. He carried a dangerous mutation, a heart defect. The odds were stacked against any offspring he might produce.

"Oh, I am sorry, but you know there are ways that genes, your DNA, can be corrected now, don't you?

"But, of course, I know. It's often in the news. Editing genes in embryos has been performed in Sweden. But it's only experimental. It will take years before the technology becomes freely available."

"Many countries use gene-editing tools, like CRISPR. Lars, I'm a scientist, I've changed the DNA of many animals…. and microbes." She squirmed, stroking her neck as if to sooth stiff muscles, then cleared her throat. "And what do you do, Lars?"

Ignoring her question again, he doled out a compliment to see her reaction. "You are smart as well as beautiful."

Mai didn't acknowledge what she had heard so many times before; she wasn't easily distracted. She persisted with a singular focus. "And your job is?"

"I run a business in Stockholm. Often, I come to Göteborg to meet with clients. And, in the harbor, I have my boat."

"A big boat?"

"Not big like an ocean liner, so I suppose you would say it's small," Lars teased.

"A big boat for a family? You can still have children." Mai tried to imagine the size of his wealth.

Lars laughed at her persistence. "My, oh my! Mai, you are relentless." Her recurring frown perplexed him. He was drawn to intelligent women who had a vulnerable side. Lars was mystified by her charm.

"Your bad gene is not a problem, Lars. I can analyze your DNA in my lab. Perhaps we could perfect it for you? And IVF clinics can implant perfected embryos in your wife," she suggested.

"But my wife is not young, she has no viable eggs left to fertilize. So, I'm afraid this is not possible…"

Mai interrupted him. "That's not a problem."

"And why is that?" He encouraged her as she honed her sales technique.

"Do you want something new? Do you want a more perfect you?" She pitched her hook, testing it on her prospective client.

"A more perfect me?" He chuckled.

"Yes. A more perfect you." Mai knew she had piqued his interest.

"Is this science fiction?" Lars playfully probed, wanting to hear more of her selling points.

"No, it's not fiction. Or fantasy. Certainly, I can help you with this," she persisted.

"Perhaps, but it's not legal. Only approved labs can experiment and edit DNA in embryos. But they're not allowed to develop into babies." He hesitated, then added, "At least, not in this country."

Mai stood up, smoothing her skirt, purposely distracting him. Lars's gray-blue eyes panned her silhouette. Her image was impeccable. But it was her performance that most impressed him. She emanated confidence with her facade of a professional business woman. Not unlike those saleswomen, the pharmaceutical reps who frequent clinics and hospitals. Intrigued, he was drawn in.

She looked around and saw no one within earshot. "Ours are not made from scratch. Synthetic babies, I tell you, are science fiction. Well, maybe someday. But why start from scratch when you already have a lot to work with? We can keep the best of you. But enhanced with extra special traits. Your choice!"

Lars continued to humor and cajole her. Not only was he captivated, he wanted to know what motivated her.

"If I had a choice, I would prefer children that resemble me. Tall and blonde, but much more handsome. And free of disease, of course."

Mai interrupted. "Removing bad genes from embryos is easy. I have a very experienced team of scientists who can do this. They can snip out DNA for your heart disease. A simple procedure. But you must want more? Most people want more."

Lars pondered for a while. What more would he want? It was an entertaining, speculative game for him. "Yes, in Scandinavia, we admire the tall and athletic. And brain power. Superior intelligence. Very healthy, perhaps with extra immunity to fight diseases." His grin beamed across his face, well aware of the fanciful dream she was trying to sell him. He knew all about enhancement; after all, his business revolved around cosmetic changes driven by the desire for youth and beauty. And he knew more about narcissistic obsessions than Mai could even imagine. "And what do you suggest?"

"High intelligence is most important. In China, the genomes of geniuses have been identified. And likely, the next generation of babies will be enhanced to make them super-smart."

"How do you know this, Mai? Are you Chinese?" Lar suspected she might be.

"No! I just know these things. I study. Do research. And my lab techniques are superior!" She deflected his suggestion and pressed on. "How about strength and athletic ability? Stronger bones and muscles? A stronger heart? And a longer life!"

He smiled and nodded, encouraging her. "Ja! Of course, yes."

"Good looks are a real social asset. Parents want children to resemble them, but only more perfect. A more perfect me. Or a more perfect you!" Mai fine-tuned her pitch as she went along, then joined him again on the sofa.

"But not synthetic babies?" Lars egged her on.

"Someday scientists will create babies without parents. Build them with three billion DNA blocks, like Lego toys. But it is not easy. Far-away, in years to come." She babbled on.

"I don't want a clone. No mini-me for me." He cupped his big hand over her thin delicate fingers but Mai seemed unfazed.

She knew she had Lars nearly trapped in her web. To lure him in, she looked deeply into his faded blue eyes. "No one wants a clone. Now we have better methods. A child like you but edited to perfection. No flaws, no diseases. But enhanced. Superior intellect. Unparalleled beauty. And strong…tremendous strength."

"How do you create this perfect human life? How can you do this? You're just toying with me."

"This is not the creation of human life. But it is the perfection of you. A more perfect you," Mai insisted.

"My perfect child. I can only dream…" Lars hummed a sigh.

"I can make your dreams come true, a son with your image and likeness! We can now take your cheek cells and edit their genes to replicate a more perfect you. Those cells can divide, as if they are an embryo. They grow and change, go through all the stages, and become a perfect replica of you." Mai was eager to impress him with her knowledge of the science.

"You're saying you have new technology?" He was incredulous and excited but he didn't let on.

"This method is our most desired, no fertilized eggs are needed. It requires the most advanced techniques and superior skills in our private labs. It's time-consuming coaxing these cells. And very expensive. Only for the wealthiest clients." Mai noticed that Lars did not bat an eyelash.

"So, my cheek cell can be turned into a perfected embryo? Not a clone of me but a perfect me! So, it is me, but enhanced. And those superior genes can be passed down to future generations... hmm." Lars was more than intrigued, he could see the potential for many millions of euros and dollars sequestered away in offshore accounts. He quickly approximated what his clients would pay for this type of perfection.

"Surely, there must be risks….. but think of the possibilities for the next generation." Lars found himself not just acclaiming but enthusiastically endorsing Mai's unusual business proposal. "What a great benefit to all of mankind. Our future is in your hands." But he was thinking about people, his clients, who would pay a small fortune for this type of service. "Tell me more."

"As you say, all of mankind. Your offspring, your sons will be a magnificently designed variation of *you*! We start with you and then your son becomes whatever you want him to be. The custom-made designer embryos can be implanted in surrogate mothers. It's easiest, and most secretive with surrogates in eastern countries." Mai paused for him to take in the possibilities.

Lars felt drawn to Mai's intellect and to what she had to offer. But he could also see a lucrative business venture. And an escape from a life less-fulfilling. He wanted so much more.

"Lars, privacy is essential for the next step in the process." She lowered her voice. "A cash deposit is required." Tearing off a corner from her notebook, she wrote a hefty amount in Swedish krona.

Lars said with a wry smile, "It's a small price for perfection."

Through Tomorrow's Door

An excerpt

By Regina Andrews

Drumming her fingers on the steering wheel of her Audi convertible, Antibes de Beaufort practiced deep breathing. She was stuck. There was no way out of it but to sit in the traffic. The narrow street in the center of the little seaside town of Bristol Harbor, Rhode Island, was completely congested.

Main Street was lined with gracious elm trees shading both sides of the quaint street. She scanned the scene, with residents of the town scurrying about their early morning business: out for a run, hurrying to the Sunshine Bakery, mailing letters at the post office, and walking their dogs along the sidewalk.

She took a sip of her latte and leaned on the horn. Enough was enough. Ann was fed up. Three cars in front of her had their hazard lights flashing. As she zoomed impatiently around them she didn't see the cyclist in her lane. He was in her blind spot. And before she knew it, he was practically up on the hood of her car.

"Watch it! Watch it!" he screamed, gesturing to her and throwing her a look of disgust as he pedaled off, frantically weaving in and out of the stalled traffic. Her heart racing, Ann looked down at her white linen suit, now dappled with a beautiful mocha design thanks to the empty coffee cup in her hand.

"You're lucky you didn't kill him," someone yelled at her.

Ann said a prayer of thanks that she had not hurt the cyclist because of her impatience. The sun sparkled joyously on the water as she inched down a side street and drove away.

By the time she pulled in to the crushed stone entrance leading to Flores Bonitas, the mansion where she worked, her heartbeat had returned to normal. When she looked at the mansion's magnificent Mediterranean design, her heart started beating more quickly—again. '*Beautiful Flowers' is the perfect name for it here*, she thought, looking at the acres of colorful gardens.

An island of daffodils lining the entryway made a beautiful statement of elegance complemented with rustic charm.

Even though she had only been the assistant curator there for seven months, Ann felt as if she had been there much longer. And she was proud that she had landed this job on her own, as Ann York, using her middle name as her last name instead of relying on her famous family name of De Beaufort. Pulling into her reserved parking space by the outdoor gift shop, she sprang out of the car, her high heels crunching on the gravel.

Something about the light in this early morning setting captivated her, never fail. Every morning she took a little detour down the rolling, sloping green lawn to pause at the water for a few minutes and inhale the divine ocean scent.

Her route took her past the southern part of the property, where a sunroom extended off the main living area. Passing the rhododendron shrubs and andromeda plantings, she maneuvered along the steep decline, her eyes fixed on the water.

Something rustling on her right caught her attention. Leaves moved and she sensed something different than other mornings in the carpet of bobbing daffodils. There, she saw him.

"Hello!"

She stopped at the sound of his voice. There was never anyone here at this time of the morning. Who was he? She turned to face him. Standing there was a man of about thirty, his sandy hair caught in the sun and his gardening jeans fitting him just right. But it was his smile that shook her to the core.

"Can I help you?" Her icy tone shot across the space between them.

"No, thanks, I'm fine."

"You are aware this is private property? The museum opens at ten."

"I punch in at seven." He took a few steps towards her.

"You work here?" Distracted by watching him move, she struggled hard to keep an icy-city-savvy-edge in her tone of voice.

"Sure do. You too?"

"What's your name and what are you doing? I have not heard of any new employees here."

"Oh, come on, stop trying to butter me up with all this friendliness and smiling! This welcome is too warm to be real. You're being too cordial—I'm getting suspicious."

Ann rolled her eyes and started back up the grass to the building.

"Hey, wait," he called. "I think you better show me some ID."

She whirled. "What?"

Catching up to her he gave a chuckle. "Only kidding," he said. "I know full well who you are. I did my homework before I started here. Your picture is on every page of every newsletter since the day you started. Nice to meet you, Antibes de Beaufort, alias Ann York." He wiped his hand on his jeans before extending it to her.

Drumming her fingers against the back of her thigh so he couldn't see, she tried to figure out how to reply. Last thing she needed was someone blowing her cover.

"How did you know?"

"I just follow what's going on in New York a bit... guess you came here to kind of get away from that for a while?"

"I did."

"I can imagine how you feel. Don't worry, my lips are sealed." He gave her a smile that looked genuine... but she couldn't be too sure.

She had no desire to engage in conversation with the stranger; yet, she had no idea who he was. He could easily be related to someone high on the town social ladder. She'd better watch her step.

Deciding to take the political highroad, she shook his hand. "Sounds good. Call me Ann. And you are…"

"Ryder Warwick." He gripped her hand firmly, keeping eye contact with her steadily. "Nice to meet you."

"Likewise. You from around here?"

"Out of town."

"Oh. Me too—but you already know that, apparently." Already Ann could tell this was not a man who was really up for a conversation.

"Apparently." His eyes twinkled for a second.

"Now if you'll excuse me, I have to get in and start what will undoubtedly be a very busy day."

He drew his palm across his beard. "Lots of high-powered stuff going on in Bristol Harbor, huh?"

"Well, it's true that Bristol Harbor is a little sleepy." How did he know? It was so quiet, it was driving Ann out of her mind. "But I am working myself to the bone trying to put Flores Bonitas on the map."

"The museum that's already here, you mean?"

"Yes, obviously. We need some more exposure."

"Oh, I get it. You mean like marketing and all that fancy advertising stuff. Something to really draw people in."

"Yes, that is exactly what I mean." She spread her arms wide. "Look at this place. It's paradise. To me, it's a terrible shame that everybody in the world hasn't heard of it and isn't clamoring to see it. We should have tour buses lined up waiting to get in every morning."

His glance skipped over the daffodils dancing in the breeze. "Nice idea, but how long do you think these would last? They'd be trampled in an hour."

"No they wouldn't, for goodness sake. We'd just have to put up a barrier, that's all, to prevent people from walking all over them."

He crossed his arms, looking at her intently. "You see? That's the problem," he said. "A barrier. Your premise is to change the nature of this place."

"Premise? What are you talking about? That's a practical answer. Part of my training."

"I'm just saying it sounds like you want to change the place. The character of the place."

"Not at all, Ryder. We can talk about this later." She turned so he wouldn't see her red cheeks. He was right, she did want to change the character of Flores Bonitas. Was she that transparent? "Nice to meet you," she called over her shoulder as she headed up the hill.

She would have to talk to her manager first thing about this new hire.

"Hey, Ann." Ryder caught up with her. Standing close, he gave her a smile. Unnerved at his nearness, she checked her footing... just to be sure she was on steady ground.

"Here." He handed her a bunch of daffodils in one hand and waved in the air with his other hand. "Before you go off on me, I just want you to know that they were cut from the garden earlier. I didn't do it, Bruce asked me to pick them up and throw them out. But they still seem beautiful to me and I thought you might like them on your desk."

"Beautiful." She dragged her gaze from his honey hair and hazel eyes to look at the flowers. "Thank you."

His warm hand brushed hers as she took the flowers from him.

She took a deep breath. “Such a lovey fragrance.” Then her smile faded. “Just to continue what we were saying, though, if there was a barrier around that garden, the flowers would still need to be trimmed and weeded. Bruce told me that already and he’s a master gardener. I’m not out to change the character of Flores Bonitas, Ryder. But I would like to bring it into the 21st century and let it progress into the place that it actually could be.”

“I know change is good. Natural progress, though, not commercialism.”

“I couldn’t agree more,” she said, then turned once again to make her way up the hill, hoping to keep her balance on her high heels. Because she could feel his eyes on her as she walked.

****

“Nice job with that side garden by the sun room. What else did you do this morning?” Bruce joined Ryder in the toolshed and handed him a brown paper bag.

“Great, you brought breakfast?” Ryder looked into the bag. “Iced coffee and what’s this?” He held up a large flat pastry. “Don’t tell me you brought me a doughboy. Bruce.. I haven’t had one of these since I moved to Nashville! I love you!”

“Hey, no funny business.”

Busy with his doughboy, Ryder didn’t seem to hear him. “These are so delicious, they’re still warm! There’s nothing like this in the world and there’s no better place that makes them than Bristol Harbor.”

“My mother made them.”

“No way! Man, we have got to get her her own food truck and get her into Nashville. She’ll be a zillionaire in two weeks.”

Bruce shook his head. “Not much chance of that happening. So what did you say you got done?”

"I stacked up the tools in the utility shed. Then I counted the bags of fertilizer for our next planting. Oh, and I met *her*.

"You did?"

Nodding, Ryder wiped the sugar from his beard with a paper napkin from the bag. "Ann York." Actually, Antibes de Beaufort, but Ryder wouldn't let on to Bruce. "The whole package." He let out a slow whistle, shaking his head.

"Didn't I tell you?"

"You barely scratched the surface, brother. Thirty seconds in her company and she's telling me how she wants to redo all of Flores Bonitas."

"She's not a bad egg, though. Just clueless, I think. What did you tell her about yourself?"

"Nothing. Not one question from her about me. Except if I'm a local guy." He spread his palms in the air. "It was all about her and her big high-powered job here in Bristol Harbor."

Bruce chuckled. "So you didn't tell her?"

"Nope. I just told her that I was a new employee here—which is true. She claims not to have known that there was somebody starting."

"She doesn't know who you are, though?"

"No, that's not really relevant anyway. I'm hoping most people don't know. Let's stick to the true story, which is I'm visiting here and working here because this is my hometown and they've asked me to come back to help spruce up this historical residence for the Fourth of July celebration."

Bruce kicked the dirt. "Okay, so we'll just forget that you're a country music superstar?"

"Just a songwriter."

"A cowboy songwriter."

"Okay, a cowboy songwriter, Bruce, but that's it. And yeah, we can forget that for now. I'm trying to forget. That's why

I am here. To get away from it all. Here in Bristol Harbor I can be myself, Ryder Warwick, and not "Dirk Kingwood."

"You really think that's going to work?"

"Maybe. Look, I'm not a performer. No one ever sees me, I'm not out on tour or anything. Coming back home here to Bristol Harbor I'm just a kid who left town a few years ago, like a lot of the other ones. The only difference is that my dad is Colonel Warwick, and he just happened to be town manager for as long as anybody can remember."

"And he loved Flores Bonitas."

"And he loved Flores Bonitas. Yes, you're exactly right. This is why I was commissioned to return here and help spruce the place up in his memory."

"But it was the Fourth of July committee from the town that recruited you, right? Not anybody from Flores Bonitas."

"Exactly. Which is why I did my best not to scare away her majesty Ann York."

Bruce covered his smile in his sleeve. "This ought to be good."

Suddenly the shed door opened, spilling sunshine into the shadowy workspace. "Here you guys are! What are you doing, having brunch? Don't tell me! I smell doughboys. Don't *tell* me!"

"Well, if it isn't Tanya, my very favorite little niece and office assistant!" Bruce held out his arms. "Come here and give me a hug!"

"I know there are doughboys in here," she sniffed, "and I need one, *please*?" Tanya hustled over and hugged him, her long dark hair swinging and her eyes sparkling.

Ryder watched as Bruce hugged his niece. The look on his face touched Ryder in his heart; it was filled with such tenderness and affection. He thought about what a really long time it had been since he had felt anything as pure as that, and it gave him a pang.

Bruce reached behind him with one hand and dangled a paper bag in front of Tanya's eyes.

"Thank you!" she squealed, swiping the bag and pecking Bruce on the cheek.

"You! That snatch was quicker than a jack rabbit in a hurricane," called Ryder with a laugh. "How you doing?" He stood up. "Ryder Warwick."

"Tanya Ferreira. Sorry my mouth is full!"

"It's charming, and completely understandable. After all, who can resist a doughboy?"

"I'm done," she laughed. "Thank you so much, Uncle Bruce! Now I have to get down to business. I just came here to say quick hello then it's back up to the office and have my morning meeting with Ms. Ann."

"How's that working out for you?"

"It's okay," Tanya said thoughtfully. "She's really a good person, but I think she's disappointed that Bristol Harbor is so quiet. After everything she comes from…"

"Well, I think Bristol Harbor is paradise, and anybody who isn't over the moon happy here has a screw loose upstairs."

"Hey," Bruce said, "that'd make a good song, don't you think, Ryder?"

"Oh, do not start!"

"It *would* be a good song," Tonya said with a smile, "but you have to make it the blues. On top of that, Ann does not get along with her manager. The only reason the manager's keeping her is because…"

"Enough gossip, Tonya," Bruce warned. "It's Ryder's first day."

"Right, I'm sorry. And I promise, Ryder, I won't tell anybody who you are, either. It's none of my business and I promise to stay out of it."

"I appreciate that. Thank you very much."

Bruce gave her a stern look. “Better get your tail up to that office and forget us clowns down here, Tanya. You don’t want any problems.”

“Right, thanks for reminding me,” she said. “And remember, you have to help us set up for the wedding! It’s the day after tomorrow! Don't forget.”

“We won’t forget, butterfly, don’t you worry.” Bruce put his arm around her shoulders.

“Okay, thanks. See you later.”

Ryder watched as Tanya closed the door behind her. The shed seemed quiet after she had gone. Finally, he said, “Nice girl.”

“She’s my everything,” Bruce answered. “Since Bethany died… I didn’t even care if I got up in the morning, couldn’t face anything. Then I realized she had lost her mother. What kind of a man was I? Sure, Bethany was my sister, but this little thing had no one anymore...”

“No father?”

“He left Bethany about six months after Tanya was born. Left Bethany to do it all by herself,” Bruce answered, shaking his head.

“I’m sure you helped. And you’re helping her now, and she knows it.”

“How are you so sure about that?”

Ryder shrugged. “I just am. I know God is with you.”

“You going to start with all that God stuff now? Because if so…”

“No, no, relax my friend. Just thinking out loud, that’s all. Now, how about we get to make a plan for this wedding, so when the queen of Sheba comes down here to question us about it we knock her out with our fantastic plan?”

***

Morning sunlight streamed in through windows onto the deep mahogany floors of Ann's office. She turned the space heater on her feet to warm the morning chill, then played her favorite pop station from her iPad.

Even though she had been there for less than a year, there was something about the office that made it feel like home to her. She loved all the architectural details of the mansion, particularly her office, which was off-limits to the public and not seen on the daily tours.

Gazing out the window, she reviewed the landscaping of the gently sloping area that led down to the water. Her eyes traveled to the daffodils planted near the entrance.

"Yes, I'm craning my neck," she said with a small laugh. "I want to see where he is."

Just the thought of seeing Ryder walking around in those jeans was enough to make her lose her train of thought about the upcoming wedding she had to prepare for. The entire property needed to be re-purposed for the event. Tables and chairs needed to be moved, twinkling white lights installed in the trees. The band area needed preparations and the entire kitchen staff had to be readied for when the caterers arrived.

But none of that really mattered to her at the moment. Ann's thoughts kept going back to Ryder and the mischievous look in his eye. Why hadn't anyone told her that someone was starting today?

And how did he know that Bristol Harbor was so sleepy? Despite its plentiful charms, Ann was itchy for more activity and more challenges…the kind that only the big city and a museum of a much larger scale could provide for her.

"Isn't it a little early for daydreaming?" Tonya came in through the side door, interrupting her thoughts.

She smiled. "Good morning. How's the world's greatest intern today?"

"I'm wonderful!" Tonya gave a little swirl in place. "I love weddings! We have one to prepare, remember?"

"Yes, I know, it's the day after tomorrow."

"Oh well, it seemed to me to be a good idea to start counting the tables and chairs and deciding how many are going to go in each area. Then we can get Bruce and the new guy to start setting them up. You met the new guy, right?"

"Yes, I did. And your idea about counting is perfect--let's go."

It was a short walk across the lawn to the storage building which housed tables, chairs, and many other items that were used for special occasions at the museum.

"Good, they're stacked in rows," Tonya said. "I have my pad and pen right here so we can just decide right now which ones are going where. I'll make a list and a sketch so there won't be any confusion when the guys set things up. Mind if I turn this on?" She pointed to a radio on a side table.

"Sure, go ahead."

They worked efficiently in silence for a few minutes, counting the chairs and making a sketch as to how many would go into the different areas of the mansion.

"Remember," Ann said, "the rental company is also going to bring their own chairs and tables, so we don't have to use as many from here."

"Got it. Oh!" Tonya lunged for the radio. "I just love this song!"

Ann, not the least bit interested, was forced to listen to it as Tonya turned it up full blast.

"Country?" Ann wasn't completely sure. Country usually wasn't her type of music. But the tune was nice and the words were…different. Not a regular country song, in her opinion. "That's really nice," she said.

"I know, huh?" Eyes wide, Tanya nodded enthusiastically. "Guess who sings it?"

"No clue. I'm not up on country music at all so I don't have any idea. None. I just know it's not Elvis."

"Well that's right, at least," Tanya laughed. "No, it's by Dirk Kingwood."

Ann shrugged. "Never heard of him."

"Dirk Kingwood," she repeated with emphasis.

"Sorry, like I said, I…"

Wiggling her index finger, Tonya said playfully, "Oh, yes you do! Dirk Kingwood is his stage name. You just met the real Dirk Kingwood this morning. His real name is Ryder Warwick!"

"Really? That's a surprise."

Tonya suddenly groaned and covered her face with her hands. "But I wasn't supposed to say anything. Ugh! Just please don't let on that you know, Ann. It's supposed to be a secret!"

The Plot Continues

An excerpt

By Dusty Pembroke

This story, The Plot Continues, *is a continuation of characters from my previous book,* The Family Plot. *These books were inspired by true life experiences and by the history and beauty of the Madeira Islands. I have combined mystery with adventure and a little history along the way. Also, what is life without a touch of romance?*

We finished our breakfast and Lizzy and I headed out into the back yard. I turned to Lizzy and said, "I think we should take a walk up to my great aunt's grave. The view is breathtaking, and you get a better idea of how the house was built right into the side of the mountain."

Lizzy agreed, and we climbed the steep walk to the impressive gravesite.

"My cousin, Edwardo, has had the land excavated and redesigned so that the path has been diverted from the cliff. Years ago, my uncle fell to his death from the side of that cliff, and Edwardo was determined to make sure no one else would fall."

The view was magnificent, and we could see for miles. Along the mountainous ridge, I spotted a lone figure, rappelling down the side of the mountain. The man stopped periodically and probed the rocks with a pickaxe.

"I wonder what that man is looking for?"

"He's probably a geologist," said Lizzy. "They often examine layers of the earth that way."

She turned and headed down the path.

She called over her shoulder, "Inez, how about us going inside and checking for that cellar?"

"I'm game!" I said, as we headed toward the house.

We had just gotten in the door when I spotted Tess, the housemaid, heading for the stairs. I called to her and asked that she get us a couple of flashlights. She giggled but ran to get them.

We stood facing two doors that were built into the wall of the stairway that led to the second floor. With flashlights in hand we slowly opened the first door. To our disappointment we found a large closet. The second door proved more exciting. There were narrow stone steps leading downward. There was also no light switch, so we followed the steps gingerly, using the flashlights to guide us.

The stairs were cut from the stone in the walls of the cliff. We made our way cautiously, as the stairs were slippery. There was a rough handrail and we both held onto it with one hand. At the bottom of the stairs an old-fashioned light fixture hung from the ceiling with a pull string. Lizzy, being taller than me, reached up and pulled it. Light flooded the center of the room. The cellar was huge and was lined with row after row of wine racks. Large wine barrels stood stacked up in one far corner. Another wall held shelves filled with different sized boxes, some of them labeled. I could tell that these were probably household items that had been stored and forgotten.

"Wow, this is wonderful!" Lizzy exclaimed.

I agreed and we each wandered off in different directions, still using our flashlights to peer into the corners and rows of shelving.

I began pulling out wine bottles and wiping years of dust off them to read the labels. I was intrigued by the different styles and shapes of the bottles. They were beautiful examples of glass art. I made my way around the room, pulling out bottles here and there. I finally stopped and looked around. Where was Lizzy? I had almost forgotten that she was with me. I started walking up and down the rows of wine racks, but I didn't see her. I walked toward the back of the cellar. There was a small low archway leading into another room. It was very dark and full of shadows. I cautiously entered the area and immediately felt a shiver of cold air. I scanned the room with my flashlight and nearly fainted when I saw a body slumped over some boxes against a wall.

"Lizzy!" I half-sobbed, half-screamed her name.

Lizzy jumped up, sending boxes flying.

"God, Inez, you almost gave me a heart attack," she said as she dusted off the front of her shirt and pants.

"I thought I had just found your body. What in heaven's name were you doing there?" I asked.

"Come and see what I've found!" she said, her voice trembling with excitement.

I picked my way around the boxes. I had to get down on my hands and knees to see what Lizzy was pointing at. There, near the base of the wall, was some writing and drawings.

"What is it?"

"I believe it's a coded message," she said. "It's a series of symbols and letters. It might be as old as the 17th century. These symbols were often used by pirates of that era. I think I recognize a few of the symbols but I'm not sure of their meaning. I'll need to do some research."

"Wow, that's amazing!" I said.

I stood up and scanned the room with my flashlight. Most of the room's walls were stone except for one section where someone had put up a makeshift wall of wooden planks with shelves and large hooks.

"Lizzy, this room must be older than the rest of the cellar. The walls in here are all uneven and it looks more like a cave than a cellar. Can you feel that cool air in here?" I asked.

I walked around the room. The floors were just wooden planks that someone had laid down. They were very uneven. Lizzy came over to stand next to me.

"It would be normally cooler in here than the other rooms; these walls would keep it cooler. Come on, Inez, let's head back upstairs. I need some paper and a pencil. I want to copy that message down, so I can do some research on it. Plus, I want my camera, so I can get some shots of it."

Lizzy didn't wait for me to reply. She left the room and headed for the stairs. As I stood there, a cold and uneasy sense of foreboding seemed to circle around me. I shivered again and bolted for the stairs, not wanting to be left alone.

"Wait for me, Lizzy," I called.

We didn't bother to stop and turn out the light but headed straight up the stairs.

"Come on, Lizzy," I said, "I'll show you the way to the study."

I opened the door to the familiar room. It was just as I remembered it, a cozy room. On the far wall a lone desk and a large ornate chair stood facing us. Above it was a portrait of a regal-looking woman. To our right, there was a whole wall lined entirely with books. On the opposite wall, a beautifully designed fireplace with large overstuffed chairs on either side of it. To the right of the fireplace, modern technology invaded the room. A computer workspace completely equipped with the latest computer and printer set up. It looked out of place in this old-world room. I walked over to the desk and found paper and pencils. I looked over at Lizzy. She was standing at the wall of books, running her fingers along each shelf as she scanned through the titles of some of the books. Her eyes were bright with excitement.

"Oh, thank you," she said as she grabbed the pencil and paper from my hand. "I'll just run down and copy what we found, and then I'm coming back in here. Some of these books are very rare and I can't wait to examine them."

She left the room before I could offer to go with her, not that I wanted to go back down there. I had an involuntary shiver just thinking about it. I heard Cassie in the hall talking to Chef Ben so I went out and joined them. Ben gave me a warm smile.

Cassie turned to me and said, "We were just going over the menu for Saturday night's party. What have you and Lizzy been up to?'

At that moment, Lizzy came racing past us and headed straight into the study. She never looked up from her phone and her expression was intent.

"What's up with her?" Cassie asked, tilting her head in Lizzy's direction.

"We just came up from the cellar, it was amazing. We found a little room in the back of the cellar that has some writing on the wall. Lizzy thinks it might be as old as the 17th century. She used her phone camera to record the pictures."

"Really? I want to see that." Cassie hurried toward the study.

Ben stood there for a minute, then with a shrug of his shoulders and a wave of his hand, he headed back toward the kitchen.

A World of Trouble

An excerpt

By Richard Maule

From his upstairs window, Thomas Maule watched the four riders galloping across Roone's Bridge. With so much snow on the hillside, he had trouble identifying the men, whose oncoming silhouettes loomed like black marks in a vicar's ledger. They wore longcoats and collars, but at that distance, Tom couldn't tell if they were clergymen or constables. In this part of Massachusetts, it didn't much matter which. He was in a world of trouble.

Tom never could keep his mouth shut. Folks thought this odd, as Quakers are wont to hold their tongues even at church, where silence is preferred to preaching. But since the coming of the witch madness, Salem had become such an oppressive place that even sacred silence cried out to be broken. Against all advice, he had published a book against the Puritan worthies, and now they were coming for him.

As he hurried downstairs, he found Naomi and the children with their faces pressed against the front window. "They've come," was all he said. At these two words, they all stepped back from the wall, the little ones huddling respectfully behind their mother. Though Tom had braced himself for this day, it still pained him to see their frightened faces. In a moment, there were hoofbeats out front and then the voices of men. He held up his hand, straining to discern what the men were saying, but all he could hear was the thumping of his own heart. He prayed and took a deep breath, trying to compose himself.

"What would thee have us do?" his wife asked, but Tom made no reply. She was staring at his lower lip which was trembling the way it always did when he was about to have words with somebody. "Curb wrath, dear," she whispered. "The Devil lies in wait."

"No, the wait's over," he said. "Take the babes upstairs… and pray."

Without a word, she nodded and followed the children, who were already halfway up the staircase. As she brushed past him, he noticed fresh tear stains on her sleeve.

The officers didn't even look up as Tom crossed his arms and took his stance on the front porch. "Bastards," he whispered to himself as he watched Sheriff George Corwin and his officers tying their stallions to the gatepost. Tom was boiling, but with lawmen in the yard, he couldn't let his anger overflow. The sheriff was brandishing some kind of document, but it was the deputies' longsticks that got Tom's attention.

"Please come no further," he said in his calmest Quaker tone, but the officers kept coming. Only when Tom screamed, "Halt!" did they freeze in their steps, frowning in unison at this shot across their bow. As George Corwin waved his warrant, Tom clenched his fists and began to mumble something under his breath. The constables couldn't make out what he was saying, but he wasn't talking to them.

"Restrain!" Tom kept whispering over and over—a command to himself, and perhaps a bit of a prayer. God wouldn't smile at his taking a swing at a sheriff.

"Thomas Maule of Salem…" Corwin began as he unrolled his document.

"Get on with it, George," interrupted Tom. "Thee knows who I am."

Anxious to finish the formalities, the sheriff paid no attention to Tom. Salem's worthies were well-practiced in making their arrests and Corwin's boney fingers didn't tremble at all as he meticulously pronounced each word of the indictment:

"Whereas there is lately published a pamphlet in quarto containing two hundred and sixty pages entitled Truth Held Forth and Maintained, by one Thomas Maule, which is laden with many pernicious lies and scandals against private persons, government churches, and against the worthies of our land…"

As the litany continued, Tom grew impatient and glanced around, first at his orchard and then upstairs where he saw worried faces in every window. He shrugged and feigned a smile, hoping to put his family at ease. It was then a single word from the warrant caught Tom's attention. *Therefore* told him the sheriff had finally gotten to the important part.

"Therefore… in his Majesty's name, the Sheriff of the County of Essex shall forthwith make a search of Maule's house for said pamphlets and shall seize and secure such that he shall find. He shall cause said Thomas Maule to appear before the Lieutenant Governor and Council at their chamber in Boston upon the nineteenth of December, 1695, current to answer to what shall be objected against him on His Majesty's behalf."

The reading apparently complete, the four officers gawked at Tom. They were waiting for some sniveling words of surrender, but Tom just put his hands on his hips and laughed at them. "Stinks of Cotton Mather," he said, "High church candlewax!"

The sheriff was neither daunted nor amused. "You'll do well to heed us, Friend Maule," he growled. "The charges are grave."

"Grave?" Tom smiled, pretending there was nothing to fear. "When are you people *not* grave? Just spit out your warning and tell me the fine."

"It's no slap on the wrist," Corwin said. "You rattled the wrong people this time!"

"The wrong people?" Tom chuckled. "I never rattle the *wrong* people." He expected the constables to laugh along, but they all just stood stone-faced.

* * *

Up in the bedroom, Naomi bit her lip as she watched. "For once in thy life, Tom, shut up."

"Is Father in trouble again?" asked Susannah, at twelve the eldest.

"We can't know," her mother sighed as she watched her husband rubbing his fist. "There's no cause for worry."

"Papa seems bent on blows," she said.

Naomi shook her head. "The Friends *never* indulge violence," she said. "Not good Quakers, anyway."

"It's mere words so far," said Susannah.

"We must pray," her mother said. "Mere words can ring like muskets in New England."

With only a slight twitch of her brow, Naomi signaled the children to join hands with her and bow, but it was hard to pray. Outside, the men's argument was escalating and even through the window glass, they could hear Father's voice rise above the others. "I'll decide who may enter my house!" he proclaimed.

Naomi couldn't keep her eyes closed now. Though it was December, she still cracked the window to eavesdrop. With icy air pouring in on their stockinged feet, the little ones continued to repeat the *Our Father*, giving special emphasis to, "Lead us not into temptation and deliver us from evil."

"Hush thee," their mother whispered as she strained to hear the men. Though the room was dead quiet, by then it didn't matter. Tom was yelling loud enough for all of Salem to hear.

When he blurted out, "By what right?" Naomi knew the cause was lost. Sheriff George had baited him to make one of his speeches, and these never ended well. For another five minutes, the men sneered and snapped like hounds when they've circled a bear. The frightened children resumed their prayer, but their mother waved her finger for silence.

“No more,” she said as she tugged the window closed. “It’s all done.”

* * *

Tom thought he was winning, of course, but when the sash slammed shut, he knew the game was up. Even his own family (his *little army,* he called them) had raised the white flag. His better instincts told him to relax his fists and be a good Quaker, but he knew Corwin would only interpret it as weakness. Just when it appeared that peace might prevail, the sheriff broke into his victory grin. As Tom’s heart sped up, his little army held its breath. He was praying they wouldn’t hear what was coming next.

“Look, you fox!” Corwin shouted as he pointed to some words at the bottom of the warrant. “It’s plain enough for a stupid Quaker to read.”

This was too much. Quaker or no, Tom wasn’t about to kiss any sanctimonious Puritan’s arse. Coming nose to nose with the sheriff, he didn’t even look at the warrant. “Roast your paper in the Devil’s fire,” Tom said. Bracing for Corwin’s reply, Tom couldn’t resist striking one last blow. “Damn thee!” he bellowed, shouting so loud one deputy dropped his club. It was just two words, but with these he sealed his fate.

* * *

Above them, Naomi pressed both hands over her lips now, bracing herself for the worst. She knew where this was going. The wide-eyed children watched as Father’s Quaker hand slowly tightened into a warrior’s fist. Tom puffed out his chest and pounded it twice, something he liked to do when he had just won an argument. Naomi had seen the gesture before. It was something he always did right before they took him off to jail. The words that followed were as predictable as snow in winter.

"I shall defend my rights!" Tom exclaimed.

"You'll have your chance to play the fool," said the sheriff, "but first you'll stand aside." With a nod, Corwin signaled his men.

Tom was raising a defiant finger and preparing a retort when a longstick struck the back of his skull. As his knees buckled, he staggered, trying in vain to find his wife's face in the upstairs window. It was good that he was too dazed to see her sadness.

Appalled at the scene, Naomi turned away. "Back from the window!" she ordered. "Gather Papa's books!"

With one clap of her hands, the children became a swarm of bees, snatching up Father's pamphlets and piling them on the floor of the girl's room. Downstairs, they could hear shouts and the muffled bootheels of Corwin's relentless men. Cabinets and doors slammed as the deputies sniffed for evidence.

Naomi sighed deeply as she hoisted the girls' linen chest and dumped its contents onto the bed. Then she began to hide Tom's pamphlets inside. There were so many, she and Susannah had to throw their weight across the lid to get it closed. "They must never find these!" she whispered as she bolted the chest and arranged the little ones across the top, much as one might arrange vases on a shelf. But with footsteps coming up the stairs, there was no time to coach them. Naomi snatched up baby John and plopped herself down in the rocker. Ripping open her blouse, she rocked frantically as she urged the baby to nurse.

"Come on, you," she chided, "latch on for Papa's life!"

For one bizarre moment, the only sounds in the room were nervous breaths and the noise of sucking, then bootsteps again, nearer this time. As if on cue, the children began to sing *Golden Slumbers* in double time – probably the most frantic lullaby ever performed in New England.

When the constables finally burst through the door, the men were taken aback. The children stopped their song mid-verse, all frozen like a row of porcelain figures. With all the skill of an actress, their mother gasped and pulled the baby from her bosom, careless with the buttons so as to distract the eyes of the lawmen.

"Has thee no shame?" she shrieked. "Private business here!"

The ploy bought a brief reprieve, but once George Corwin stomped in, the eyes of the constables went back to the task at hand. Two searched under the beds while a third began to rummage through the girls' dresser.

* * *

Hearing the crying, Tom disobeyed orders and ran upstairs. As he burst into the girls' room, Naomi rushed to his arms, smelling of perspiration and tears. It was then Corwin raised his hand.

"No more," he said. Everyone in the room was surprised and became so quiet you could hear a pin drop. Tom thought they might have weathered the storm, but before he could exhale, the sheriff spoke again. "I know where the books are," he said. Corwin's assistants were breathing hard as they arranged themselves in front of him. "Use your eyes," the sheriff sneered, "and your heads." He seemed to have spotted something across the room. "Tell me," he said as he pointed to the pile of linens on the bed. "What's all that?"

"Clothes?" asked the youngest deputy, sounding very much like a schoolboy trying to guess the correct answer.

"Does it look like clothing?" Corwin asked.

"Well, no sir," he said, "It's blankets, bedding, and such."

In breathless silence, everyone watched as the sheriff picked up two well-folded bedsheets. "These," he said, "why would anyone fold linens only to toss them in a careless heap?" His snakelike eyes flashed about as he approached the children who sat trembling on the chest. "And what if we removed this little post of guards?" he said.

"Lay thee no hand on my babes!" Tom said as he stepped between Corwin and the children. As the deputies jumped in to restrain him, Naomi began to weep.

"I'll do what I must do," Corwin sneered. "Even search your good wife if I need to."

Enraged, Tom struggled to free himself, but there was nothing to be done. "Go to Mother," he muttered. As the little ones hopped down and clustered themselves around Naomi, all of them looked worried, except for little Sarah, who had closed her eyes to recite the 23rd Psalm. "Yea, though I walk through the valley of the shadow of death, I will fear no evil…" Tom held his breath as the officers pulled back the lid to expose the books.

"Queer bedding," Corwin chuckled in triumph. "We've got him dead to rights this time."

Tom tried to feign surprise, but the sheriff was right. "Religious tracts," Tom said, grasping at straws. "Left by some Baptist," he added, but he knew Corwin would have none of it.

"A *burly* Baptist, I would think," smiled the sheriff. "It would take a robust man to hoist such a library." Then he picked up a book and read the title page aloud. "Truth Held Forth," he said as he toyed with the latch on the chest. "Maybe you should've called it, The Truth *Well-Hid*."

Tom longed to swing a fist at the sheriff, but, short of cheating, there was nothing he could do to win this game. "I've not read it," was the best lie he could offer.

"Just stop!" shouted Corwin as he put his index finger on the cover. "The book bears your name." At this, Tom became as quiet as a dead man. Naomi's eyes were full of sympathy as she wiped away her tears, certain that her husband would soon *be* a dead man.

"My Tom's a good man," was all she could offer, but the sheriff had other things on his mind.

"Have we got them all?" he asked.

"Something like three dozen books," said one of his men.

"Don't estimate," Corwin said. "I want the number. Each is a nail in Friend Maule's coffin."

"Be gone!" snapped Tom, "You have what you came for."

"Oh… not yet," Corwin said. With only a twitch of his chin, he commanded the men to take Tom in hand. "You're under arrest," he shouted. "A thousand crowns won't buy you out of this one."

Tom felt every riser on the staircase bruise his back as they dragged him out to the front steps.

"It's nonsense," he mumbled as they hammered iron cuffs on his wrists and ankles, right in front of his own wife and children. Susannah shrieked, but one glance of Mama's eyes put her to silence.

"Keep supper warm," Tom laughed as they led him away. "I'll kiss some backsides and be back by nightfall."

* * *

Naomi tried to smile, but she wasn't as confident as Tom. "Get inside, children," she said as she followed the men out to the front gate. She went to kiss her husband goodbye, but Corwin's lackeys held her back. Her tears had dried now, but there always seemed to be fresh ones to take their place.

"Mind thy words, Tom," she said, but she knew she was wasting her breath.

"They can't jail a man for writing a book!" he exclaimed.

By now, a cluster of neighbors had come out to watch them take Tom away. He shook a few hands as he went, tipping the brim of his hat to the rest. Naomi, however, was busy surveying their eyes. In some she saw judgment, in others, sadness.

As she offered a simple nod of thanks to the sad ones, Tom looked up and smiled at her one last time. Naomi had more she had wanted to say, but now she could only stand there, her moist eyes expressing the deeper secrets of her heart. Tom's labored smile became a grimace as with one tug, they yanked him away by a long chain.

She swallowed her sobbing then, not wanting him to worry. As she walked back toward the house, she yearned to look back at Tom one last time, but she didn't think her heart could stand it. Even the squawking of the crows couldn't drown out her babes as they wept on the front steps. She quickened her steps, eager to comfort them, but mostly just wanting to escape the pointing fingers of the neighbors. But in New England, there were so many fingers, and never anywhere to run.

My First Demon

By L.A. Jacob

I summoned my first demon when I was 12.

That summer, I stayed with my Aunt Jane, who was a witch. I studied some of her books on paganism, but that really New Agey, mushy stuff didn't interest me. I wanted revenge.

Christoforo Arcuri—known ironically as "Mousey," because he was huge—had been beating me up ever since I started school. He tipped my desk over onto me the first time I met him. He beat me up even *after* I gave him my lunch money. He stole my books and ran around the playground, making me—the short nerdy kid—chase after him.

I tried to fight back once, but I was told I "hit like a girl" and got a black eye for my trouble.

Even my older brother Phil got into the act, sometimes just watching, laughing at my antics. Sometimes he'd go up to Mousey and tell him to cool it and then he'd retrieve whatever item Mousey had stolen from me. Phil would then constantly remind me of these times whenever a chore came up that he didn't want to do.

It was time to take things into my own hands. If I couldn't fight Mousey on his turf, then I was going to fight him on mine.

He hadn't been studying the hierarchy of demons since he could read. He hadn't gone on sabbats and to rituals with a witch and a coven since he was eight. He didn't know that I knew magic. Nobody knew, except Aunt Jane and my sister Evelyn. Evie kept it from Phil and my parents, and would probably let herself be tortured before she ever would admit that I was a witch. Not a warlock. There's no such thing as warlocks.

In the middle of a forest outside of New Haven, and under the watchful eye of my Aunt Jane and the moon goddess, I first drew the containment circle, with the sigil of the demon inside it. Surrounding it were the sigils of three angels that bound the spirit to this plane. They would also make the spirit appear "in a comely fashion" according to the *Lesser Key of Solomon.*

Second, I drew the protective circle, which held me safely inside. This was put down in case the demon got loose from the angels, or if I drew something incorrectly. And I wasn't about to draw anything incorrectly. I had practiced for months.

The demon Andromalius appeared before me as a man bathed in white light—beautiful and naked, with a snake curling around him.

He spoke without his lips moving, a gentle voice on the wind. "Who summons me?"

"I am Michael," I said, for once glad that I had a powerful name.

The demon looked down at me. His face, his whole countenance was gentle.

"What is your wish, oh Master?"

Demons were wily, my aunt had warned me, and they often flattered the summoner. I needed to be strong. I had to stick to my purpose.

"You will punish Christoforo Arcuri."

"Who is this man?"

I nodded to the center of the circle. There was a school picture of him that I had cut out from the classroom photo we all took together. I also added the torn-off cover of his science book that had drawings all over it. I knew I needed both a picture and an essence of him, and that was all I could get my hands on.

The demon turned and went to the items. He stared down at them, studying them.

"Set me free, and I will do as you will."

"No. You will do as I will. I bind you, Andromalius. I bind you. I bind you."

Each time I said the words, I clapped my hands. It would sound like thunder to the demon, and would tie invisible chains from him to my will. When—and only when—I knew Mousey was taken care of, would I cut the invisible chains in a ritual to unbind him.

Until then, he was mine to do what I wanted.

Andromalius' snake dropped, and both the demon and snake hissed at me.

"You will punish Christoforo Arcuri. He is a wicked, wicked boy."

"Punish this boy." He flipped the picture over, and caressed the book cover. "Then you will release me."

"Yes," I said, though I didn't say where I was going to release him.

The snake climbed up Andromalius' leg, and he took the creature in his arms. He stepped forward to me. For a moment, I could see his true form: a large, angry snake. And then he was gone.

I said the required prayer for the dismissal of the circle. A hot breeze momentarily caressed my face. I turned around to see my aunt, sitting at the base of a tree off to the side. I smiled at her.

"I did it."

She struggled to get off the ground. She was short and wide at a time when most people her age were thin and trim. She got to her hands and knees and I helped her up the rest of the way.

"Thanks, Mikey." She looked up at the stars and then the moon. "Ah, we'd better get home."

After we cleaned up the area to make it look unused, we started walking the mile or so back to the car.

"How did it feel?" she asked me.

"I could do it. I could do anything!"

She smiled, rustled my hair. “Just be careful, Mikey. What are the Four Pillars?”

“To Know, To Dare, To Will, To Be Silent.”

“So we’re going to let the spell work on its own.”

On the way home, we stopped at a convenience store to pick up some candy.

At her apartment in the assisted-living complex, we walked in to hear Uncle Mark guffaw loudly at the TV. He saw us come in, and switched on the light in the living room, as he liked to watch TV in the dark.

“Hey, hey, how’re my little witches?”

“Wonderful!”

Aunt Jane tossed him a candy bar. He caught it on the fly and patted the chair next to him. Aunt Jane took off her coat and said, “He did a great job.”

“Did you see it?” Uncle Mark asked, as I went to sit on the couch.

“Uh huh,” I said.

“What did it look like?”

I described Andromalius to him as best as I could, and he nodded. He wasn’t a witch, but he let Aunt Jane have her way with the pagan stuff. He understood, like Aunt Jane and I did, that demons weren’t evil; they were spirits. However, if left to their own devices, they could be malicious and evil. It was up to the magician to teach them and keep them on a tight leash.

And as I described Andromalius, my breath caught. I know my eyes widened. Aunt Jane looked at me.

“What’s wrong?”

“I didn’t tell it what to do. I said ‘punish’ him.”

Aunt Jane waved a hand. “He won’t kill him. They never do, unless you tell them to.”

My aunt Jane was not a believer in the Rule of Three: whatever you do comes back at you three times worse or better. I, even in my young age, believed in something more like the typical Westerner's belief of karma.

I hoped Andromalius didn't kill him. I didn't want to die.

I slept over at Aunt Jane's that night and Phil came to pick me up in the morning. We lived four blocks away from my aunt's high-rise, in our own three-bedroom house just outside of New Haven. Phil was three years older than me, but he was only two grades ahead.

He came to the house wearing a t-shirt and shorts, his waistband down to his hips, showing his knit boxer underwear.

"Pull up your pants," my aunt said, as she gathered my stuff to bring home. "He's already had lunch."

"Okay," he said, sniffing.

"You want some, too?"

"Nah," he said.

"It's lasagna."

Phil got that distant look that meant he was thinking.

"I'll give you some in a container."

As soon as we were out the door, he thrust the lasagna at me. "You carry it," he said, and walked ahead of me, brooding. He was 15. He didn't want me around.

I got home and saw that my father's car was not in the driveway. Phil was already home; I could tell by the cast-off sneakers inside the mudroom. I picked them up for him and placed them on the shelf, then took off my own sneakers.

I smelled baking. It was Sunday, and my mother was cooking for the week. She saw how to do it in one of those women's magazines a few weeks ago and was trying it on us. However, by Wednesday, we were tired of frozen food.

"Hi, Mom," I called, and came into the kitchen.

"Hi, Mike. What's that?"

"Lasagna." I handed over the container.

"I doubt it's low-fat," she said with a snort, and tossed it in the garbage. She and I were about the same height. I was of average weight, but my mother was always getting us to try and lose weight. "Are you going to clean your room?"

"Yes, Mom," I said, slightly dejected.

I always ended up cleaning my room on Sundays. I wanted to cook with her.

She knew it and said, "After you're done, we'll make some cookies."

"Okay!" I went out of the kitchen, into the living room where Phil sat on Dad's recliner, watching some videotaped wrestling. I headed to the stairs.

"Hey," he said to me. I turned around. "Don't forget to pick up the clothes."

Feeling a lot like Cinderella, I went upstairs to work on the room. I vacuumed, dusted, picked up the clothes, brought them down to the laundry, and put them in the washer. I made the beds, and then went to join my mother.

She was sitting at the kitchen table, looking through her *Taste of Home* magazines. My father just walked in the door as I said, "Okay, Mom!"

He stood in the mudroom, taking off his hat. A tall, overbearing man, with a paunch from beer and bread, he yelled into the kitchen, "Marge?"

My mother jumped up as if she was on a leash. All of us kids had learned to do that. Or we got smacked.

"Where's my blowtorch?"

"In the garage," she said.

"It's not where I looked. Didn't I use it last year to peel the paint off the window in Evie's room?"

"I don't think it's there anymore," she said, going over to my father in the hallway. She put her hand on her hip and regarded him. "Maybe you left it in the cellar with the paint."

"I'll check there." He walked by my mother without even a kiss, a hug, or any type of endearment. It wasn't surprising. He also walked by me without acknowledging me and went into the living room.

I turned to my mother expectantly. "What kind of cookies?"

She pulled out a magazine and pointed to a page. "Here. I think we have all the ingredients."

Hershey's Kisses cookies! One of my favorites!

I gathered all the ingredients and started mixing the cookie dough while she sat at the kitchen table and smoked, looking through her magazines. This was the best time ever during the week.

My father didn't find his blowtorch so he had to go to Ace Hardware to get a new one. He brought Phil with him because I was still baking cookies.

By the time my dad got back, he was grumpy. I had baked the cookies and was enjoying them when he snapped, "Get outside and come help me."

I glanced at my mother, who only tilted her head toward the door. There went the happy time for the weekend. I skulked outside. He was setting up a ladder against the garage, with Phil and me watching him. He stared at me as if I was stupid.

"Hold the ladder!" he yelled, and I ran to do his bidding. "Don't pull the rope," he said, carrying the blowtorch and a chisel, and started up the ladder.

Phil leaned against the car, his arms crossed, looking from my father to me. He grinned at me—a malicious grin—and then headed back into the house.

My father saw him go into the house. "Phil!"

Phil peeked out. "Yeah?"

"Get out here. You think I trust your brother?"

Phil came back, his shoulders hunched.

"Hold the ladder," my father ordered him, and he held it on the opposite side.

I held onto the ladder, staring at the rope between us, wondering what would happen if I pulled it. Would my father fall the ten feet to his death? On days like today, that didn't sound too bad.

As he scraped, curls of paint fell on us. We would let go of the ladder to brush them off, then he would yell at us to keep holding the ladder.

Phil glared at me. "This is all your fault. If you weren't such a girl, you could hold the ladder yourself."

"I'm not a girl!" I yelled at him.

"Faggot."

"Jerk."

"Gay faggot."

"Stop it!" yelled my father. "Jesus Christ, I'm almost done."

I held about ninety percent of the time, while Phil just put his hands on the ladder, looking bored. Finally, the ladder started to shake as my father came down. I held it tighter, and so did Phil. My father pushed past me to get his feet on the ground.

He went back up with a paint bucket this time. We had to hold the ladder until he was done.

"The work is done, master."

It wasn't a dream. My eyes snapped open. In the dark of my room, I could see Andromalius, the white snake coiled around his naked body, as he stood in the area between my bed and Phil's.

Phil slept like a stone.

"Release me." Andromalius stood, waiting.

I eased out of the bed, and whispered. "Come with me." There was no way I could do a banishment ritual in the middle of my room.

I tiptoed in the dark down the hall, past the living room, and out into the garage. Andromalius followed me like a shade gliding along the floor.

The first thing I did was use chalk to draw a protective circle. That was for me to stay in after I released him, so he wouldn't come after me. Then I drew his circle with his sigil in it, along with the sigils of his three binding angels.

I stepped into my circle and pointed him to his circle. He hesitated. Those three binding angels were what stopped him.

"You will not come after anyone I know or care about?"

"Certainly, master," he said.

I erased the three angels. He stepped into the circle willingly.

"What did you do to him?" I asked the demon.

"He had a water Jet Ski accident and is paralyzed from the waist down."

He'd never be back in school again. I couldn't help but smile.

"Cool," I said.

Then I raised my hands and began the prayer that summoned forth the three angels.

"You are to release me!"

The three angels, that actually looked more like white eagles, appeared outside of the circle. Flapping their broad wings, they attacked Andromalius, talons and beaks tearing his spirit apart.

When nothing but the echo of his scream remained, the door to the garage opened and Evie stood in the doorway. "Mikey?"

"Yeah?" I quickly started rubbing away the circles on the ground.

"What're you doing?"

"Nothing," I said. "Practicing."

Summer ended soon enough and fall came. School started and I went in with some trepidation. Mousey had not arrived the first few days of school, which turned into the first few months. I was free.

That is until we came back from December break. As I got on the bus, I sat next to a boy that I always sat next to. The boy never spoke to me. He kept looking out the window, even when I would try to talk to him.

Then, that one day after December break, a bigger boy grabbed me out of the seat and punched me in the ribs. I couldn't breathe.

He threw me to the floor. "I'm sittin' here from now on," he said. "Go somewhere else."

I struggled up, but no one would let me sit next to them. Finally, a girl at the very far back of the bus felt bad and scooted over for me.

So it wasn't just Mousey. It was going to be other kids. More kids. Different kids.

It would never end.

Macchiato

By Edward Taylor

"Dress like you've never worked a day in your life." Benjamin's eyes squinted as he struggled to read the text that caused his phone to chirp. The stillness of the morning made his ringtone sound like a loudspeaker as he stood outside the front door of his hotel. The old neighborhood was eerily vacant. Many of the town's workers were already out to sea before first light, and the rest of the labor force had yet to wake. It had been years since he had walked the streets where he grew up, but this wasn't a trip he wanted to make. His hotel was like something out of a horror film. The owner had clearly given up on maintenance years ago, since few people had cause to visit their backwater paradise. Worse yet, the nearest coffee shop was a twenty-minute walk away.

His blood pressure shot through the roof the longer he stared at the message, and Benjamin shoved the phone into his jacket pocket. The temptation to reply with a biting retort was almost overwhelming, but he knew there was no winning with his brother. Fighting back would just make things worse, and he wanted the experience to be as painless as possible. Only a few more days and he'd be able to fly back home to Seattle, once again able to enjoy the company of the people he chose to spend his time with. Friends who felt more like family than the relatives who mocked him for not following in their footsteps.

Looking down at his clothes, Benjamin grimaced before scanning the street for signs of his ride. He knew he was going to catch hell for his outfit. His synthetic down jacket kept him warm during the frigid fall mornings, but it was far too expensive to be practical for the daily toils to which the locals were accustomed.

The brand was synonymous with pretentious yuppies wanting to dress casual while still displaying their bloated bank accounts. Top-quality hiking gear that was more often witnessed while walking down city streets than traversing a trail. Still, it was better than nothing, and it was a far better choice than his typical casual attire.

The honk of his brother's truck horn was jarring. Benjamin had lost track of his surroundings, and was startled at the sudden burst of noise. "Get in, loser," his brother shouted from his truck's window, a satisfied smile on his face.

"It's too early for this, Dan," Benjamin replied, annoyed as he opened the passenger door.

"Oh Christ…will you lighten up for once. By the way, nice outfit Benji…is there some fancy ivy league college we're going to have to visit later? I'm not saying Pops was dumb, but that's the last place I'd expect we'd have to go. You should have warned me, I would have dressed to blend."

"Lighten up? We buried Dad three days ago, and you want me to crack jokes?" Benjamin closed the door and continued as he buckled his seatbelt, "How many times do I have to tell you that I hate that nickname."

"Everyone's called you Benji since middle school, how can you hate it?" Dan asked.

"Everyone here calls me that…it's not a name I brought with me to Seattle," Benjamin snapped as he crossed his arms and stared out the window.

Raising his eyebrows in response to his little brother's sudden temper tantrum, Dan put the car into drive and made his way out of the hotel's meager parking lot, a lot that was long overdue for repaving. Even the tiniest bump was felt as his modest pickup bounced from the slightest change. Benjamin grabbed the handle above the window and groaned in protest, but settled down as Dan turned onto the relatively smooth road. The two estranged brothers sat in awkward silence, already out of common interests to discuss, despite not seeing each other in years. Dan nervously tapped on his steering wheel.

His truck was nothing to brag about, but he loved it regardless. It wasn't old, but it didn't have all the bells and whistles that manufacturers were installing these days. That was what Dan liked most. Ever since lawyers across the country fancied themselves as truck people, trucks have never been the same. What was once a model of pure utility had been reduced to yet another status symbol. Accountants across the country continued to demand fancier amenities as they fought to keep up with the Joneses. High-end suburbs were littered with souped-up rigs that were only used to commute to the office. Luxury trucks were too costly to risk using them for their intended purpose. Worse yet, the trend had made even modest pickups more expensive.

"I was thinking coffee?" Dan finally asked after five minutes of silence.

"Sure," Benjamin answered, embarrassed at how emotional he had become.

Burying their dad wasn't easy, but he'd struggled with cancer for several years, and the boys felt guilty that their strongest emotion was relief. It was a depressing thought, but it was almost a blessing that he went senile when he did. His final years were spent in his recliner with his live-in caregiver tending to his every need, but when you'd visit he'd tell you about the amazing catch he found that morning. Despite being long retired, his fragile body could barely get into a boat, never mind the other rigors of the craft, yet he was convinced he was still making a living as a professional fisherman.

Dan found comfort that his father still thought he was doing what he loved. He could see the joy in the old man's eyes as he told him the same stories he heard as a child, and Dan bonded with his father as he told him what he had managed to pull in that morning. The local fishing industry had fallen on hard times, but Dan didn't see the point in distressing his father and would lie about how well the business was doing.

On the other hand, Benjamin visited less once his father began to degenerate, the old man unable to remember his youngest son moving to start his own internet-based company after graduating from college. It didn't help that most days their father was convinced they were still teenagers, and would constantly guilt Ben for turning his back on the family business. It was a sore spot that put a rift in the family that in many ways still existed. Benjamin's relationship with his father never fully recovered, but in his dwindling years an olive branch was extended. Dan couldn't deny the disconnect between them, but he loved his brother. They were simply from different worlds. He wouldn't care if he didn't get the sense that his younger brother felt he was better than the place he was born.

"Chocolate frosted or jelly?" Dan asked as he pulled up to the local coffee shop's menu board.

"I don't want anything, they don't have anything I like," Benjamin replied. "Just a large cappuccino."

Dan rolled his eyes as the menu's speaker sprang to life. The employee's voice was far too pleasant for someone forced to hawk coffee and donuts for meager pay so early in the morning. "Hey, Becky, it's Dan and Benjamin."

"Ben? I had no idea you were in town…I'm so sorry to hear about your dad. How have you been?" Becky asked through the speaker.

"Wait, Becky Price?" Benjamin asked.

"There another Becky in this town?" she replied with a giggle. "Hey, just pull up and order at the window. I'm as bored as a hooker in the Vatican back here."

"What?" Dan burst out laughing. "Analogies are clearly not your strong suit."

"Just pull up, fish breath," Becky quipped playfully.

The truck inched forward as Dan pulled up to the window. "You should have warned me," Benjamin mumbled, then cut short at the sight of his old flame staring at him through the drive-thru window.

"Well, don't you look...metropolitan," Becky said with a grin. "Nice jacket, that must have set you back a shiny penny. So, what can I get the famous Alvey brothers?"

"You wouldn't happen to have any chocolate croissants, would you?" Benjamin asked awkwardly.

"Oh my god...Becky, we'll take two black coffees and two jelly donuts," Dan cut in.

"Boy, you sure have gotten fancy in the past twenty years. Can I whip you up a macchiato?" Becky asked.

"Can you? That would be lovely." Benjamin was near ecstatic.

"No." Becky was barely able to contain her laughter and exchanged a look with Dan before she turned to complete their order. "Two black coffees it is."

Returning a moment later, Becky handed them their drinks and a bag. They sat and chatted for a few minutes, reminiscing about old times. Noticing Benjamin wince at the taste of the acidic medium roast coffee, Becky handed him a few creamers while his brother teased him for being a baby. Becky simply smiled as she took a sip of her own drink. It was strange to see her after so many years. The two of them dated all throughout high school, and never crossed paths again after he went off to college. Another truck pulled up to the menu behind them, and the reunion came to an end.

"Seriously Dan, what the hell!" Benjamin exclaimed, then sipped his now tolerable coffee.

"Do you want the donut or not?" Dan mumbled as he held one of the donuts between his teeth and extended the bag towards his now irate brother.

Defeated that his diet was going off the rails so early in the morning, Benjamin snapped the bag away. Still chewing, his lips now coated in powdered sugar, Dan continued, "Sorry man, it's the only coffee shop in town. She was happy to see you, why are you so annoyed?"

"It's just embarrassing, that's all," Benjamin replied, then took a bite, keeping the bag under his chin.

"That you dated the local donut girl for four years? Dude, get off your…" Dan began but was interrupted.

"What…no! That has nothing to do with it!" Benjamin lied. "I just wasn't ready is all. Listen, let's just focus on what we're here to do. No more detours."

"All I did was get us coffee…it's not like I went out of my way to torture you. You think I want to make this longer than it needs to be? I'm losing out on money right now by not being on the water," Dan said.

"How's the business going?"

"Terrible." Dan paused and took a sip of coffee, clearly trying to downplay how upset the thought had made him. "Everyone is in a bind right now, the fish just aren't there. It's not just us, a few of the other nearby ports are having the same problem. It doesn't help that the government is slapping down more regulations on us every year. Liberals are going to be the death of us…I swear it."

"Let's not go down the political route," Benjamin said.

"Yeah, I agree. You'd think with all that money you have now, you'd be a stauncher conservative than me, but somehow you're still drinking that lefty Kool-Aid." Dan laughed. "We're a little better off since we have a few boats in the water. Everyone else only has one."

"I still wonder how Dad pulled that off. We're the only company in town with more than one boat. Like you said, Dad wasn't dumb, but he never struck me as a man hungry to build an empire. Everyone else never made enough to expand, or they simply didn't want to."

"That's Pops for you." Dan put the car in park as they reached the end of their father's driveway. Stepping out of his truck, he brushed away the light dusting of sugar decorating his work clothes. "I know you think you're a fancy businessman in the big city now, but you got it from somewhere. Never knew why you turned your nose up at us after you moved."

"I didn't turn up my nose at you," Benjamin replied, irritated, then returned to his rapidly cooling cup of joe.

With his key already in the lock, Dan turned to shoot his brother a look before opening the front door. "You tried to order a macchiato and a pastry at the coffee shop you used to go to every morning before school. You know exactly what that place is, Ben. You hate hearing your old nickname, when we all had them back in the day. On top of that, I know you're genuinely upset about Dad, but you've looked at this week as a massive inconvenience. You try to hide it, but you're counting the days before you return to your metropolitan bubble." Dan was blunt as he swung open the door and stepped inside.

"You're not being fair…" Benjamin was at a loss. His brother's words, while curt, were accurate. If he tried to convince himself otherwise he'd only be trying to sell himself a delusion. For the first time since he had arrived, Benjamin felt guilty. "Listen, I'm not ashamed of you…I'm sorry. Maybe I have been a little pretentious all these years."

Searching for a light switch Dan countered, "A little?" He smiled, then noticed that his brother's words were genuine. "You'll always be my little bro, you know that. So, we're different, who cares? Listen, Dad was hard on you when you left. I kind of get how he felt, but at the end of the day, it's your life. If pulling in nets wasn't what you wanted to do, then no one should stop you. I know I don't show it, but I'm proud you were brave enough to get what you wanted. There're a lot of people in this town who can't say that."

"Thank...thank you. Wow."

"I have my moments, I guess. Listen, I'm sure the few times I visited you back in the day, I was a judgmental little snot, too. I'll have to actually try one of your fancy coffee drinks when I visit sometime," Dan joked.

"What about sometime next month?" Benjamin asked.

Dan stopped and looked at his brother for a moment while he stood in the clean but cluttered living room of their late father. "You serious?" Dan asked.

"Absolutely. It's been years since I invited you to visit Seattle. Come and stay for a week. I have room for Alison and the kids, too. I'll actually show you around properly this time."

"Well…then you'll have to show me where to buy one of your fancy coats so I can fit in over there," Dan said with a warm smile.

"Just tell me what color you want and I'll have one waiting for you."

"Good…the guys will be jealous of my flashy outfit when I get back," Dan joked. "Thanks. The kids will love it, we haven't gone on a trip in years. Want to get the more interesting step out of the way first?" Dan pointed to the basement where their father kept his safe.

"Call me Benji…yeah, let's see what Pops has been hiding down there all these years."

The aging steps creaked under their weight. They had their work cut out for them as they prepared to deconstruct the culmination of seventy years of hard work left behind by a man who was considered the most successful in their tiny little town. "He told me once he got a loan from the bank, the only townie brave enough to take the leap." Dan said, as they reached the chaotic basement that no one had stepped foot in since their father's health deteriorated.

"That's odd," Benjamin said. His brother gave him a curious look. "They never gave loans to operations like Pop's…it was too risky. One bad fishing season and the investment could fold. Boats don't hold value like houses."

"Well, we both know Pops could be persuasive, that's how he landed Mom," Dan joked as he reached the large safe at the far end of the basement. "How about you do the honors?"

Dan handed Benjamin a crumpled piece of paper with the safe combination and leaned against a dusty table nearby. Channeling his old high school locker days, Benjamin opened the steel door to reveal the contents inside. To no one's surprise, it was what you'd expect to find. Old manuals, their late mother's jewelry, and his dad's old pistol were the first things Benjamin noticed. In a red velvet box, he found his mother's wedding ring and handed it to Dan, who smiled. Their father tried to be the hard as nails type, but they always knew inside he was a softie. "Huh, this is interesting," Benjamin said as he handed Dan what must have been a forty-year-old newspaper clipping. "Wait, there's more of them."

Benjamin handed his brother the rest of the weathered pieces of paper as he continued to study the safe's contents.

"Benji…you remember that bank robbery a few towns over that was all over the news when we were little kids?" Dan asked.

"Yeah, one of the few things of interest that actually happened around here. It was never solved, right?"

"No, it wasn't. These are all clippings of the coverage. Why would Dad save these? I know it was interesting and all, but it's still strange. I wonder if he tried to solve it when the police gave up," Dan hypothesized.

“Dan…” Benjamin’s voice trailed off.

Dan looked up to see Benjamin holding several stacks of bills, which looked as though they had been in the safe for some time. The color completely drained from his face, Benjamin swung the door as far as its hinges allowed so Dan could see inside. Pushing aside an old blanket had revealed a large stack of money at the bottom of the safe, and a rolled-up document was lying casually on top. “Pop’s business was this successful? I thought he kept the company money in an account at the credit union?” Benjamin asked.

“He does…” Dan was at a loss for words.

Benjamin leaned into the safe and grabbed the mystery document. Unrolling it made his face grow paler. “Dan…Dad told you that he took out a loan from the bank, right?” Benjamin asked.

“Yeah…” Dan couldn’t hide the confusion in his voice.

“I don’t think it was a loan,” Benjamin replied as he turned to reveal the document. The years had caused the image to fade, but it was clear that it was a blueprint with the schematics of a bank that looked exactly like the one discussed in the news clippings still in his sibling’s hands.

Dan stood up straight at the revelation and both brothers stared at each other wide-eyed, not knowing how to respond. “Well…” Dan began in a haze, “Maybe the old man wasn’t as boring as we thought.”

We Are Stardust

By Hannah R. Goodman

Sharon lay in the backseat of her brother's '65 Chevy, trying to find a comfortable position amidst all the camping gear. Reaching behind her head, she readjusted the rolled up sleeping bag and then leaned back against it again.

Her eyes were halfway to closed when the car lurched forward.

"Dammit, Scotty!"

"Sorry, sis! I'm a little jazzed!"

"Forget this." She shoved the sleeping bag back and then climbed over the seat into the passenger side.

Just then the rev of a motorcycle engine filled the car. She craned her neck out the window to get a better view of who was on the bike. It was a young man, with longish, dirty blond hair. He wore a white tee shirt and his tanned arms were bumpy with muscles. The car lurched again and a bubble of nausea arose in her. She sighed and rubbed her stomach, closing her eyes for a moment, breathing in and out for a few breaths.

"Sweet ride!" Sharon opened her eyes. Scotty was pointing at the motorcycle, now just inches away from their car, glistening in the hazy August heat, steam coming off the chrome.

She breathed in the smell of exhaust and rode another wave of nausea.

"Sis, you're bumming me out." He wrinkled his nose at her. "You're not gonna toss it, are you?"

Sharon shook her head and closed her eyes again. Fresh air was what she needed. The car was stuffed with three days' worth of camping gear, and her twin brother rode the brake a little too heavily. With crawling traffic and the stop and go, her stomach was lurching all over the place.

"Man, I love this song!" Scotty turned up the sounds of electric guitar. "Out of sight, sis!"

Sharon stared at the bike next to them and got an idea that would cure her carsickness. She reached for the door handle. "I'm gonna catch a ride with that guy. I'll meet up with you there."

Her brother started to protest, but it was too late. She was out the door and tapping on the shoulder of the hunk on the bike.

"Hey, groovy ride."

As the guy turned and looked at her, she noticed an intricately decorated gold cross dangling from his tanned neck. He noticed her looking at it and said, "I made this." She reached out and touched it gently. "Hop on," he told her.

She smiled back at him and swung a leg over, realizing she forgot her shoes. She gripped his shoulders, which were firm. "Take the breakdown lane. Let's just fly."

The unspoken rules of the moment. Freedom. Peace. Love. She'd been on a protest and sit-in tour with Scotty since they graduated, traveling all over and hitting the major cities and marching in each one. Who cared about college and the status quo when the Age of Aquarius was upon them? All that mattered was making love, not the stupid war.

If this were just a few years ago, she would have never gotten on the bike, barefoot, with a long-haired guy who had a gold cross—that he'd made himself—around his neck. Mother would pitch a fit. And yet there was good little Sharon, riding all the way to a hippy music festival in the middle of nowhere New York.

So much had changed in a year, now with Scotty on his way to Nam in just a few days (unless she could convince him to drive with her to Canada), she didn't care about any of the mainstream crap, the expectations of her mother and father to finish college and find a husband along the way—a nice Jewish boy who would be on his way to law or med school. There were lots of things to discover and learn more about, she realized, as she and Scotty did the protest tour. There was Women's Lib and Black Power. There was free love and LSD. The rules of yesterday didn't apply to today, just like that Hare Krishna guy said at the last rally they went to at Brown University.

"What's your name," the guy turned back and asked her as they sped alongside the lines of cars. She told him and asked for his. "Joseph," he told her, adding, "I make crosses," and held up a small wooden cross hanging from his neck. Sharon figured this was important to remember, though she didn't know why.

They sped along the breakdown lane, passing car after car. The traffic seemed to have completely stopped.

They continued all the way, until up ahead they could see swarms of people swaying and dancing to far-away sounding music that gradually became closer and louder. They slowly passed people playing guitars, drinking beer, smoking joints. Joseph hadn't said anything else to Sharon, and she said nothing to him. They pulled the bike onto the grass where other bikes were parked. He got off first and then held her hand to help her. Her stomach was calm but her heart hammered a little at the sight before her. Overcast sky and swarms and swarms of people all around. People making out and making love. People in tents and sleeping bags. They walked together a couple hundred feet, all in silence, and then before them the land dropped down and there was the stage. Richie Havens going to town on his guitar, singing *freedom* over and over. *Sometimes I feel like a motherless child,* his voice gravelly and pleading. Sharon's whole body felt the vibrations of love and music. Joseph grabbed her hand, and they stood side by side, watching. She reached into the pocket of her pedal pushers and pulled out a thickly rolled joint. Wordless still, Joseph pulled out a lighter and they smoked it together.

"Does it get any better than this?" Joseph asked the sky.

Sharon began to dance, still holding his hand and still smoking the joint. She swayed and let her long brown hair cascade around her bare shoulders, and she felt a pulsing sensation up and down her body, like she was coming apart and back together again.

"Hey!" Joseph yelled out, forcing her to lose the groove and open her eyes. She followed his gaze, and up ahead a truck was slowly moving, a large Mack truck. "Oh, God!" The sound of a thud and a crunch as it rolled over what looked like an oversized sack on the ground, but then something popped out of the sack, an arm and a hand.

They gasped together, their bodies reeling back at the shock of what they had seen together, at the same time.

"Mother of God," Joseph whispered and his hand became limp in hers.

The nausea returned, coiling up in her belly, squeezing in her gut until she felt the breath leave her body. She dropped the joint and fell to the ground.

"Sharon?"

Her eyes were slits and she could barely make out the face in front of her but she recognized the voice. "Scotty?" She spoke but realized the words didn't make a sound.

As a face came into view, she saw Joseph, tanned skin glistening with sweat. Droplets fell on her but she realized they were drops of rain.

"What happened?" she asked but she already knew.

Joseph's friendly face hovered over her, covering the rain briefly. "You just fainted." He touched her forehead and her cheek. "You okay?" The image of the lump and the hand jutting out came rushing to her.

"I told some guy to run over to the trailers to tell the cops what happened. They're gonna take care of it, okay. It's gonna be okay."

She nodded and slowly rolled herself up with Joseph's help. As she steadied herself, she felt something against her collar bone and put her hand to it—the wooden cross. They stood together with her leaning into him, and watched as a helicopter appeared and hovered over the mound below. It made her think of the countless hours of the six o'clock news, watching something about Vietnam, and how they show the boys being lifted up in their body bags, and Sharon wondered where Scotty was now.

The next two days went by in a delicious haze of off-and-on rain. Joseph bought a few bottles of wine, and they smoked hashish and slept in a section of the site called Groovy Way, sharing the tent of a newly married couple. As the rain stopped and the ground grew muddier, the smell of cow manure became strong. Food was running out, and in between the music and the smoking, they ate free cups of granola handed out by some of the men in food trucks. On the last night, Joseph splurged on one-dollar hot dogs. They didn't talk much and although they made out some, and Joseph put his hands on her breasts, it wasn't about getting it on.

And now they stood back at the original spot where they first heard Richie Havens open the concert. Jimi Hendrix, in a white fringe jacket and an orange headband tied around him like an Indian, plucked out the chords to a familiar tune which quickly became apparent as "The Star-Spangled Banner." Sharon let the tears stream freely and fully down her cheeks and wondered where Scotty had parked the '65 Chevy and if he ever even made it to Woodstock.

Always to the Never-End

(or, the joy of writing)

By Paul Magnan

It flared in my hand, a bright thermal explosion that extinguished into nothing as my fingers curled around it. Despite the heat, my skin did not burn.

Who would've thought it was so easy to kill a star?

Cinders drifted from my palm as I released my grip. Tiny orbs, bereft of their gravitational master, fell from their orbits.

They froze and died.

I heard no screams.

It wouldn't have mattered even if I had. The star's placement had been all wrong. The planets…well, there is no help for them, faultless though they may be.

Color and movement surrounded me. Massive rivers of photons flowed ceaselessly between spinning galaxies. Gases coalesced and formed new stars, while old ones sputtered out, or exploded into noiseless bright light that incinerated nearby planets and blasted distant ones into empty space.

There was so much that needed correcting.

This system, for example. It had three blue planets. That's too much life, too much sentience. I reached out, cupped a black hole, and carefully dragged it into place. I don't like using black holes, but sometimes I have no choice. I placed it near two of the living planets and allowed the gravitational pull to suck them out of their solar orbits.

Once a planet has been torn from its life-giving path around a star, it dies quickly. These two were no different. The planets passed through the event horizon and disappeared.

Once again, I heard no screams.

But with genesis, everything was distant. It had to be. If empathy was mixed with creation, nothing would ever get done.

***

The motions of the world were labored, asynchronous. There was too much clutter. It's my own damn fault. I put everything in place.

A multitude of wires hung before me, shiny and sharp. I would need to be careful.

A thin, serpentine man leaned against a light post and watched those around him with pale, calculating eyes. He had such promise, but as the world sprang up around him it became obvious he would have no influence in the greater course of things. He was a distraction, a loose end. He had to go.

I grabbed a wire and yanked. It pulled loose from him and coiled at my feet. He looked at me in shock and then faded from the street corner.

My fingers dripped blood. I ignored the pain. Things were going to get worse before they got better.

There she was, the crux of this world, holding the hand of a young girl, possibly her daughter. However, her actions as of late have digressed from the initial catalyst that gave her motivation and the means to reach the end. She had several wires attached to her and I manipulated them. Agitation flashed in her dark eyes as I tried to finesse her back to the correct path.

I was only partly successful. One wire needed to be pulled. I hesitated. I had grown inordinately fond of it. But I had known, even as I created it, that it was wrong. Now it was an obstacle blocking the woman on her set course.

She recognized the wire I took, and in desperation shook her head. A piece of my heart split away, but I could not stop. I jerked the wire; agony flared as my flesh parted. She screamed as the wire snapped from the young girl who had been holding her hand. The girl looked up in confusion before falling away into nothingness.

The woman gave me a look of betrayal and ran off, but at least it was in the right direction.

I looked at my palm. It was cut clear to the bone.

But the world was back on track.

***

She was so light, yet she meant the world to me. Still I lowered her into the trunk.

Her eyes, so big and moist, her trembling lips, tore through my soul, carving it bloody.

You'd think I'd be used to this by now.

Tears slid down my face. I wanted to say something. But there was nothing to say. The decision had been made. To postpone it would merely prolong the pain. I've learned, and relearned, that lesson many times.

I loved her, but she had been rejected. I had to move on.

The lid was heavy. I lowered it and eternal shadow crossed her face. She cried out and her tiny hands reached for me. I nearly lost my nerve, but I squeezed my eyes shut and pushed down. Her last plea for life was cut short as the lid locked into place.

I slumped to the floor and cried, like I always did.

I took the trunk and laid it on top of dozens of identical ones. Her brothers and sisters. My forgotten children.

Despair rocked me as I counted their number. So many more of them here, never to be seen again, than there were out there, enjoying the attention of their aunts and uncles.

More gestated in my mind.

There was plenty of space here. I dared not follow that thought any further. This was bad, but sterility was worse.

Within me, stars swirled haphazardly. I dove in. After all, these worlds weren't going to create themselves.

The Man

By Thom Ring

The woman saw her out there every day, the little girl always in the yard, playing in the sandbox – or on the rusting hulk of a swing-set left there by tenants years ago. The child was the only person the woman ever noticed out there. Not that it was a proper yard for a child to play in. It was tiny, for one thing. The woman could see every inch of it, every clump of grass, every broken bottle and bit of trash, every deep hole dug by the dog that died out there last winter.

The little girl certainly spent a lot of time alone. She played well alone. Sometimes the woman didn't even hear her out there. But she'd look out her kitchen window and there she was, playing quietly, always in the same clothes, always in what looked like a faded boy's tee shirt over jean shorts. The girl must have had a drawer full of jean shorts. She always was wearing them.

Then the woman saw the man. She knew he'd just moved in, knew someone had, anyway. When she first noticed him, he was smoking a cigarette outside his door. His hair was long, unkempt, flying out in every direction from his head. It didn't look as if it ever saw a drop of shampoo. His beard was long and equally out of control. The man's clothes appeared dirty and ill-fitting.

She started to see him out there every day – or hear him. His presence usually was announced by a desperate, disgusting, hacking cough that sometimes seemed to go on forever.

She gave him little thought, but then one day she saw him talking to the little girl as she sat on the rusty swing-set's lone seat. It made the woman uneasy. What did this man – this dirty, distasteful man – want with that little girl?

A few days later she saw the man give the little girl a push on the swing. She saw him stumble over behind her, give her a tiny push, and then do it again, and again, pushing a bit harder each time. She heard the little girl laugh. She could hear it, hear that man making the little girl laugh.

The little girl went inside. She headed for the stairs that led to her mother's upstairs apartment as the man disappeared into his.

It was a relief that was short-lived. The next day she noticed that when the little girl appeared outside, the man emerged only a moment later. As if he'd been waiting for her. Now he stepped behind her to give her a push as soon as she hopped on the swing. The little girl smiled at him; the woman could see it clearly even from her second-floor window. She heard the laughing and giggling. She saw the man smile back. It betrayed intentions that the woman could scarcely imagine.

She saw the man give the little girl a piece of candy, which she readily accepted, as she did the sandwich he offered her a day later.

When the woman saw the man take the little girl into his apartment she reached for the phone, but the little girl reappeared only a moment later, clutching a juice box. What would a grown man, this low-life of a man, be doing with juice boxes? Still, there was no evidence he'd done anything, nothing to reveal his true intentions. She'd wait.

Two days later, the time came. She saw the man heading into the yard – with two other little girls following him. Now the woman had to act. She made the call.

Not soon enough, the police arrived. The officer headed directly to the backyard, as the woman had advised them to do. She peeked out her window, trying to hide behind the ruffles of her kitchen curtains.

The police officer could be seen gesturing toward the children. The man shrugged. She saw him laugh. He laughed directly at the officer. Carefully, quietly, the woman reached down and slid the window open just a few inches. Now she could make out what the man was saying.

"Come on inside. I'll show ya," she heard. "I got some hotdogs we're gonna grill, and ice cream. I even got some broccoli."

"I hate broccoli," said one of the girls.

"Yeah, but you wait," said the man. "I make it good, I put cheese on it."

"I like cheese," said the other girl.

She heard the police officer laugh. She saw the man lean over, exchanging a confidence with him. Then he reached out with his right hand as if to point to the building's second floor. The woman quickly ducked behind the curtain.

Whatever the man's story, the officer evidently bought it. In a moment he was gone, leaving the man with the three little girls.

The woman was shocked the officer had left the girls behind. But then, within the hour, another police car arrived at the apartment house, revealing that indeed the first officer had not been fooled. Right behind it was another car, identical to the officer's but painted white, with no lights or markings. A woman emerged from the car, looking serious in a gray business suit.

The pair entered the yard, looking around briefly before heading toward the stairs. The woman thought to correct them but decided to keep to herself. She didn't want the man to suspect she was the one who alerted the authorities.

The police officer knocked on the door of the little girl's apartment, evidently checking in on her. The door opened, and the two of them disappeared behind it. The woman could see the door of the man's apartment and worried he'd make an escape before the officer came downstairs.

The officer and the woman seemed to take forever at the little girl's. Then, when the door finally opened, the woman walked out, holding the little girl's hand. She was followed by the police officer, and a young woman. She was barely dressed, in dirty, bedraggled clothing. She seemed asleep on her feet. The officer struggled to keep her from falling down the stairs.

Five minutes later, the man came out of his apartment and headed for the swing, two little girls giggling as they trailed behind him drinking from juice boxes.

Adversity and Prosperity

Shadows of One Another

By Hank Ellis

The annual Wilson pilgrimage to the great outdoors was finally here. John, Karen, and their two boys Peter and David had been making plans for the last eight months to camp with friends in central Maine. Everyone was excited.

"Are we ready yet?" asked the impatient twelve-year-old.

"C'mon Dave, we've been waiting this long, a few more minutes won't hurt," replied Dad. "Why don't you and Peter get the rubber raft. We can use it on the lake."

The excited boy trotted off in search of his older brother while John hooked up the popup tent trailer to the station wagon. Karen was almost done packing the remaining food and clothes for the week-long camping trip. The family was thrilled to be leaving early on a beautiful Friday afternoon in the middle of summer.

Another thirty minutes passed and they were finally ready. The car pulled out of the driveway around 1:00 p.m. Maybe it was an omen, or possibly strike one, but no one in the Wilson family would have seen it that way. Only a half-mile down the road, John had to stop because the safety chains to the trailer were dragging on the road. No big deal—he pulled safely to the side of the road, draped the chains securely between the trailer and the station wagon, and they were back on the road.

John and Karen discussed the rendezvous they had set up with friends in South Portland as they traveled toward central Maine. The family sang songs, played games, and munched on snacks to pass the time. After an hour and a half into the trip, another warning, or possibly strike two, showed up in the rear-view mirror.

"Sorry dear, I need to stop. The vent top on the camper is up in the air and it's getting blown around pretty bad," said John as he pulled over onto the shoulder of Route 495. Fortunately, John quickly remedied the situation and they were back in business. Unfortunately, they only managed to move another mile down Route 495 before the car started acting funny. "Oh, now what? The car isn't shifting and I think the transmission just went," announced the frustrated husband and father as he pulled back into the breakdown lane. "Well, it's still moving forward, but only in first gear. Maybe I can get to the bottom of exit 20."

The boys weren't saying a thing and Karen didn't want to add to an already tense moment as the car rolled to a stop at the bottom of the off-ramp.

"Now guess what?" said John. "I can't go forward or reverse. Here we are almost in the middle of the off-ramp and I can't move. This is great!"

"John, I see a Mobil Station a little way down Route 85. I'll go get help," said Karen. Even before she finished her statement she heard a man shout from an adjacent car.

"Hello, miss! Can we help you? This is a tough place to get stuck, especially on Friday evening."

"Thank you," answered Karen. "You're a life saver."

"John, you and the boys stay with the car and I'll go see if we can get a tow."

Karen quickly jumped into the adjacent car with the charitable driver and his two daughters. "I'll be right back," she yelled as they moved toward the Mobil Station.

"Well, this is a great place to stop," said Dad as he glanced into the rear-view mirror to check on the boys. "How are you guys doing?"

"We're good," answered Peter. "Do you think we can fix it?"

"Not sure, kiddo, it doesn't sound good." As they continued to talk about their predicament, John repeatedly motioned approaching vehicles to go around. Only ten minutes had passed since Karen left and already a tow truck was pulling alongside. "That was fast!" exclaimed John. "Where's my wife?"

"She's next to us with the man who gave her a ride," answered Dave.

In the craziness of the traffic at the bottom of the off-ramp, everyone switched vehicles. Karen and John rode with Billy, the tow truck driver, and Peter and David rode with Billy's friend in an old Firebird that had 'Bad Boy' written across the windshield. Karen explained to John that the man who gave her a ride was nice enough to wait around until she got the help she needed.

"So now what do we do?" said John.

"I don't know. I guess we should contact Al and Cathy to let them know we won't be able to spend the week with them."

"I wish there was something else we could do. We've had this planned for so long," said John. "Maybe we can rent a car that will tow the camper."

John called three rental companies and none of them allowed towing. Then he tried U-Haul as a last resort. "Nothing in Milford, I'm going to try Worcester," he said. After trying seven times from the towing company's phone he finally located a U-Haul dealership in Worcester. "Hey sweetie, they have a fourteen-foot truck that could tow a vehicle. I explained our predicament to the woman on the phone. She quoted a good price from Worcester to Bangor. But they close at seven and it's already four-thirty."

"Maybe we can rent a car to get over to Worcester," said Karen. "But we need to get moving. It's late. I noticed a rental place near the Mobile station."

John locked the car and the entire family walked to the nearby rental office at Mobil's competing gas station, Granite Gulf. It turned out that Granite Gulf owned the company that towed the station wagon to the repair shop. Since money was always an issue with this young family, John and Karen hoped that Granite Gulf would simply lend them a car to pick up the U-Haul truck.

As John walked toward the young man behind the rental counter, he quickly glanced at the name tag above his left shirt pocket. "Hi Bob!" said John. "I know this is a crazy request, but our car just died and your towing company has it in the other lot. Is there any way you could lend us a car for an hour or so to pick up a U-Haul truck in Worcester?"

"I'm sorry," replied Bob, "that's not a crazy request, but I can't do that. Let me see what we have." After several minutes of searching he spoke up. "We can rent you a Ford Escort for twenty-five dollars a day. That's the best we can do."

"Give us a minute, will you?" answered John. "I just want to talk with my wife."

"Well, what do you think, sweetie? Do we go to Maine without the camper and most of our provisions and buy a tent? Do we go home? Or, do we rent a U-Haul to carry everything that was in the car. There's a lot of stuff in there."

"Oh, John, I'm not sure. But we need to do something soon because the towing company is going to close up. And whatever we do, we need some sort of transportation."

"We do need transportation. Let's get it," replied John.

After completing the rental transaction, everyone piled into the Ford Escort and headed north to Worcester in search of the U-Haul store. The first store gave a price that was twice the quote given on the telephone.

"That sounds awfully high," said John. *Am I in the right store*? he thought.

"Let me call the main office. I can double check the price," offered the store manager.

"No, that's okay," answered John. "We don't have the time."

Back on the road again—but this time they quickly found the correct U-Haul. It was now almost six. It turned out that Sonja, the woman who quoted a special price, did so out of the kindness of her heart. Because the reality of committing to this rental was finally upon them, John asked Sonya for a moment with his wife to reconsider everything.

"Hey, sweetie, here we are again. Should we do it?" asked John.

The beleaguered couple ran through all the positives and negatives. There seemed to be too many disadvantages involved in not going. The deposit on the campground would be lost and the balance still due. The deposit on the room at the Best Western might be lost. Friends were scheduled to meet them at the Best Western around six. Not only would the Wilson family vacation be ruined, but Al, Cathy, and Chris would be disappointed if the Wilsons didn't show up. But even this special offer on the rental price was a lot to consider. Money did not come easily.

Karen smiled. "I think you know the answer."

"Yes, I do," answered John, as husband and wife hugged and kissed each other in front of the U-Haul store. "Let's do it," he answered, confirming what his wife already had in mind.

As John checked the back of the U-Haul truck it became clear that the taillight hookup between the camper and the U-Haul truck was incompatible. "Now what do we do?" asked John. "We need signal and brake lights on the back of the camper. It'll be dark soon."

Sonya came through again. She showed John a kit with two attachable lights and wires long enough to reach the U-Haul truck. The kit and a roll of strapping tape to attach the lights cost another twenty-five dollars.

"What do I owe you?" asked John as he pulled out his credit card. A quick scan of the transaction indicated that Sonja had forgotten to include the travel lights and strapping tape.

"You forgot the lights and tape," said John.

Sonja looked up and grinned. "Don't worry, you take them."

"Really? Thank you so much."

"Yes, thank you very much," replied Karen.

"You're very welcome," answered Sonja. "Have a great trip."

The decision was made and the Wilson family was committed once again. Dad and David took the U-Haul and Mom and Peter drove the Escort. They stopped at a Friendly's restaurant because they hadn't eaten anything since the light snacks they had in the car. Hunger, mental exhaustion, and frustration had been traveling with them for the last several hours. But none of these unwanted intruders would be appeased because the family waited in the restaurant for fifteen minutes with no waitress.

"Let's go," said Dad. "We'll find someplace else. We still have a lot to do." Everyone was so tired and hungry they didn't put up a fuss. Although frustration won the moment, good fortune won the hour because the family found a Wendy's fast food restaurant while traveling back to Milford.

The towing company was closed when the family returned. John pulled the U-Haul close to the disabled car and everything was transferred from the car to the truck. This included the two bikes that were tied upside down on the roof racks of the car. Despite the complete off-loading, the cargo hold of the truck was almost empty. Once the transfer was complete, John backed the truck up to the camper hitch. After trying several times, he came to realize that the ball on the U-Haul, although seemingly the same size as the hitch on the camper, would not fit entirely into the hitch. To work safely it was necessary for the latch on the hitch to fully engage and sit in the down position to ensure that the hitch would stay on the ball. No matter what he did it wouldn't go fully on the ball.

"This is ridiculous," mumbled John. "Can anything else go wrong?" But instead of giving up in total frustration, and probably as a distraction, John shifted his attention to the task of attaching the tail lights to the camper. At this point Karen and David decided to go to Granite Gulf to call Al and Cathy at the Best Western Motel. It was now nine-thirty and they were probably worried.

Back to the hitch. *How could we get this far only to realize that we still can't haul the camper to Maine*? thought John. *There's no bringing the U-Haul truck back to Worcester. The store is closed. But what am I going to do?* "Hey Peter, how are we going to fix this problem?" asked Dad. "The hitch on the camper won't fit on the ball of the U-Haul."

The fifteen-year old thought a moment and responded. "Why don't we put the ball from our car on the U-Haul?"

Peter's statement struck his father like a cold shower. Suddenly, the tiredness, frustration, and clouded thinking were gone. Yes! There were two other holes next to the ball on the U-Haul hitch, probably for that purpose. Pulled back from the depths of frustration, Dad replied with a big grin, "Kiddo, you're a genius!"

It looked like it might work. All they needed now was a way to get the ball off the car hitch. Tools were king—but did they have the right ones? John searched the car and camper for the only tools he had. He smiled to Peter as he pulled a vise grip plier out of the camper and held it in the air. "I've got this. Let's hope it works."

Unfortunately, he needed two. The entire ball turned when he turned the 1½-inch nut with the vise grip. But this was a good sign. There was still hope.

By now Karen and David had returned and everyone piled in the Escort and went to the Gulf station in search of a large wrench or another vise grip. An attendant informed John that all the tools were locked up, but another station down the road might be able to help. John was skeptical, but he was out of options. Everyone piled back into the Escort to try again. As the family headed south on Route 495, Karen thought they were headed in the wrong direction. John agreed, and the course correction was made at the next exit where they turned back north on Route 495. It was now very dark and late and frustration was returning.

"Let's go back to the camper," said John. "I know I already looked, but I might have a small vise grip inside the camper."

As they pulled into the dimly lit parking area, John changed his mind. "I'm beat, guys. I don't think there's one in there. And even if there is, it's probably too small. Plus, we would have to raise the top on the camper to check the drawers inside. Let's try something else. Do you guys remember the huge vise in front of the office?"

"I saw it, Dad," said Dave. "Why?"

"I'm hoping it's functional. Let's check it out," said Dad as everyone turned and faced the towing office. The boys ran over to view the massive devise. "It doesn't work, Dad," yelled Dave as his father approached the useless decoration.

"Well, it was worth a try. Check some of the tow trucks. Maybe there's a wrench or some pliers in one of them. The doors on the trucks are probably locked, but sometimes there's a tool box outside behind the cab." The boys scoured several trucks with no luck.

"I've got jumper cables," declared Peter.

"Sorry, kiddo, but they're no help. Let's go back to the Gulf station."

The family piled back into the Escort and traveled five hundred feet down the road to the Gulf station to ask the attendant if there was a Wal-Mart or hardware store nearby. Unfortunately, it was almost 10:00 p.m. and those stores probably wouldn't be open. The attendant suggested that the Mobil Station might have some tools.

"Let's give it a try," said John. "I don't know what else to do." Back in the car and up the road only six hundred feet, the family quickly realized that the Mobil Station was strictly a gas and food mart. "Why don't you guys stay here. I'll give it a quick check. Maybe they have something," said Dad.

As he returned from the store he held some pliers in the air and shrugged his shoulders with a 'who knows' look on his face. "Only four dollars, they're small, but they might work. Here we go again!"

Quickly back to the disabled station wagon, the hopeful and desperate man opened the jaws of the pliers as wide as they would go and placed them around the hitch ball. Somehow, using his huge feet to secure the handles of the pliers, he managed to turn the large 1½-inch nut with the vise grip. Amazing! They were back in business.

The station wagon ball was transferred to the U-Haul bumper next to the one that was permanently attached. The camper was attached to the U-Haul and the lights were hooked up. Everything worked—it was a miracle, at least in the eyes of the Wilson family. It was also 10:00 p.m. Dad and Peter drove the U-Haul and camper to the Gulf station and Mom and David returned the Ford Escort.

As the four of them sat in the wide front seat of the U-Haul, it was clear by the looks on their faces that the family was excited to have overcome the challenges of the day. They finally left Milford, heading for South Portland around 10:30 p.m. After leaving the highway at exit 7, backtracking several times, and asking a toll attendant for directions, they arrived at the Best Western at 1:30 a.m.

The hot summer night air drained their tired bodies as the four of them jumped out of the truck. “I can’t wait to hit the bed,” said Peter as Dad rolled up the gate on the back of the huge truck.

“Grab your night stuff and clothes for tomorrow,” said Dad. “Mom and I will check in.”

The night manager was very inefficient, or perhaps it was embarrassment, because the motel gave away the room despite the earlier call indicating they would be there. All the manager could find was a king-size bed that barely fit in the room. John, Karen, and David slept on the bed with Peter stuffed on a cot that barely fit between the bed and the wall. On top of it all, the air conditioner didn’t work. But tiredness overcame the cramped and heated quarters as the family finally got to sleep around two-thirty in the morning.

Karen got up early, took a shower and went searching with David for Al and Cathy. John followed her example, and grinned as he looked through the window to the pool outside the motel. There they were. Al, Cathy, and Karen sitting by the pool while David and Chris were enjoying the water.

“What a sight for sore eyes!” yelled John as he walked outside to greet everyone.

“So, how’s Milford?” kidded Al. “I hear you want to move there.”

“It’s nice,” John countered sarcastically. “We especially like the area around exit 20.”

“Where’s Peter?” interrupted Karen.

“Take a wild guess!”

“I know—he’s still sleeping.”

“You’re a psychic,” said John.

Karen and John retold the tale of adversity while David and Chris played in the pool.

“It is so good to see you folks,” said John. “I’m amazed we made it this far.”

"I have to hand it to you guys," said Cathy. "I'm not sure we would have done the same thing if it had happened to us. We probably would have gone home."

"Thanks," replied John. "We kept wondering the same thing. But one thing led to another and here we are. Sorry to shift subjects, but did you guys eat yet?

"No," answered Cathy. "We figured you folks would get here very late so we wanted to let you sleep. Since it's late, let's check out of the motel and go next door for something to eat."

All the adults agreed while the boys slowly dragged themselves out of the pool. As Karen, John, and their wet son David headed back to the room to pack, they found Peter wandering the corridors looking for everyone.

"I thought you would still be asleep," said Dad. "Let's pack up and head over to the restaurant."

Peter glanced at David's wet bathing suit but never complained about missing his opportunity in the pool. "Sounds good to me!"

The relaxing breakfast and reunion with close friends was a godsend. The adults continued to catch up on all the latest news while the boys joked around. Unbeknownst to the adults, the kids ate all the jelly packets on the table. "What are you guys doing?" asked Karen. "We do feed you, you know! Breakfast will be here in a few minutes." The three of them sheepishly apologized as they turned to giggle at one another.

As the meals arrived, Karen asked if they could have more jelly for their toast. The waitress thought nothing of it and asked if anything else was needed. As she left to retrieve the jellies, the boys started to giggle once again. "If this is their outlet for all the stress that occurred over the past twenty hours, it's a small price to pay," said Karen.

"About three more hours and we should be there," said John as the family climbed into the truck. Unfortunately, it took longer than everyone thought. The U-Haul and camper finally pulled into the campground around 3:30 p.m. Driving toward the waterfront campsite, they noticed people pointing at the truck and laughing. Karen rolled down her window to hear one person say, 'They sure bring everything with them,' and another voice said, 'I wonder if they brought the kitchen sink.' John looked at Karen, shook his head and smiled. "If they only knew what we've been through."

Al guided John as he backed the tent camper into position. The truck was unhitched and moved to one side. Al and Cathy set up their tent while John raised the pop-up camper. They hung a large tarp over the picnic tables on the adjoining sites while Karen and the boys removed everything from the back of the U-Haul. When all was done, the boys quickly found the lake. And so the week began.

The vacation was terrific despite the continual shifting of adversity and good fortune. The second night of the trip was cold and John developed a sore neck, which lasted several days. And the repair shop was having little luck locating a replacement transmission. But on the positive side, John and Karen found a local U-Haul dealer very close to the campground. He told them they didn't have to return the truck to Bangor. This was great news because the family had already used up their allotment of miles and any additional miles would cost fifty cents per mile. As the pendulum swung back, John's trick knee became swollen from moving the camper into place. But as fortune would have it, he had packed his knee brace and would do just fine.

Repeatedly, the good and the bad kept changing places. Fortunately, the ugly never showed up. On Tuesday, John returned the U-Haul to the nearby rental company. Left without transportation, the Wilson family piled into Al and Cathy's Ford Taurus. It was quite an experience traveling with seven passengers in the car. Four rode in the rear seat and three rode in the front. But despite the squeeze, everyone was still friends at the end of the week. From swimming and kayaking on the lake to sightseeing, hiking, and riding go-karts, the camaraderie was special. But doubt kept its place in the group whenever Karen or John contacted the repair shop. They were still having trouble locating a transmission.

On the day before they left, Karen and Cathy rented another U-Haul at the shop near the campground. In fact, it was the same truck the Wilsons had rented in Worcester. This memorable week was finally coming to a close. But fate was not finished with the families yet, as a huge storm blew in through the evening. It seemed that this was protocol for these fine families whenever they went camping together. The storm filled the sky with lightning and was accompanied by a quick downpour. John got up and went outside around two in the morning to check on the tarp. Peter got up as well and went outside.

"What are you doing up?" asked Dad. "This isn't the safest place to be, especially in the middle of a lightning storm."

"I know, but I couldn't sleep and I heard you. How did the tarp do?"

"Apparently, pretty good, otherwise we'd be soaked right now. Give me a hand pushing this water off the tarp," instructed Dad. As they moved the sagging load of water from the tarp, Dad asked about the experience. "Since we're heading home tomorrow, what did you think of the trip?"

"It's been fun," replied Peter.

"Even with all that happened on the first day?"

"Yeah, even that. We worked like a team. Everyone did something to solve problems."

"We sure did," said Dad. "I want you to know you saved the day when you solved the hitch problem. I was at wit's end."

"Thanks, Dad, but it just came to me."

The next day was sunny and hot. Because everything was wet, both families waited before packing their gear away for the trip home. When it came time to leave, Al, Cathy, and Chris headed toward Claremont and the Wilsons headed toward Rhode Island. John, Karen, and the boys made it home around 7:00 p.m. John backed the camper into its parking space and the open U-Haul was left in the driveway. Because it was so hot, the family only unpacked a few items and went inside to recover. No one shut the front door.

"What's going on over there?" said Carol to her husband Tom in the house across the street. "There's a U-Haul in the front driveway, the door is wide open, and I don't see John and Karen's car."

"I can't imagine," responded Tom. "If you're so worried, why don't you go check it out?"

"I think I will," said Carol as she crossed the street to the Wilson house. "Hello! Is anybody here?" she called out through the open door.

"Hi, we're up here," said Karen. "C'mon in."

Carol climbed the stairs to find the entire family slouched on the sofas in the living room. "Wow! You guys look beat. I thought someone was breaking in. I told Tom that I'm not letting that happen on my watch."

Despite their tiredness, the entire family chuckled at Carol's remark.

"Thank you for watching out for us," said Karen. "It seems that someone has been watching us the entire week."

The next day, John and Karen returned the U-Haul to a shop that was only three miles away. Then Karen called the repair shop in Milford, only to discover that someone had lost the keys that were left under the floor mat. The shop towed the car into the repair bay so they could start the work. It wouldn't be ready until Tuesday. In addition, it would be necessary for someone to bring them the keys so they could check out any remaining adjustments and to test drive the vehicle.

John and Karen drove to Milford on Tuesday afternoon. Testing the vehicle revealed that everything worked except the downshifting from second to first. Brad, the owner, said he might have to get another transmission.

"You've got to be kidding," said John. "We drove sixty miles just so you can tell us that?"

"Just let me make a few more adjustments. I might be able to get it going."

"Okay! We're going to Wendy's for a drink and some air conditioning," answered John. "We'll check back."

Two and a half hours passed and the frustrated couple returned to the shop. "How's it going?" asked John. "Any luck? We saw you driving the car a few minutes ago."

"We might have it. The electronic controls on the transmission need adjustment," replied Brad. "Give us a few more minutes."

Amazingly, by 5:00 p.m. everything was all set. The Wilsons charged $1,125 for the transmission and tow on their overused credit card. As they traveled back to Rhode Island in their separate vehicles, they both wondered how they were going to pay for everything. Karen pulled into the driveway before John and checked the mailbox. *What's this*? she wondered as she headed into the house. John had stopped to get gas for his vehicle and was running behind.

You've got to be kidding! she thought to herself. *Wait till I show John.*

John pulled into the driveway about ten minutes behind her. Even before he had a chance to get to the front door, she ran out, waving a piece of paper in her hand. "Wait till you see this!"

"After that bill and all the money we spent on the U-Haul rentals, I hope it's money from a long-lost relative. We're hurting," he replied.

Karen smiled. "Well—not that good—but almost. It seems we overpaid our escrow for the past year and the bank is returning the overpayment. It's a check for twelve hundred dollars. The angels are watching!"

"They sure are," replied John. "The timing on this is incredible. I love you, sweetie."

"And I love you," replied Karen.

A House of Knives and Scissors

By Yvette Nachmias Baeu

She pauses at the cemetery gate before walking through. Her heart is beating so rapidly she is sure she can see it. An overwhelming feeling to turn back comes over her, but her feet are rooted to the spot where she stands. There are voices, sounds, and rumblings in her head.

Mary Linn Wolfe, a woman in her late fifties, is still lithe and attractive with an intense narrow face, cloudy blue eyes, sharp, penetrating features, and skin tightly stretched over quite good bones. Her ungenerously thin, blond-streaked hair is well-maintained, though she constantly fidgets with it. It points to her lack of composure. Dressed in a pair of fine leather boots and a well-fitting grey wool bouclé suit, she is an image from a time when women wore gloves and hats and nylon stockings. The beautiful jewelry she wears catches the light of the fading sun. This, in her opinion, is the attribute that fine jewelry must possess. If it does not shine, it is not worth having. On the middle finger of her left hand, she wears a four-carat diamond ring.

Visiting the gravesite of her grandmother is unusual. It is difficult to remember the last time she had come. The fact is, this detour was not planned. Driving through New Jersey on her way back to her current home in New England, she will pass the neighborhood where she grew up. She knows if she takes the next exit off the highway, she will begin reliving that time all over again. Is that really what she wants to do? The closer she comes to the exit, the closer will be her demons, and she knows she should avoid them. In the final run, she simply cannot help herself. When she passes the railroad station, she blinks, finding the past still intact. Her difficult memories roil around and confront her as individual episodes arrange themselves in her mind. She heads for the cemetery to present herself to her family, all of whom are long gone. She is the remaining link to this sorry but remarkable family. Grandmother Lindbrook made sure that the family would have the benefit of a family plot. Whatever love went missing in life would at least come to a cohesive end. Mary Linn buried her mother and her sister here. Where her father lies is a mystery that has never been solved.

Standing in front of her grandmother's grave, she wonders whether her grandmother had been aware of how her grandchildren were made to live. Had she any idea at all? In the fragmented stream of memories available to Mary Linn, she recalls the imperious woman who had a secret. Her grandmother's marriage to Howard Lindbrook had produced two daughters. One of those daughters, her mother, Ann Lindbrook, the other, her Aunt Georgina.

Grandmother Lindbrook was Mary Asheton before her marriage to Howard. Mary Linn was named Mary after her grandmother, and given the middle name Linn to link the past to the future. As for her last name, she often said that she never really came with one. Well, of course, she did, but she was never sure what it should be, since her father left when she was born. When Mary Linn married, she took her husband's name to settle that question. Both Mary Linn's sons bear the name Scribner, so they will have another story to tell, but they, too, will live in the shadow of the family dynasty. After her husband Grayson Scribner died, she wanted to call herself by some other name. While the early death of her husband was painful, she felt it might be time for her to find her own identity. She kept her first name because she needed to. Perhaps she was trying to mend the branch that broke off completely from that particular tree. She briefly considered the last name of her so-called stepfather, *Shiner*, or possibly her real father, whose name she only learned when she turned fourteen.

Mary Linn often told the story this way: "My father walked out on the family just as I was being born. He abandoned them and me because I had been born." Matthias Woolferstone (with two O's) was her father's name. So perhaps she would call herself Mary Linn Wolfe with one O, dropping the other O because he had dropped her. Her mother would sometimes talk venomously about him, but at other times she would call him a prince. He was a tailor! A princely tailor, because he made clothes for princely people, just as his father before him had. The prince had left her and their children. He was also a drunk. Her mother frequently looked Mary Linn in the eye and skewered her with the accusation "*he left because you were born.*" That phrase stuck with her. She was a six-pound baby girl who had the power to send men away.

Now Grandma, Grandpa, Mother, Aunt Georgina, Father, Stepfather, as well as her older sister Maddie are dead. Maddie's sons have managed to stay alive. One of them lives prosperously somewhere in Australia, the other is rapidly following in his mother's unfortunate tradition. He is addicted to anything consumable.

It is not surprising that there are no flowers on Grandmother Lindbrook's grave, nor any on her mother's or Maddie's. Who would put them there? She didn't bring any, either. She picks up a small stone and puts it on her grandmother's headstone. She has no idea what the significance of this gesture is, but she has often seen it done in movies. Maddie's grave is next to their mother's. She stares down at the inscription on the headstone, *Madeline Woolferstone, 1938-1976. She died for want of love.* Mary Linn looks at her left hand and slowly removes the ring. It had caused so much hateful talk and months of legal battles, all of which Mary Linn had finally won, but the two sisters never spoke again. She digs a small hole with the heel of her boot and buries the ring in front of Maddie's headstone while a gust of wind gathers dried leaves and settles them on top of the covered patch of earth. Moving on, she greets her mother, whispering the words, "I forgive you," wanting to let go of the bitterness that remains from a youth that had been constructed by all these women.

Staring down at her mother's grave, she lets the breeze that has begun to strengthen encircle her as she falls to her knees and cries, "I forgive you. I am trying to forgive you," saying the words over and over again. When she returns to her car, she is determined to leave her story there in the bedroom of the dead. Turning on the ignition, she looks straight ahead, but the road is a blur, and her face is wet with tears. She pulls into the now-deserted train station recalling another defining childhood moment.

The businessmen had been picked up in their family station wagons: wives, children, and the family dogs all there to meet their husbands and fathers at the commuter train. Mary Linn remembers the scene. The wives slid over to the passenger side. The husbands took their place behind the wheel, put their briefcases in the back, reached over and gave their wives a kiss on the cheek, just a peck, not a real movie kiss. Then they looked back at the children, patted their heads, and the dogs barked for attention. They drove off and everything grew quiet again.

She vividly recalls that day, waiting for hours for her father to come to see her. He promised he would come. She thought he would come and save her. She wanted him to save her. But one after another, the trains from New York came and went. He never showed up.

The station parking lot is silent now, except for Mary Linn's wail, "*Why didn't you come*" which turns into shouts and attacks on the steering wheel. There is no one there to hear or listen to her. Mary Linn begins to gasp, swallowing breaths, trying to compose herself. She breathes deeply in an effort to calm herself down. She stares blankly at her memories, slowly starts the car and heads for home.

***

I arrive at Mary Linn's house on a summer's afternoon. I want to hear her story if she will tell it. People have strong opinions about her. We had been friends for years, but for a long time, I lost track of her. What I remembered was that she lives in a house that she and her husband built. I knew she had two sons and a husband, a professor, who passed away some time ago. I learned that now she is a practicing psychologist. There are many opinions about her. People have strong feelings. I want to make some sense of why she has the ability to make people angry and why she often alienates them. Now that we have resumed a tentative friendship, I want to find out the reason she makes people want to take sides. I would like to be a friend but have some reservations.

By the time I get there, everything about the day feels like it has already been used. We sit at the lone table on her deck sipping wine. The fishpond's waterfall gurgles continuously in the background and I look out at the backyard admiringly. Though calling it a yard seems wrong. It is more than a yard, it is a garden and even more than that, it seems to me it is a statement of endurance, of obsession and love, reflecting the need on Mary Linn's part to be the best. The flow and natural choreography of Mary Linn's garden had been carved out of the forest of second or third growth trees so prevalent in this area. Now it is a beautiful flowing vista of flowers and trees surrounded by a soft green cover.

I can almost feel the scrutiny of Mary Linn's obsessive weed picking, like a continuous tic that tugs at this small masterpiece. I observe her face looking over her beautiful canvas. It is not a tender, loving, or peaceful gaze, but a critical searching, as if she can see every small imperfection in herself, through every weed that has not yet been pulled out, in every bed of flowers that might not be thriving. Her need to enjoy the beauty she has created is hamstrung by her overwhelming need to be perfect. The wind picks up and the trees begin to sway. The sun has started to cast shadows on the perfect lawn. In the background, I hear the mournful sound of a cooing dove. The landscape strikes no false notes.

We have been sitting here for about an hour. When we finish one bottle of wine, we casually start a second. Her monologues and stories have always been told so vividly, and she has an uncanny ability to caricaturize and mimic her subjects with pointed accuracy. I hope to capture that quality by recording as much of her story as possible. I believe her story is worth hearing. I cautiously direct her to begin. "Talk about anything," I suggest. "See what comes." Her stories have often transported me into the dank cell of her mind she sometimes lives in, but still I coax her into sharing more. Picking up her glass, she takes another sip of wine, lights a cigarette and begins.

"I always thought of my grandmother as her fine china and the rococo silverware she kept in the carved hardwood drawers, lined with felt that smelled of cedar and mothballs. The fine old-fashioned china and linen have now come down to me, though I rarely use them. I see my grandmother now only as the sepia photographs, somewhat frayed and faded in the top drawer of my bedside table. She was a woman of wealth and class, who could not stop herself from dipping into the brandy bottle or for that matter, developing rushed and clandestine relations with delivery boys. She was a secret drinker. She thought no one knew her secret because she topped off the bottles every day with the brandy brought in by a parade of delivery boys from the liquor merchant. I learned about my grandmother's secret life quite by accident when my mother, complaining about her life in a fit of tears, sniveled out grandmother's terrible secret. Grandmother Lindbrook's reputation was shredded by my mother's tongue. My mother often railed against everything when she was low on cash and full of booze. It was her way of expressing her hateful dissatisfaction with her life. My mother's outbursts were loud and vicious. These fits usually happened after a particularly hard day of drinking. She was not a nice drunk. At five feet eleven inches, she could do and often did, quite a bit of damage when she took herself to the local bars. She would start fights and brawl like the best of them. I recall that I sometimes accompanied my stepfather when he bailed her out of jail after she got arrested, or when he managed to drag her out of a bar before she was.

"Then there were those afternoons when we had to dress up like proper little girls and visit Grandma Mary. My mother's family, the Lindbrooks, was an old American family, living in an appropriately large house with room upon room filled with the modern trappings of the day, and stuffy remnants of the past. Whenever I visited my grandmother, I had to practice the manners and eccentricities often found in families of good breeding.

"My mother would parade us in front of her mother as if to say, 'see what a good mother I am?' She would fuss over us and tell us that we were to be very quiet and we must be very good. She would prepare us for the afternoon's visit with a litany of don'ts and, of course, I managed to do most of the don'ts. I was instructed not to touch anything, not to talk too much or too loudly and I was not to stumble and fall, and under no circumstance was I to chew with my mouth open. She cautioned us never to take more than one piece of cake and when we did, we must only nibble on it.

"It was imperative for Mother to remain on the good side of her parents because they were her primary source of income. Grandfather gave my mother and stepfather money to buy a house. It was a nice house in a neat little suburb in New Jersey. A town replete with front lawns, young families, dogs, and station wagons. It never occurred to Grandfather that Mother might not have enough money to furnish it, so while the outside looked respectable enough, the inside was nearly bare. What money did come my mother's way was often used to sustain her drinking habit and that of her current boyfriend."

Mary Linn stops. She fiddles with a pack of matches, gathers up her hair and fixes it behind her head with a comb. I do not say anything because I do not want to interfere with her mood. After a time I can see another memory surfacing as her face takes on a faraway look.

"I used to sleep in Mr. Nelson's barn when I ran away from home after getting beaten up. I would often run away for as long as I could. Eventually I would give in and go home, because I got cold or hungry or tired—mostly hungry. That's why I have this thing about food now. I'll keep food until it is rotten and even then I have a hard time throwing it out. Ask my sons. It's the subject of many of their jokes. It is from being hungry most of my childhood. I'd do things like pull the grass out, because if you pull the shaft out slowly, you can eat the bottom of the blade, which is soft and moist. I ate a lot of stuff like that. Once I found a chicken farm, and I'd take the eggs, but I never took the ones they could sell, just the broken ones."

There is another long pause before she begins again. I have receded into the background of her consciousness.

"When my parents beat me, which started in the fourth grade and continued until I got old enough to protect myself, and old enough to leave home—nobody intervened. 'Mind your business' was a theme at the Al-anon sessions I used to go to in my attempt to get my family's drinking problem under control, or at least for me to survive theirs.

"You know how people say, mind your own business? Well, I just can't do that. My instinct is to say, 'don't just sit there, do something!' But at Al-anon they would say, don't do anything, just sit there. One has to accept things as they are."

There is a slight pause in her thoughts. She looks over at me, wondering if I understand her.

"Here is an example of what I mean. Say you are on a train, staring out the window, watching the scenery go by. Just for the sake of discussion, you see a tethered cow out in the field, and there is no grass around the cow. The ground is bare. You have no idea how long the cow has been out there. Here is what I would be thinking—*someone should move the cow*. The question is, should I be the one? Should I bash the window out, jump off the train, yell at the farmer, and move the cow? Apparently not! What I was instructed to do is observe and do nothing. Meanwhile, I know the cow needs to be moved. I can continue to watch the scenery, look at the lovely flowers, sit there, and do nothing. Well, damn it, that is too tough for me. I try to control myself. I must not stop the train. I must not start to cry or scream that the cow has no food! That sort of action will get me nowhere. The truth is, I am not fully alive unless I am moving everyone's cow. I know I can't run everything. I need to mind my own business. Like the policeman who was minding his own business when there was clear evidence that I had been beaten by my drunken stepfather. Mind my own business, like the neighbors that watched while my stepfather, drunk as a lord, chased me out of the house and flung a shovel at me, causing me to lose a bucket of blood. The neighbors were minding their own business when I fell down. What did they do? Nothing! Nothing! Like the teacher who refused to see my bleeding legs. It wasn't their business. Well, for better or for worse, I am not like that! My God, if that cow needs help, I will make the conductor stop the train! I am going to find the farmer and make that son of a bitch move his cow!"

Mary Linn looks at me, as if to scrutinize my reaction to what she has just said and then begins to laugh at herself. We are both laughing at the images she has created. But she grows quiet and looks at me cautiously.

"Here is something else I have never told anyone. Some nights I would creep up to the neighbor's house and look into the window while they were having dinner and pretend I was part of their family. I always wanted to be a part of a real family, part of other people's lives. I wanted to be a ME."

There is a long silence. I notice the light beginning to change, as if her story has brought down the day and made the nightfall.

"Well, Mary Linn, I say to myself these days, 'you have not done a very good job of living.' I am a middle-aged grandmother now and I still have no idea who I am. Isn't it laughable? I find myself embracing the image of a poor little rich girl who can't find any reason to be happy. Other times I am an angry bitch who will forever feel devalued and ignorant and apologetic. At the same time, I will get angry because I realize I don't know much of anything. I defiantly hide that weakness because I hate feeling ignorant. I continue to accuse those wretched people who were my parents for all that I am now. I barely had a chance to go to school. Now, I have so few references. I don't have any idea about what the people around me are talking about. The fact that I managed to earn a master's degree after fifteen years of struggling did nothing to make me feel any smarter. Someone else might have been proud of this accomplishment. I just beat myself up because it took so long."

Her monologue has been flowing now without any prompts from me. She does not notice that I have been stunned into silence. I had no idea she came from a house of knives and scissors that had cut her so deeply.

"When I was just a young girl, I overheard my Aunt Georgina say to my mother, on one of her infrequent visit to our house, 'It's a good thing Mary Linn is smart, because Maddie, that's my older sister, certainly has all the beauty in your family.' It came as a shock to me that other people could decide what I was or what I had—and do it with such ease. When I heard that, I cut my hair off and began wearing men's clothes. I liked the way that felt. I could remain my own secret. The fact is, I spent most of my life using my looks to get along. I needed to prove that Aunt Georgina was wrong. To that end, I flirted mercilessly with anyone at all, but I always assumed people would see through me. I discovered that there were cunning ways to get what I needed. I would snare men into loving me, but that only worked for a while. What I still hadn't figured out was that I wanted unconditional love and respect, regardless of how I behaved. I wanted to be loved for no reason at all."

Mary Linn's emotional floodgate is now wide open and I sense that while I am sitting across from her, I have become invisible. I am paying attention to what she is saying, knowing that she needs someone to listen and confirm. I nurse my glass of wine and long for a cigarette.

"Foolishly, my sister and I thought we might become heiresses, even if we were malnourished heiresses. We worried that we would develop rickets or low brain function before we could eventually walk into the light of inherited wealth. Through some legal trickery, we were not included in the Lindbrook will. Aunt Georgina's sons, our cousins, got the lion's share of the estate. With grandmother and grandfather gone, and their legacy given to our cousins, my sister and I still hoped Mom would leave us something—like her four-carat diamond wedding ring. When she died, that ring became a battleground between my sister and me. The little that was left of my relationship with my sister was permanently destroyed by that ring. I fought her for it in court and I won. I still don't know what made me fight so hard. Maddie certainly needed it more than I did. However, Maddie was irresponsible, unemployable, and unrelentingly self-destructive, and if she had succeeded in getting that ring, she would have pawned it for twenty dollars to buy her next line of crystal meth. Beautiful Maddie was dying an addict's death, because even her beauty wasn't enough to get anyone to really love her."

As her stories spill out into the evening, I wonder if time is the measure of one's life. Her time is tangible now as she stared straight ahead. The young girl that she had once been seemed to materialize before my eyes.

"I am 58 years old, and still unable to figure out who is living in my soul. I have spent all these years trying to understand my past and change my future. I continue to feel the sharp pain of my childhood and I am overwhelmed. Isn't it time I got past it? While I am able to understand and help other people, I know I am still not steering my own ship. I often wonder, who the hell is?

Where There Was Darkness

An Excerpt

By Deb Zanelli

Marcus woke and turned to face the window. The curtains were pulled open to show a brilliant sun. Throwing the sheets to the floor, he stepped to the window and opened it. Fresh air washed over a face that was no longer unnaturally pale. Hospital sounds retreated as his memories returned. His past was covered in blood. His father had been torn apart. Marcus's head exploded. Then there was darkness. There had always been so much darkness. Marcus had awakened in an unknown place, one that smelled of death. The floor was slick with blood, his blood.

"It's too loud." Marcus forced the memories aside. Walking to the closed door, he listened to sounds he knew he should not be able to hear. His dusty hair hung about a face with sunken cheeks. Gray eyes narrowed as he listened to a nurse telling her boyfriend to deceive his wife one last time. It would always be one last time. Marcus heard it in the seductive tones of her voice.

He felt the johnnie stretch across his muscular chest and arms, and pulled it away to lessen the strain.

There was the smell of food being eaten by the old lady down the hall. He sniffed, shaking his head, smelling her years, the aging blood. He moved to the window, too swiftly, and pushed his hands into the sun.

To the quiet bed, the empty room, he whispered, "What have I become?"

The door opened behind him.

"How are you feeling, Mr. Rollins?"

He was smiling when he turned. “I am not Mr. Rollins. Please, I am Marcus and I guess I’m fine.”

“Don’t you know?”

“I don’t know anything.”

She returned his smile. “Your burns aren’t infected, so you can go home. Your friends are coming to get you in a few hours.”

He looked down at the gown he was wearing. “I have clothes?”

“In the closet. Maddy left them for you.”

“I didn’t hear her.”

“You were sleeping.” Dimples crawled into her rounded cheeks. “I’ll be back a little later.”

He watched her walk, her bright white uniform tight against ample hips, and he wondered if she had seen his darkness.

“I remember.” Gregor’s face swam before him. A light breeze pushed the curtain aside and once again he saw the sun.

A timid knock turned him from the light.

“I’m sorry to bother you again.” He saw her frown, concern etching her brow. “Are you all right?”

He could not face the concern in her eyes, and turned away. “I will be.”

“I’ll be right back.”

Her steps were too loud as she ran down the hall. In only moments he was dressed. One finger, and the window opened wide. Before the nurse could return he was on the street.

***

Chief Daniels was happy to see the desk before him littered with nothing. Looking into the mirror, he was pleased to see a thinner version of the man who’d sat behind the desk only a few weeks ago. His short hair was combed back, white but plentiful.

He smiled, thickset eyes over cheeks that had been heavier. His wife had often compared him to a bulldog.

He turned his smiling face to the ringing phone.

"Chief Daniels here."

"This is Abigail Hawkins, the nurse from Memorial Hospital. I was just in Mr. Rollins's room and he looked, well, he looked suicidal. I went to get the doctor. When we returned he was gone. I thought it best to call you, that you might know where he'd go."

"Thanks." He hung up the phone more loudly than he intended and received frowns from the officers sitting outside.

"Sharon." He did not wait for a reply. "I'm heading out, don't know when I'll be back."

He drove too quickly, grateful the streets were quiet. "I know where you're going."

The abandoned factory was a place of lost dreams, and now a lost soul.

Marcus was sitting by the chimney, a long piece of filthy glass held tightly in his trembling hands.

"What are you doing?"

Still staring at the glass, he snorted. "I should have known she would call you, that you would find me."

"So, you gonna answer my question?"

"I think you know the answer."

"Humor me."

"I'm here to finish what I tried to do the other morning. I have no life here." He spoke to the gravel at his feet. "I don't even know where to start."

"I'm coming over and no, I won't try to take the glass from you. Let's talk. If I can't convince you there'll be a time when I won't be there to stop you." It took Chief Daniels a few moments to lower himself to the wall. "Tell me. I'll try to understand."

"It seems," Marcus continued to look at the dirt, "that I have both too many and too few memories. It's all backwards. To live, I need to forget the things I remember, to remember what I forgot." The pause was unfilled as the silence grew. "Did you wonder what I did to escape?"

"I think I have a good idea and no, you don't have to tell me."

"I had tried so many times." A growl sliced through the air. "This." Marcus pulled the collar of his shirt open, showing a large jagged scar that ran from just behind his ear and ended below his Adam's apple. "Glass." The weapon shook in his hands. "Just like this one. I slit my throat. How could he save me from that? That's when he gave me his blood. He fed me, but never enough. I was always hungry, that unearthly hunger." His voice grew harsher. "I knew then what I had to do. I let him think I was glad he saved me, that I loved him. He didn't trust me until," his voice faded away. "I let him. I am so ashamed."

"He took me with him to make my first kill, to kill Maddy. He didn't know I had found that rat blood would do. Rats were plentiful."

Glancing at his quiet companion, he saw only compassion. "I was stronger than he knew."

Once again the quiet grew loud. Marcus shifting on the wall was the only sound. "You have nothing to say?"

"What can I say to that? I know you spent the next twenty years hiding. Rescuing people when you could."

Finally there was a smile, but it was not happy. "I did save some, but for the years I was with Gregor, I prayed he would leave me alone. He only did that when he had killed. The saved do not cover the cost of the dead."

"Now that I do have something to say about." Chief Daniels's voice grew harsh, colder than Marcus had ever heard. "You didn't make him kill those people. Don't do that to yourself. Hell, who *would* want to be tortured? My son Connor," he said, joining Marcus in his absorption with the dirt, "was sixteen when he died. Cancer, damn thing ate him alive. When I'd take him for treatments there were kids going into remission. I wished it were my boy, not them. Some got sick again. My wishes didn't make those kids sick."

"He was your son."

"It was your life." Marcus turned away.

"Cancer's a different kind of monster, but it's still a monster. If I wanted to be an insensitive prick, I'd say at least you got to outlive yours."

"It is…"

"I'm not saying it, I am not an insensitive prick, but I wanted you to see how we twist things around, make it harder on ourselves." He turned away from the chiseled profile and his bulldog face softened to that of a pug. Chief Daniels almost reached over, but he could see that Marcus would not appreciate the contact.

"Maddy," his voice caught, "thinks she loves me. She knows only the man hunting the monster, not the person. I don't know who I am, beyond what Gregor made me."

"The things you don't know are not who you are, they're just the trimmings. You are still the man Gregor couldn't destroy. She knows what she needs to. Give yourself some time. We'll figure out the rest."

"We?"

The chief barked out a laugh. "I'm in this for the long haul. Can't you tell?"

"Chief…"

"I told you to call me Ray."

"Ray. There is something I must tell you. I can still hear more than I should. I am too fast and too strong. I see better than I should."

"How about blood?"

"I can smell it but I do not long for it. I am hungry but blood is not on the menu. It is not so much that I don't know who I am, as it is that I don't know what I have become. What if the hunger returns?" The glass, still clutched in his hand, glinted in the sunlight. "I find it not so easy to kill myself now. I see her face, feel the hope I had when I woke. If I do not do this now, later I may not be strong enough. You would have to do it for me."

Chief Daniels shifted on the wall, as thoughts crossed his expressive face. "If you ask me to, I will. I won't let you live that nightmare again."

"You would do that for me?"

"For my friend, yes."

"I have no place to live. I can't go back to Maddy's and I can't get a place to live without money and I can't get money without a job. I have no skills, no education."

"Well, I can address those issues, but one at a time. I know a landlord who would be willing to let you rent an apartment for very little. The Baltic Country Gardens is looking for help. Once you get a regular income, you can hire a tutor."

Laugh lines crinkled around his mouth. "You have thought of almost everything."

"What did I miss?"

Marcus looked down at his clothes, now stiff with the dust swirling about the factory. "Clothes. This is all I have."

"You can get new clothes."

"I have nothing to purchase them with."

"How about the money Lenore gave you."

"I spent very little. Didn't need food, can't get a motel room without identification and travelling, well, no one wants to sit near a monster."

"You were never a monster." Chief Daniels rose, angrily stepping over to stand before him. "Drop the glass."

"You sound like a cop."

"I am a cop."

He dropped the glass.

"So what about the money?"

"I gave it away."

The chief raised one eyebrow. "Why and to whom?"

This time the smile was more than vague. "I thought it was better used by those less able to get what they need. There is a shelter. I have a connection." The smile faded and he once again looked away. "The shelter is named for me. T.O.I.C.S."

"Tell me what T.O.I.C.S. stands for."

"The one I couldn't save." The grey eyes that returned to Ray Daniels's face were softer than he'd seen before. "I don't like to talk of that. The doctor there saved me. It was not just the wounds. He is an honorable man. His kindness gave me hope. I gave him the money."

"I'm not rich, but I'd be happy to get you some clothes."

"I am not sure if this is truly a memory, but I think my father would not want his son to accept charity."

"I should think your father would not want his son to kill himself or run around naked, either. There is no sin in accepting a friend's help and if it hurts your pride…"

"What little I still have. I guess if you promise to let me pay you back."

"So, I think I have given you enough reason to try to live as hard as you've tried to die. And for Maddy, give her time. I think there's a future for you two. If not, there are other women."

"No one else would understand me so well. I could not tell who would believe."

"If she loved you, she would. But first there's helping you grow up." The upraised hand forced Marcus back to the wall. "I am a rather plain-speaking guy. In some ways you're a hundred years old, okay, more like my age. In some ways you are still that fifteen-year-old boy just discovering his manhood and in other ways, well, I can only guess that you are a normal, lusty thirty-year-old. It wasn't all that long ago for me. Couldn't get enough of Louise then."

The color rose in Marcus's cheeks. "You have succeeded in making me do something I have never done. No, that's not true. She was the banker's daughter. We were poor farmers. Not a good match. But she was pretty. I think it was in the barn. Her father was not so pleased. He sent her home, taking me with him to mine. My father and mother were waiting by the door. He told my father that I had attacked his daughter."

Chief Daniels held back his laughter. "I'm sure you weren't attacking her."

"She was willing. When my mother left the room, my father told me to pick a better spot next time. I think I was embarrassed but I don't remember." Once again he looked away. "You see, my memories return in snippets. I am awkward. I don't speak as I should. I think making friends will not come easy."

"I'm absolutely certain women will find you quite charming. You're not bad looking, brood withstanding. So shall we go? This place is depressing."

"I think I can guess at the landlord. Would he be named Ray Daniels?"

"You got me." Ray held up his hands, surrendering. Turning to examine the horizon as the colors faded, his hands fell to his sides. "My son, when Connor got sick, he asked me to build him an apartment. He wanted to live a normal life but he couldn't go far from us, not with the treatments. We built one in the back of the garage. It has everything you need. It's small, but free until your income is sufficient. There is one caveat. My wife will want to feed you. She still cooks for three and it would be good for her to have someone to care for." He expected a scowl, but found himself looking at a small smile curling Marcus's lips.

"I have not been cared for in a long time."

"Just don't let her mother you too much." He dusted the back of his pants.

"I am gladder than I thought I would be to leave this place. I didn't want my dust to be with his."

It didn't take long to get to the car and Chief Daniels laughed when Marcus opened the back door.

"You're a friend, not a prisoner. Front seat, please."

Once again Marcus blushed, the color looking good on his serious face. "The front. Perhaps I have come of age. Can I turn on the siren?"

Chief Daniels looked into smiling eyes.

"You said I was still fifteen, wouldn't a boy that age want to do that?" Chief Daniels nodded. "Did you tell Louise you're bringing home a guest?"

"No, and you're not a guest."

"I think my mother would have been angry if not warned of a visitor."

"I'll go to the door first. Now, my wife is a good cook, but whether you like the food or not I expect you tell her you do."

"Ray, I must ask this. What is it you want from me?"

A purplish look took over his face. Bushy white eyebrows drew together over dark frowning eyes. "If I didn't think you'd go straight back to that piece of glass, I'd throw you out of the car. I don't want anything."

Staring out the side window, Marcus refused to meet Ray's angry eyes. "I have not met many who didn't want something. I'm sorry."

"What about Lenore?"

"She wanted a trophy. I was to escort her, to be paraded as her lover, her fiancé, to anger her friends." He looked away. "In some ways I played the part. She tried to be kind, but there was a price. I did see kindness." His smile was lopsided, joined by a slow shake of his head, "It didn't come where it was expected. The old woman, the whore, they were kind."

"What about Maddy?"

"I think she wanted the nightmares to stop, to love a man in such desperate need of love, a relationship with the ending already known."

"Look at me." He waited. "I know that is not correct. Maddy didn't want anything from you. She wanted to give you the love she'd felt since she was nine."

The crunching of gravel was loud, and Marcus looked up to see they had driven to a small Cape Cod-style house. The garage was almost as large as the house. The grass, a brilliant green, needed mowing, but the flower gardens bordering the door were well-tended.

Chief Daniels saw Marcus looking at the door, its soft buttercream yellow a contrast to the robin's egg blue of the house. "Lou said yellow means welcome. I think it means paint me."

"You haven't changed your mind?"

"Look, kid, I got thick skin and I understand perhaps better than you realize. I won't walk away and I hope you won't either. Give me a few minutes. I'll wave you in."

"It is nice, with the gardens."

"Louise loves to garden."

"Perhaps she'll let me help. I like the smell of the earth, of growing things. You can take the vampire out of the farmer, but not the farmer out of the vampire." He looked to the chief's face. "Was it funny?"

"Not bad. Keep trying, it'll get better."

As Chief Daniels walked to the side door between the house and garage, the curtains closed and the shadow disappeared.

"She was watching." Marcus found that by concentrating on the buzzing garden bees, he was able to block out the conversation he did not want to hear. "Can I control it?"

"I am chastised but you are welcome. Just give her that goofy smile and she'll love you forever."

"Goofy?"

"Quite." Eyebrows once again rode high in his broad forehead. "Want to fill me in?"

"Talking to myself. I think I learned how not to hear what I should not. I will practice." He unwound, climbing out of the car. "Seems your seat does not have enough room for my long legs. It's good I'm skinny."

"You won't be for long. Louise will do her absolute best to fatten you up."

"A fat vampire."

"You're not a vampire, so stop that right now."

"Yes, Daddy."

"I'm gonna spank you."

He quickly turned away, once again staring at the garden lush with color. "You have made me happy in a way I haven't known in a long time."

Marcus was introduced to a woman whose auburn hair, streaked with white, topped a somewhat angular face. Brown eyes flecked with grey examined him.

"So you're the man who's been driving my husband crazy."

"I…"

"Don't worry. It wasn't your fault." A smile softened her features. "Being a little crazy is good for him. Come in. I shouldn't keep you standing on the stoop."

"We surprised you. I'm sorry. It was impolite."

"Shush, boy."

"I'm not a boy. Old as your husband, I think."

"You look younger." She grinned and her eyes lit with mischief. "Let's try to figure out your true age. When were you born?"

"No idea," Marcus shrugged.

"That's okay, I have my ways. You were fifteen when..." She saw his grey eyes grow stormy. "Forget it. It's not important."

"I was. He had me thirteen years. I hunted him for twenty. I think, even without finishing high school, I can do the math. It was my favorite subject." For a moment he looked confused. "I liked to help my father with the books. I am about forty-eight now. Surely that is older than you."

She grinned and shook her head. "You didn't tell him our ages. That means I can lie to him. I won't, but first you must promise not to tell anyone."

"Of course. You're twenty-nine."

"I'm five years older than you. And Ray, well, he's a couple of years older than me."

"Fifty-three, fifty-five. We're young."

"You are. Those twenty years don't count. You didn't age and no one is gonna believe you're forty-eight, so to all but a few you're five years older than Maddy. You were there when she was attacked. You can pass for thirty-four."

He peeked past her into the kitchen. "Smells good."

"Lunch is almost ready. Ray, why don't you show Marcus the apartment?"

"This way, young man. The door's right off the kitchen."

"Did he live here long, your son? I'm sorry. I see that it makes you sad to think of him."

"No, I mean yes. It makes me sad but it's a fair question. Connor never moved in. The cancer spread too fast. He'd be happy to see someone live here. He'd like you. This is the kitchen. It's small but it has everything. The stove even has an oven. Connor loved baking cookies. There's a coffee pot and microwave. A set of dishes, silverware for four, some pots and pans and a decent amount of utensils come with it. No dishwasher."

"I'm a dishwasher." He stopped, sucking in his breath harshly. "My sister dried the dishes. She always made me wash them."

"The table's a drop leaf."

"Drop leaf?"

Ray's eyes crinkled. "It's kind of fun having to explain everything to you. Pull up the sides and a table for two becomes a table for four. The kitchen opens to the all-purpose room. It's a bit oddly shaped, but big enough. That couch is a day bed. As a living room, there's a bookshelf big enough for a TV. There are side tables and a footstool. As a bedroom, there's a closet with some place for hangers and some drawers. Closet's small. Conner was going to leave a lot of his things in the house."

"I don't have a lot of things. It will have much room for me." He grinned. "I think I didn't say that quite right."

"Good enough, I got it. Over there is the bathroom. Toilet, sink, and shower. There's a cabinet for the toiletries you don't have."

"I think we should buy soap." Marcus wrinkled his nose. "I shaved with a knife and used it to hack at my hair. I went to a barber once. He was too afraid to take the razor to me. He went to the back to get something and I took the razor. I've often wondered what I did with it."

"We'll add a razor to the shopping list. Over here is a stackable washer and dryer. There was a time when I thought my son would get better and I wanted him to be able to care for himself."

After a few quiet moments Marcus pointed to the washing machine. "I must learn to do laundry. I will need soap; there's so much to buy. I would like to get coffee. It smells good. It seems I'll never have enough money to repay the debt I owe you."

Chief Daniels looked out the window to the backyard. "I'm going to confess, now that I have you here, I do want something from you. I want you to have the life you deserve, the life I couldn't give my son. You're so different, you're dark where he was light. You need to learn to laugh. Even at the end, he couldn't stop laughing. I couldn't give him what I wanted to, but perhaps I can give at least a little bit to you. Will you take it?"

Marcus walked over to look out at the vegetable garden Louise carefully tended, her love evident in its lack of weeds, the large fruit blossoming in the rich soil. "I think I would like very much to be a part of your lives, almost a son. But now, if you don't want to see a crying vampire, who will be too embarrassed to eat your wife's wonderful meal, we should say no more."

"Good. Think I was getting a bit ladylike. One more thing." Ray pointed to a door facing the back yard. "It opens to a small patio. It's pretty private, except when Lou is tending the vegetables." He chuckled. "Don't know why she grows them. She doesn't like to eat them. Never could figure her out. There aren't any front-facing windows because the garage is there. Other than our coming and going it should be pretty quiet. What do you think, you want the place?"

"It is a palace. I have never slept in a place of my own." Marcus turned, looking at the day bed. "Does it have a pillow?"

"Of course."

"I have for many years wondered what it is like to sleep with a pillow."

A strange look took over Ray's face. For a moment he did not speak. "Glad you like it. Done deal. Now if I understand the rocking feet and the growling stomach, I would say you're hungry."

"I am."

"Don't worry. You're gonna be fine. I have a feeling about this. Lou made potpie, love that stuff. I always overeat, then she says I have to go on a diet. See if you can figure that one out."

"Like the place?" Louise asked as the men entered the kitchen.

"It is wonderful. I have a favor. I should not ask more of you."

"Ask away."

"Could you teach me to cook? I'm sure you are a good cook. Your husband looks well-fed."

Louise laughed, nearly spilling a glass of water she held.

"Already ganging up on me." Ray turned to Marcus, trying to look angry but only managing to look amused.

Louise spoke directly to Marcus. "I'll teach you, but first things first. You need a shower, a shave, and a haircut, then coffee, and laundry training." She turned to her husband. "You're taking him shopping. He needs food, personal items, and clothes. And fresh underwear."

Marcus moaned.

Her voice softened. "I don't know if Ray told you that I used to be a nurse. I know you haven't eaten in a long time. I'm not certain it's the same thing, but after a long period of starvation, a person needs to be careful how much they eat. See how their stomach handles it. I'm going to give you a small piece of pie. No salad, not yet. Raw vegetables can be tough on a stomach. If you keep the pie down, you can have more for dinner. There's plenty. Eventually I'll make you cookies and maybe apple pie. Unlike my husband, you could stand to gain a few pounds."

"Speak for yourself. Ouch!" Ray turned to the woman who had just slapped his forearm. "Been working out? That hurt."

She turned to Marcus. Placing her hand over his, she made him turn toward her. "I'm sorry. This is hard on you, I can tell."

"I feel like a…a spy, perhaps that is the word." He shrugged. "What you have is special. I guess I am jealous."

"Time to eat. Don't let it get cold."

Marcus ate, forcing himself to slow. It was so good, and warm on his tongue. The rich sauce rolled down his throat. He stared at the plate. "This is something no one should miss." He looked into Ray's eyes. "Worth living for."

The Soul Experiment

By Kevin Duarte

A white limousine entered the parking lot of the Gateway shopping plaza. The sun shone brightly in the Utah sky, evaporating the previous night's rain from the asphalt. Markarian Damascus and his driver, Greg Harper, exited the vehicle. Damascus was tall and fit. But his specialty was his aura, his presence, his confident demeanor, and his ability to influence the people he addressed.

The shopping plaza bustled with energy and activity, but Damascus completely ignored the shoppers and instead scanned the overpass that ran along North Temple Highway. The concrete structure provided one of many places the city's homeless could find shelter from the weather. It was mid-morning, and the occupants of this makeshift community were either still slumbering, or lethargic, even though their only recent activity was panhandling at the car show near the plaza the day before. Their efforts and energy were conserved for self-preservation. Survival was a skill the members had acquired because of circumstance and sharpened due to necessity.

Damascus lifted his head, basking in the luminescence of the sun above him. He carefully slipped off his overcoat and tossed it into the vehicle, revealing his exquisitely fitted Kiton blue mélange suit. A blue-and-white pinstriped shirt and floral medallion-print tie accompanied the ensemble, while his Artioli dress shoes completed it. Damascus looked down and brushed himself off. This was not a formal meeting, unlike the one he had arranged and attended just hours ago with the government officials at the Capitol. Although he had planned everything to the last detail, the encounter this morning would be the quintessential exercise in circumstance, and he hoped it would not be a waste of his precious time.

Damascus needed volunteers. To make this endeavor work, he knew that to acquire them, he would have to appear to sincerely care about the people he was addressing and make them feel that his intentions were trustworthy and genuine.

"Take the gun," Damascus instructed his driver, Harper.

Harper pulled open the jacket of his chauffeur's uniform, displaying a shoulder holster filled with an SVI Tiki-T pistol. Damascus had picked it out for Harper himself, not because he knew anything about guns – Harper was the expert in that regard—but because he wanted one of the most expensive pistols money could buy. Paying over four grand for a gun that was never even fired, not even on a practice range, was not what Damascus considered a waste of money. With Damascus, it was not about the functionality of the weapon, it was another illustration of his status.

As the two men started toward the overpass, Damascus noticed a scattering of clothing, tents, and makeshift cardboard structures that augmented the shelter provided by the overpass. Once out of the sunlight, the air became damp and humid, and the smell of human occupation permeated his nostrils. He tried to control his reaction to the stench, but his face contorted, and his nose flinched at the offending aroma. Damascus saw a bottle of Mad Dog 20/20 amidst fast food carry-out bags. The label read "Electric Melon" but the bottle contained a warm, bright yellow liquid with thin, congealed streaks of bright red blood. The owner of the bottle rolled over when Damascus walked by, his body covered in a mish-mash of clothing much too big for a man his size. The blankets rolled off the man, and new aromas added to the vile mix.

Damascus waved his hand in front of his face, trying to fan the scent from his nose.

"How do people choose to live like this," Damascus asked Harper rhetorically.

"We can leave whenever you're ready, sir," replied Harper.

Damascus started to turn, but his attention was drawn to the sounds of a radio. The shape and structure of the underpass amplified sounds that would normally dissipate, allowing him to hear the radio clearly.

"*Government officials met with executive members of The Center this morning, granting them unrestricted jurisdictional liberties while conducting scientific research. One of these projects, called 'The Soul Experiment,' is set to proceed as planned. Some Mormon leaders protesting the meeting insisted that there is no scientific way to prove the soul exists. But members of The Center claim they can prove otherwise. Reporting from the state capital, this is...*"

The radio crackled and the volume dwindled. Damascus scanned the area to find the failing device, as he knew it could not be the transmission. He spotted a group of three raggedy individuals with dirty faces and even dirtier clothing huddled around a radio. Accompanied by Harper, he headed toward them and saw one of the men slapping the side of the radio. The broadcast would clear up for a moment, then fade out again.

"You seem to be the engineer of the group," Damascus said to the man.

Startled, the man turned toward the two visitors, then cowered away. Men in suits always seemed to be a threat to the homeless.

Another man came walking toward the group. He stood almost six feet tall. His blue eyes peered through Damascus and Harper as he passed between them. He was not deterred or intimidated by the men in suits. The only outward evidence of his homelessness was his heavily worn clothing and his long brown hair.

"What's the problem, Barry?" asked the man.

"Hey, Anthony," said the man with the radio. He seemed more comfortable now that Anthony had joined the group. "The radio's getting all quirky and stuff."

Barry lifted the radio and shook it. The speakers came to life for a moment and then were silent again.

"Mind if I take a look at it?" said Anthony. Barry handed it to Anthony, then lowered his eyes.

Anthony opened a latch underneath the radio and pulled out the square 9-volt battery. "Anyone have a stick of gum?" Anthony asked.

One of the three reached into his pocket and pulled out a pack of gum. He hesitated, then showed it to Anthony. The man was slim and his face was gaunt, but he had surprisingly white teeth. The pack was flat and almost empty. There was one piece of gum left. With the slightest hesitation, he handed the pack to Anthony.

"Thank you, Steve," replied Anthony with a smile. He took the last piece of gum, unwrapped it, and tore a slim strip off the wrapper. He folded the piece back in the foil and returned the pack to Steve. Anthony folded the strip and placed both ends so they touched the terminals of the battery. He waited for a moment, and nothing happened. Anthony looked at Barry and shook his head.

"If the battery had enough juice, the wrapper would burn at the fold," instructed Anthony. He licked the terminals with his tongue. "Very little tingling. The battery's shot. I'll try and get you a new one."

Damascus and Harper glanced at each other, intrigued. Damascus leaned into Harper and said, "This might be our man."

Anthony replaced the battery, handed the radio back to Barry and silently walked away. Barry wrapped the radio in a blanket and stuffed it into a shopping cart next to the cardboard box that Steve called home. Damascus, trailed closely by Harper, followed Anthony for a few steps, then called out to him.

"What can I do for you?" asked Anthony. He stopped and faced the two men.

"My name is Markarian Damascus. How do you know these men?"

"Because, like them, this is my home," replied Anthony.

"You seem quite talented for a homeless person."

"On what do you base that assumption?" Anthony struck back.

"It's the impression I get from you," started Damascus. "You seem very resourceful, and you present yourself with a sense of confidence not often found in people who have come upon such hard times."

Anthony looked around at his group of friends, scattered among blankets and cardboard. They existed among pieces of rubble. To some, they were just as valuable. He looked up and down at Damascus, scanning the clothing that he guessed cost as much as a decent used car.

"I'm sorry, but I doubt you know many people who have fallen on hard times," Anthony rebuked.

Damascus ignored the comment and continued. "It's like you have a purpose. A spirit that transcends your circumstances and seems to drive you. I can almost feel it right from where I'm standing."

"Oh really…" replied Anthony, not flattered by the comments.

Damascus added, emphasizing each word, "It's almost measurable."

Harper let out a single, subdued chuckle and turned his head.

"I doubt that," Anthony replied.

"As do most people, my friend. As do most people. But I still think you'd be perfect."

"Perfect for what?" replied Anthony, his guard raised to a new level.

"You seem to make a difference in these people's lives," said Damascus.

"I try," replied Anthony.

"Must be difficult without resources," added Damascus. "Any family? Friends? Other than the ones you live with here," Damascus carefully added so as not to offend Anthony.

"I already have everything I need right here," said Anthony, patting his chest. "It's the only thing I've ever needed, and something that no one can ever take from me."

Harper looked away again, feigning interest in a pigeon that was flying beneath the overpass.

Anthony continued. "When I came here, things seemed better. Up here, you'd think that being surrounded by mountains would make you feel like you were trapped inside them. But I see them differently. It's as if the mountains lift me up. Everything seems cleaner, fresher, and clearer. Seems closer to God."

"That's just elevation," replied Damascus.

"Yeah, well, it had better be all I need," said Anthony. "Because right now it's all I got."

Damascus had heard enough. He cut right to the chase. "I'd like to offer you a chance to change things. First with you, then with your friends here, and then for many, many others."

"How many others?" replied Anthony, his skepticism increasing with every word that slithered out of Damascus's mouth.

"The world, my friend. I think together we can change the entire world."

Anthony paused, letting his guard down for a moment. Damascus had found a common ground with Anthony.

"What could you need from me?" asked Anthony.

Damascus replied with a jovial ring in his voice.

"It's not about my needs at the moment," Damascus sang. "Let's let the change start with you. It will be a show of my generosity. What can I do for you?"

"How about a sandwich?"

Damascus laughed. "That's for the short term."

"That's pretty much the increment we live by here," replied Anthony. "Our lives are day by day. I lost two friends here last winter. All they needed was some food and shelter."

Damascus stepped back, and with an overly dramatic motion that could have been considered condescending, almost bowed.

"As with all things, we progress in stages," said Damascus. He snapped his fingers, then turned toward his driver, his voice radiant. "Harper, some food for our friends here." Damascus turned his head back to Anthony, leaned into him, and softly asked, "How many friends do we have with us today?"

Anthony chuckled. "There are seventeen 'friends' here."

Damascus turned to Harper and ordered, "Make it happen."

Harper pulled a cell phone from his pocket and started dialing. He quietly wandered away from Anthony and Damascus, leaving the two men to talk in private. Harper knew that Damascus had nothing to fear from Anthony.

Damascus noticed Anthony's demeanor change. Although he had been trying to gain Anthony's trust, his actions had somehow appeared condescending to him. He felt he had accidentally jeopardized his overall plan and needed to focus on the goal.

"Why are you doing this?" Anthony asked. He hated charity because he felt it was never of itself. There was always a motive, a hidden agenda, and Anthony felt that Damascus had one. He just needed to figure out what it was.

"Does it matter?" replied Damascus. His demeanor was contemplative and quiet now. He needed to project a reserved manner because he felt that this worked better to convince Anthony of his intentions.

"Actually, it does," replied Anthony.

"You're right," conceded Damascus. There was always a motivation. Generosity was seldom given from purity. There were always expectations. And he had to make sure that Anthony did not discover his. "I'm doing this because the greatest thing we can do is be a gift to others. We should be a blessing to one another by giving what we have to those in need."

Anthony looked at Damascus's suit again. "I doubt you got to where you are by giving things away."

"We progress in stages," Damascus reiterated. "It took me awhile, I won't lie. And it was a hard road, but once I succeeded, I made sure to incorporate certain values into my organization."

The restaurant delivery truck arrived at the overpass and found Harper waiting. Harper took the food and handed the driver some large bills. The driver fumbled through a wad of wrinkled money to make change. Harper turned toward Damascus, who was thoroughly engaged in conversation with Anthony several feet away. He turned to the driver and said, "Keep the change."

Anthony distributed the food to his friends. The first few people he approached were wary of the offer, but the aroma of the food and the warmth of the hot sandwiches overcame them, and they soon huddled around Anthony for their share. As hungry as they were, they maintained a sense of order and courtesy, especially when Anthony repeatedly informed them there was plenty to go around. These were his friends, and they had an intrinsic sense of camaraderie gathered through circumstance and situation. But when push came to shove, civility would take a back seat to survival in a heartbeat.

After everyone had received something to eat, Anthony offered Damascus and Harper one of the remaining sandwiches.

"No, thank you," declined Damascus, waving his hands. "We are fine. More for our friends."

Anthony shot him a stern look, then offered the sandwich again with an outstretched hand. The friends stopped eating, some in mid-bite, and watched, as if suddenly becoming suspicious of the food. They looked at each other, then at the food, then peered at the two men who refused to partake of the meal that had been distributed to them so freely.

Damascus dispelled their suspicion. "Harper and I will get something before we head back."

Anthony shook his head and rolled his eyes. Handing out the last sandwich, he then sat down and unwrapped one he had taken for himself. He managed one bite before Damascus started his pitch again. He kneeled down next to Anthony, trying to create some semblance of privacy from the others.

"My offer still stands, Anthony," Damascus said. "Do you want to make a difference?"

"We just did," replied Anthony, raising his sandwich. He turned to his friends, who returned the gesture with smiles brimming across their faces.

"I mean a real difference," replied Damascus.

"Who doesn't?"

"Then come join us."

"What's in it for you?" asked Anthony.

"Everyone has worth and potential," started Damascus. "It's our duty, our privilege to provide love and respect for those who might have fallen on hard times. I'm offering you a chance, Anthony. You'd be a fool not to take it."

Anthony grew silent, and Damascus could see that he was contemplating.

"I'll tell you what, Anthony," continued Damascus. "Come with us. You can look around and see what my organization has to offer. See if it's something you might want to consider being a part of." Damascus stood up and shrugged his shoulders for emphasis. "If not, no hard feelings. And as compensation for your consideration, I'll send a different truck back here to feed your friends every day this week. What do you say?"

Anthony huffed a conceding breath. He looked around at his friends and thought that if his efforts could afford them even a temporary reprieve from their dire situation, it would be worth it.

"Okay," Anthony replied. "I'll do it."

"Wonderful," replied Damascus with a smile as he clapped his hands together.

Anthony wrapped the remainder of his sandwich, gave it to the friend closest to him, and then rose to his feet. "What do we do now?"

Damascus snapped his fingers and Harper immediately appeared at his side. He handed Harper a small roll of cash from his pocket.

"I have some more business to attend to in town," said Damascus to his driver. "Take Anthony and put him up in the motel nearby so he can get some rest."

He turned to Anthony and placed his hands on his shoulders. "We'll pick you up this evening, and then all grab something to eat before we head back."

The three men walked across the parking lot toward the limousine. Damascus held the limousine door open, allowing Anthony to enter. They drove to the motel where Harper checked Anthony into a room. Harper returned to the limo, where Damascus was using his handkerchief to wipe down the leather seat where Anthony had been sitting.

"Is he checked in?"

"All set, sir," replied Harper. "You gave me way too much money for a dump motel like this one."

"I know," Damascus replied, his face contorted with disgust. He tossed the handkerchief into the front seat next to Harper.

"Drop me off at the Capitol for my next meeting. Take the rest of the cash and buy Anthony some clothes." Damascus sat back in his seat and urged Harper to head out of the motel parking lot. "When you get back to the motel, make sure he's taken a shower. We have an hour's ride, and I don't want him riding in my limo again smelling like shit."

The limousine returned to the motel that evening. Neither Damascus nor Harper exited the vehicle. They waited a few moments while Anthony made his way from the lobby. He opened the door to the vehicle, entered, and Harper drove off.

"You clean up nicely," replied Damascus. He sat in the seat facing the front of the limousine, forcing Anthony to sit with his back to Harper. "The new clothes seem to fit you well."

"Yes, thank you very much for them," replied Anthony. He turned his head and gazed reflectively out the window. "Amazing what a difference a shower and clean clothes can make."

Damascus sat back and extended his arms to his sides. "Tomorrow will be the start of something big."

Harper knocked twice and slid open the window behind him. "We're about 45 minutes away," he announced.

"Where exactly are we headed?" asked Anthony.

"Why, The Center, of course," replied Damascus proudly.

"You run that facility?" replied Anthony, intrigued.

Damascus smiled and said, "I own it."

Damascus looked at his watch and nodded to Harper who observed him in the rearview mirror. With one hand on the steering wheel, Harper reached into the center console and, with his mouth, pulled off the protective cap of a hypodermic needle. He reached through the window and injected the needle into Anthony's back between his shoulder and neck. Anthony flinched, then fell over unconscious in his seat. Harper tossed the needle to the floor and adjusted his rearview mirror.

"He's out," confirmed Damascus. "Call the surgical team and let them know we're on our way."

Harper picked up the car phone and dialed. The call was answered immediately and lasted less than a minute.

"They're ready for you, sir," reported Harper.

"All that's left now is the experiment and some simple math," said Damascus.

"Math?"

"It's how we'll measure the weight of Anthony's soul," Damascus replied.

"Speaking of numbers, I'll make sure to stay under the speed limit," said Harper as he checked the side view mirrors of the limousine. "Don't want to get pulled over by the police with an unconscious body in the back."

"It's just the police," remarked Damascus. "Won't make a bit of difference."

Anthony's head reeled with pain as he opened his eyes. He felt the cold chill of the metal table against his naked body. The clothing that Harper had bought for him to wear had been removed. Turning his head, Anthony noticed tools arranged on a roll-out table that looked as if they came from an automotive shop. He heard a symphony of fans and vacuums, and realized that he was in a type of clean-room. The room was filled with medical monitors, vacuums, air-ventilation systems, and walls made of the thickest glass. There were robotic arms on tracks and microscopes near metal tables.

In the middle of the room was a menagerie of metal parts placed in an open container. The parts, Anthony noticed, lay on a scale. A technician, dressed in a clean-suit, complete with slippers and two layers of gloves, zeroed out and calibrated the scale, and then with the help of a pulley that looked strong enough to pull the engine from a car, placed all the pieces into the bucket. The technician noted the weight on a tablet, then nodded to a doctor who came into Anthony's peripheral vision. Before Anthony could ask the doctor what was going on, he felt the pinch of another needle in his arm and quickly fell into unconsciousness.

When Anthony woke the next time, he was surrounded by a team of men in full clean-room gear. His left shoulder and hip felt extremely painful, and when the doctor saw him grimace when he came out of the anesthetic, he looked over to Damascus, who was also wearing a clean-suit. Damascus nodded, and another needle was thrust into Anthony's right arm. Instead of knocking him out, the Demerol immediately eased the pain.

"How do you feel?" inquired Damascus.

"The shot is working," replied Anthony. "My left side was very uncomfortable. What did you do to me?"

"Necessary modifications," replied Damascus. Damascus turned to the doctor, whose expression seemed to contradict the response. The doctor almost turned away, but then faced his patient.

"Can you move your arms and legs?" asked the doctor. The doctor looked at Damascus, then back at Anthony. "Right side first."

Anthony lifted his right arm and bent his elbow so that his hand was in front of his face. He turned and examined it. The flesh was cleaner than it had been even after his shower at the hotel. Anthony bent his leg, lifting his knee off the cold steel table. He slid his foot and secured it against the table about a foot from his hip.

"Now remember the effort it took to do that," replied the doctor. He looked down slightly and hesitated.

"And put forth the same effort on the other side," interjected Damascus. Eyes widening, Damascus waited for the results of the efforts. Gears clicked and whirled, and Anthony watched as a metal appendage lifted off the table, and at the end of the appendage there was a mechanical hand with two digits fewer than the flesh and blood he had lifted on his right side. The pain in his shoulder immediately returned. Anthony looked over at what constituted an elbow as it bent in front of him. He saw the metal appendage attached to his shoulder, which was brown and stained from iodine.

"What the hell did you do to me!" Anthony screamed. The doctor took a step back from the table. Anthony turned to Damascus, reaching out with his metal hand.

"This is part of the project," Damascus reassured Anthony. "It's the most critical piece. *You* are the most critical piece."

"But why did you take my arm?" Anthony focused and tried to move his leg. Gears clicked and whirled again and as Anthony looked down, he was greeted by the sight of a leg made of alloys, cables, and small mechanical devices that responded to his nerve impulses. His eyes widened with both disbelief and rage. "My leg, too?"

"Don't struggle, Anthony," urged Damascus. "You'll cause bleeding, and we don't want anything to contaminate the equipment. If you get blood on the components, it could skew the results, and we don't want that."

"What results?" replied Anthony. "I want my arm and leg back, damn you!"

"They are of no more use to you," replied the doctor, gathering enough courage to approach the table again. "The nerves in your limbs are beyond repair."

"What did you do with them?" demanded Anthony. His rage increased, and his mechanical arm responded to the impulses by thrashing about. Damascus, wearing two layers of gloves along with the clean-room suit and mask, tried to hold him down.

"They've been disposed of," replied Damascus as he leaned into the mechanical arm and forced it to the table. The doctor readied another needle. Tapping the needle to remove the air bubbles, the doctor stuck it into Anthony's right arm. As Anthony started to succumb to the tranquilizer, he turned his head to his right, and saw the remains of his arm and leg in a flat plastic container on a table next to him. Iodine stains ran down the triceps of the arm, and the foot of the awkwardly folded leg draped over the edge of the container. As the room began to spin around in his head, he heard Damascus address the doctor.

"He must survive the rest of the procedure," demanded Damascus as he released his hold on the mechanical arm, which suddenly lost its strength. "We must preserve his soul or we will have nothing to measure and nothing to show for our efforts!"

"I'll do my best," replied the doctor.

"You had better! I've invested a lot of The Center's money on this experiment."

Anthony succumbed and his eyes closed again.

When he awoke, Anthony did not feel any pain. His mind focused instead on the swirl of red that seemed to infiltrate his peripheral vision. It was as if he were wearing thickly hued sunglasses even though he did not feel anything on his head.

But then, even his head felt strange. He tried to take a deep cleansing breath, but where his chest used to be, there was a heavy, square slab of the finest alloy metal. His mind commanded the appendages that replaced his arms to lift up and touch the metal surface. It looked cold and lifeless, but he could not feel it. He could not feel any skin. He gazed over at the flat plastic storage container and to his absolute horror, he saw the remains of all that made him human. His torso, cut in two down the middle, lay across the plastic box, leaning against a smaller piece of flesh adorned with long scraggly brown hair.

And his eyes.

His real eyes.

And in the window of the clean room, Anthony could see the reflection of two glowing orbs that had taken on the duties that were once fulfilled by his real eyes.

"What do we do with his body?" replied the doctor.

Damascus peered at the mound of flesh, blood, and bones, streaks of iodine smeared across the incisions that removed the flesh from Anthony's body piece by piece. Anthony's temple for his soul had been disassembled and was lying worthless in a plastic container.

Damascus looked at the remains. "Burn it. Every bit of it. Let's get him on the scale," said Damascus, with renewed eagerness.

Anthony's surrogate body was much too heavy for Damascus and the doctor to lift. Two assistants, also wearing clean-suits, hooked the replacement body to a chain attached to a lift. One assistant hit a switch, and the body slowly lifted off the table. Rolling along tracks across the ceiling, the lift carefully moved Anthony to the scale on the side of the room. Anthony hung helplessly in his metal prison, arms dangling uselessly as he was rolled over and placed onto the scale. The digital readings flashed on a nearby monitor.

The doctor's brow creased, and he looked uncertain. Damascus noticed the expression and inquired.

"Doctor?" asked Damascus. His concern was a fiscal one; he had spent a phenomenal amount of money to assemble this soul-prison, and he planned to promote the results as part of a televised special on the new cable access network.

The doctor spun from the monitor and looked at Anthony's surrogate body. "The weight is different."

"Perfect!" exclaimed Damascus, clapping his hands and rubbing them together. "That's wonderful news! Well done, doctor. You realize what this means? We've scientifically concluded the weight of the soul?"

Anthony rolled his head to the side, peering helplessly at Damascus through his red-infused vision as he realized the horrible extent of the experiment. Despite the shock of losing his flesh-

and-blood body, he couldn't help but feel curious about what they'd discovered about his soul. Then, a wave of disgust washed over him.

"That's just it," the doctor replied. "The weight is different from before the transfer." He paused. "It's lighter."

"Lighter?"

"It could be the margin of error from the scale," replied a technician.

"We just had it calibrated!" insisted Damascus.

The doctor looked at the monitor again as if to find different results.

"Options?" inquired Damascus.

"We would need to perform the experiment again to disprove the readings are a result of the scale's lack of precision. We don't need a body as elaborate as Anthony's, but we'll need something."

"How many times would we need to duplicate the experiment?" replied Damascus.

"A dozen, at least."

"Would seventeen work for you?"

Anthony's surrogate body flinched. *Seventeen*, he thought in horror.

The doctor thought, then replied, "Certainly."

"Get the engineers started on the next host," said Damascus as he headed for the door of the clean room. "I'll get you the bodies."

The Lady Next Door

By Victor C. Rudowski

MEET OUR NEW NEIGHBOR

The lady next door taught me how to kill.

I was eleven years old when I first met the lady, our new neighbor. I remember the date very well because I had just celebrated my birthday two days earlier, which was on a Saturday. So our first meeting would have been on the following Monday. My previous birthdays were just a blur, even though I know my parents made a big deal for each of them. There was something magical about my eleventh birthday because I received my first two-wheel multi-speed bicycle and I still think that it was one of the best birthday gifts ever. Most of my friends already had their two-wheel bikes like mine and I really wanted one so bad. My new bike made me part of the "gang." One might say that getting the bike was my first experience with "keeping up with the Joneses." I had already learned to ride by using some of my friends' bikes and now having my own bike made me "one of the guys." Riding my old 18-inch bike that originally had training wheels and no gears to shift was beyond boredom once I learned to ride without the training wheels.

Tony our mailman told us that the lady's name was Madeline Fitzgerald. I remember my parents saying that the lady got a "real steal" when she purchased the house. The previous owner was Mrs. Carlton who went to live with her son because she was old and couldn't take care of her house anymore; I knew this because I heard my parents talking about Mrs. Carlton and her situation. She was always nice to me and I really missed her when she moved away. I used to run errands for her to the corner store and she always gave me fifty-cents as a thank-you for my effort. The new neighbor did her own errands so my weekly income went from a dollar to zero. That sucked!

A few days after the lady moved in my mom spoke to dad about maybe making an apple pie for our new neighbor to welcome her into our neighborhood. So with Dad's OK Mom made the pie and on Sunday morning the three of us walked next door to formally meet and greet her. Early in my childhood I began to realize that my dad wasn't the most sociable person in the world, so I was a little surprised when he and mom reached out to our new neighbor, while not having argued about it. Maybe he was mellowing in his attitude towards meeting new people. We spent about twenty minutes talking with our new neighbor, mostly grown-up talk that totally bored me. She seemed like a nice person, but for an eleven year old kid, most older ladies seem nice. She asked that we call her Maggie rather than Madelyn.

As I tell my story the reader should know that I'm now thirty-five years old, having just celebrated my birthday a week ago. Unfortunately I'm living on death row at Terra Haute Federal Penitentiary, awaiting execution by lethal injection. Looks like I won't be celebrating another birthday. Three appeals of my conviction were denied over the past six years and my execution date has been set for June 15th, four weeks from today. I was told that my execution will take place at ten PM and there will be twelve witnesses in attendance, six of whom would be a friend or family member of the three people that I murdered and for which I was convicted. When I began my murderous career I foolishly believed that I would never be caught because I was so good at my business. Maggie taught me well and was always successful with her "eliminations." It took me ten years from age twenty-two to thirty-two to earn my reputation and be fully trusted by some of the most powerful men and women in America.

Enormously rich people accumulate enemies and people like myself are sometimes hired to eliminate their enemies. During my ten year "apprentice" period I removed fifteen individuals and earned almost two million bucks for my efforts. After being fully accepted into the "Elimination" club I was able to earn one-hundred and twenty thousand dollars for each elimination. For the record, my name is Dexter J. Cannon. During my childhood my family and friends began calling me Dex and the name stuck. I think that it's a pretty cool nick-name.

I was originally serving time at the federal prison in Florence, Colorado, but was moved to the federal prison here in Terre Haute, Indiana after my final legal appeal to the U.S. Supreme Court was denied. The justices refused to hear my case, so my last guilty verdict was upheld. I read somewhere that Terre Haute is the only federal prison that carries out death penalties. Why was I here in Terre Haute on death row? The answer is simple: I was convicted of killing an FBI agent and his wife and child. When the Elimination Club assigned a case to me, I was never told why the victim was to be eliminated. I was given basic information such as name, address, work location, and most importantly, a few pictures of the victim. I was also given sufficient expense money to locate, identify, and dispose of the victim. That's all. Do the deed any way you can and do it quickly. I was paid in cash via UPS delivery as soon as the victim was eliminated. I didn't even know the guy was an FBI agent. I didn't need to know. You should understand that I never intended to harm his wife and son. They were at the wrong place at the wrong time. Too bad for them.

There isn't much to do when you live in a 10 X 9-foot cell with a window that is 8 inches wide and an electric door that can only be opened by electronic remote control. Fortunately each death-row cell does have a 15 inch color television and a radio, together with a sink and toilet. If you're into reading, of which I am, there is an almost unlimited number of books that prisoners have access to. The warden allows us to have up to five books checked out at a time. They give us a one inch thick computer listing of books that are available and this list is updated weekly. There is only one list and it is passed around from cell to cell every three days. If you order a new book then you must also return a book. In one of the books that I read I learned that it costs our government $740,000 a year to maintain each federal prisoner and $1.26 million to maintain that same prisoner on death row. I spent six years in the prison in Colorado and just a year and a half here in Terre Haute. So it has cost the government approximately $4.44 million during my residence in Colorado and $2.5 million here in Indiana. WOW! Getting caught and prosecuted becomes an expensive liability to the government. I think the mentality of the "Old West" justice system was much better when they said: "Let's give him a fair trial today and then hang him in the morning." I guess the judicial reasoning back then was: if the sheriff arrested someone then they must have done something wrong. "Cowboy Justice" was served really fast back then.

KILLING IS EASY

Killing is easy when you have no conscience.

I have read that one out of every twenty-five people are considered to have Anti-Social Personality Disorder (APD). I'm one of them. I was born without a conscience. I know you are wondering why Maggie had such a negative influence on my life. Well personally I believe that she had a very positive influence on me. Why? The answer is quite simple—she was also born without a conscience and learned how to act out false human emotion when needed. Remember the saying: "It takes one to know one." She, more than anyone, understood the problem with my psyche and guided me along to maturity. She taught me numerous tricks to interact with "normal" folks during times of stress and anguish.

Maggie became good friends with most of the neighbors and she was always nice to the neighborhood children. I came to learn that she had never married, although she did date a lot. When I first met her she was thirty-two years old and she is still alive as I tell my story. I believe that she had much more influence on my life than my parents. To this day I don't believe that my parents fully understood my problem, or were even slightly aware of my problem. When my parents recently visited me here in Terra Haute they still could not understand why I did such an evil deed to total strangers. I chose not to tell them of my hidden profession because they were always great parents and should not be burdened with the truth. It was not their fault that I was diagnosed as a APD. In the human gene pool it can happen to anyone. It's not my parents' fault that I'm one of the four in one-hundred human beings who has no conscience. I guess some little gene got mixed up and helped me become what I am today—a cold-blooded killer.

There was an incident in my childhood about one year after Maggie had moved next door. This incident revealed the problem that I had, and only Maggie recognized it.

Sometimes on Saturday afternoons a bunch of us kids would play street hockey in front of Billy Stevens' house, which was just one house away from my home, and directly across from Maggie's. The makeshift goals were set up at the bottom of each of the driveways. Maggie and most of the parents enjoyed watching us play. We had two teams of five players each, plus a goalie. The goalie on my team was Jimmy Correia. He was a good friend and everyone liked him. He lived four houses down from Maggie. Usually the driveways where we played were empty of vehicles but on this particular Saturday, Jimmy's dad had left his pickup truck parked toward the end of the driveway, maybe about three feet from the back of our hockey net. His truck had a trailer hitch that was used to pull their 20-foot boat. Jimmy's house had a two-car garage, but sometimes his dad left the truck in the driveway.

Each game was about a half-hour in duration and one of the adults kept track of the time. Sometimes we didn't have a referee during our games so each of us had to be honest about calling penalties. Occasionally one or two adults acted as referees for us. I guess they just wanted us to play fair.

On that day our game was tied three to three with about two minutes left when the incident occurred. Our good friend Tim Johnson was on the other team and just in front of his own goal when he lofted the puck over everyone's head. It was too high and was going to travel well over our net, probably into the bed of the pickup truck. To this day we don't know why Jimmy ran backwards and jumped to try to stop the puck. He should not have even tried because the puck was just too high. He jumped up backwards, reaching for the unreachable puck. He landed flat on his back and his head struck the silver ball of the trailer hitch. The sound of the impact was unforgettable. We didn't know that at that moment Jimmy died instantly. The force of his fall detached his brain stem from his spinal column. Of course we wouldn't know that fact for at least ten days after all of the post-mortem medical tests were completed. By then, Jimmy had already been buried and I was just a few weeks from my fourteenth birthday. I do miss Jimmy but I don't grieve for him. I'm incapable of grieving for anyone. After that incident Maggie taught me how to project false grief.

I HAD NO TEARS FOR JIMMY

I could not cry for my good friend.

We didn't have cell phones back then so one of the parents had to run back into their home to call the police and rescue squad. It was obvious that Jimmy was hurt bad. We didn't know that he was already dead. Everyone had gathered around his limp body and two of the adults were trying to revive him by shaking his shoulders and pumping on his chest. I remember seeing his mother running across the street from their home. She was screaming for somebody to help him. Another adult began CPR and mouth-to-mouth on Jimmy and kept it up until the police arrived, quickly followed by the rescue squad. All of the guys on both teams had very troubled looks on their faces. Some were even crying. I felt nothing. It was like I was floating above the crowd, watching the event and being invisible. At that time I truly didn't understand that I lacked the normal emotional concern when another human being has been injured or killed. Maggie told me years later that this obvious lack of concern gave her the first hint of my condition.

I can remember numerous instances where me and my parents would be watching a movie on TV and there would be a sad scene where someone was injured or died and Dad and Mom would feel so sad for the person or animal in the film. I never could feel sad although I quickly learned to fake it after having been asked a few times why I didn't feel bad or sad. One example was when a friend's pet dog was run over and killed by a speeding car. Mom and Dad had tears in their eyes and talked about how horrible it was to lose a loved pet. I didn't feel anything. My brain told me "so what" and that's always been my attitude and internal reaction to such an incident. Over time I've learned to fake my external reaction for the audience. "Oh my god. That's terrible" is often my reaction in such situations. In reality I'm laughing to myself and silently thinking "Who cares? Not me."

There was a memorial service for Jimmy the following week. He died on a Saturday morning and was buried the following Thursday. Of the twelve kids playing street hockey that day, four of us were in the same grade as Jimmy. On Monday morning at school the principal had professional counselors speak to all of the classes a few times and anyone who was personally troubled by the incident could have a special session with the counselors.

Only one of our friends needed such help, and it wasn't me. Grief has always been a total stranger to me.

Both my parents had critical work commitments on that Thursday and were unable to attend Jimmies church service. They asked Maggie if she would take me to the service and she gladly agreed. That day, she and I had our first real conversation concerning my condition.

We attended the service and then joined the funeral cortege to the cemetery. At least two-hundred people made that journey to bury our friend. There were many tears that morning, none of which were mine or Maggie's. I really didn't care whether I attended, but she thought it best for us to follow the crowd. Acting like everyone else is a quickly-learned skill when you have no conscience. While driving to the cemetery, Maggie asked me a few questions about Jimmy and our friendship together.

"Did you and Jimmy spend a lot of time together, besides playing street hockey," she asked.

"Well I've always known him. He was one year older than me but we were in the same grade at school. He told me that he had scarlet-fever and missed the entire fifth grade."

"I noticed that you didn't cry like the rest of your friends when you watched the police and firemen trying to help him. Why no tears?" she asked with a serious tone in her voice.

"I don't know. I can't cry when people get hurt or die on television. I've cried many times when I hurt myself. I really cried bad when I accidentally banged my head against our garage door last summer. The door was half open and I bent down to go underneath it. I didn't bend low enough and "bang" I hit the door, fell down and passed out for a few seconds. When I woke up my forehead was bleeding and it hurt real bad. In fifteen minutes I had a 'goose-egg' like you wouldn't believe. Man, did I cry then. I had a tough time trying to explain my stupidity to my parents."

She laughed and asked: “So you cried from the pain, right?”

“Yeah, I guess so. I cried for being so stupid too.”

“Did you need stitches because of the bleeding?”

“No. It was just a bad scrape and it stopped bleeding after a few minutes and it healed in a couple of weeks. I walked around with a stupid bandage on my forehead for a week and a half.”

“Do you know that I perform volunteer work at the Community Animal Clinic?”

“Yeah. Mom told me about that. She said that you go there once a week to help out with cleaning and taking care of the sick animals.”

“Yes that’s true. Would you like to come with me some time to see the animals?”

“Sure. That sounds like fun. Can I hold some of the animals?”

“Of course you can. I’ll talk to your mom and dad to make sure that its ok to take you, maybe next Thursday, now that school is out. OK?”

“Sure. That will be super.”

The service at the cemetery lasted about thirty minutes. Everyone had tears in their eyes and Jimmy’s parents and his younger brother and sister really cried awfully hard. His parents thanked everyone for attending and asked them to pray for Jimmy. I did pray for his soul but felt no sympathy in my heart. I just didn’t possess the ability to care.

SHE’S NO FRIEND TO THE ANIMALS

I learned a new word last week: “Euthanize."

The following Thursday as we were driving over to the pet clinic she told me that the abandoned animals that were at the clinic were on a 90 day time table to either be adopted or euthanized. I didn't know what that word meant and told her so.

"Well after 90 days we need to kill the animal. All of the people who work there refuse to harm, let alone kill any of the pets, so I do it for them."

"How do you do it?" I asked.

"We have a small single-window chamber that holds about three average size cats or two dogs. I place them in the enclosure, close the door and then turn on an electric pump that slowly removes the air from the chamber. They die from lack of oxygen."

"Do they scream and try to get out?" I asked.

"Oh no. They slowly fall asleep and die in about fifteen minutes."

"That sounds easy to do. What do you do with their bodies after they die and why do the other volunteers refuse to do it?" I asked, trying not to seem too interested in the process. I really was interested and wanted to see how the process works. More importantly, I wondered if it would bother me to watch because I was finally coming to grips with my lack of conscience and wondered if seeing the pets being killed would have any effect on me. Evidently, Thursday was "kill day" at the clinic.

"We place the bodies in individual cloth bags and call a company that will cremate the bodies. The ashes are then spread on the grass of a memorial pet cemetery across town.

Maggie unlocked the door to the clinic and held it open for me to enter. She closed the door and asked me to follow her to the kennels. While walking through the various rooms I noticed that there were no other volunteers working. Maggie told me that they would be in around 1 PM.

"I need to check each kennel to see if there are red tags affixed to the doors. The red tags indicate that the pet inside will be euthanized today."

On that day there were two dogs and one cat waiting to die. We did the dogs first. She took one and I took the other, both mutts. Like she said, it took about fifteen minutes for them to die. She then gave me both of the cloth bags and told me to put the dogs in them. She had a roll of paper towels that she used to clean up pee and poop that the two dogs left behind. I guess when they die their bodies totally relax and they poop and pee when they finally die. The cat died the same way, only faster.

FINALLY THE TRUTH

Maggie gets paid big bucks to kill people.

We spent the afternoon together at her house and I finally learned the truth about her profession. We were watching a comedy on TV and when it was finished she shut off the TV and asked me to move from the recliner and come sit next to her on the couch. She said that she had something very serious to talk to me about.

"What did you think of me after seeing what I had to do to the animals?"

"I didn't think it was such a big deal. Someone has to do it. It didn't bother me at all," I told her. I felt the same way I did when my friend Jimmy died in that freak accident.

"Can you guess what I do for a living?" she asked as she reached out to hold my hand.

"Not really. I know that you travel around almost every month. Mom said that you do some kind of investment counseling, whatever that means."

She squeezed my hand and said in a hushed tone of voice "I kill people for a living. Does that surprise you and do you think I'm a bad person?"

It took me a moment or two to think about how to answer her. Should I lie and say that is a terrible way to earn a living.

Should I just get up and go home? Or should I be honest and tell her the truth?

"Well to me it sounds pretty cool. Do you get paid a lot of money to kill people?"

"You bet your little ass I do. I have over three million dollars in foreign banks and another two million in domestic investments. By that I mean American investments."

"Oh my God, that's great. I'm almost seventeen and will graduate from high school next year. I'm not sure that I will want to go to college if I can get in on something like you do."

"Well first of all, college is exactly what you need to complete if you expect to work for the people that I work for. They want smart people. No high-school dummies will ever work for them. What I do is very serious and you need to be very smart to get away with murder year after year after year," she said with a very concerned look on her face.

"Your parents told me that you are very good at math. Is that true?"

"Yeah, I really enjoy it. It just comes easy to me. In fact I help a lot of kids in my classes and sometimes they give me a few bucks."

"That's good. An Accounting Degree would serve you very well in this profession. You could work for a couple of years at a large firm and then open your own practice and do taxes. That type of job will give you the freedom to manage your time and perform a few elimination jobs each year."

"Elimination jobs? Is that what you call them?"

"Yes. When you receive a verbal contract or speak of the work we do, we always refer to contracts as "Elims," she stated.

Fourteen years have now passed since that fateful day when Maggie revealed her profession and explained how killing can be a very profitable enterprise. I'm now 31 years old. I did pursue a degree in accounting and had a job with a huge accounting/investment firm. I was there for three years doing taxes on the side to build up a clientele so that I could eventually leave the firm. Ten years ago, even before I graduated from college, Maggie began teaching me the art of elimination. And it truly is an art. Killing someone and not getting caught is very difficult and requires patience, stealth and an ability to blend easily into the framework of society. She taught me how to use all manner of handguns, knives, blunt instruments, gas and poisons, and most importantly, disguises. Each "Elim" is different and must be planned and quickly completed. I spent two years of evening classes learning self-defense and have had to protect myself a few times. Naturally, I won all physical challenges. Maggie also taught me how to break into homes and apartments using fake keys and other tools. I learned that it's easier to go through a door than through a window. Of course windows are not an option when your victim resides in a high-rise building, which is frequently the case because a large percentage of our victims are wealthy. I was about one year away from being an independent employee, which would have put me in the same category as Maggie. The last time I saw her was a week or two before I was captured. We went to dinner together and discussed some of our recent "Elims." What else can two sociopaths talk about when they are enjoying each other's company—sports, religion, politics? Hell no. We talk about killing because we are so good at it. In my last "elim" I made one big mistake and will now pay for it with my life. I spent a ton of money on legal fees and have almost one million dollars spread between a Swiss savings account and an investment account. Since I'm still single I have willed those funds to my parents. They're in good health and can surely use the money. It's not their fault that I was born without a conscience. My personal needs were never a big issue with me. My double-wide trailer in Sarasota Florida and my five-year-old Volkswagen Jetta will also be left to my parents. Maybe they will move down to Florida from their home in Rhode Island. I miss Rhode Island.

JUSTICE AWAITS ME

Let me tell you about my last elimination.

I tailed my victim for a few days before I decided the best way to kill him. I didn't know that he was an FBI agent and I never saw him with his wife or child. I found out later that the wife and son were away visiting the grandparents and returned home early on the evening that I planned to kill him. Maybe I should have waited a day or two and then picked a better environment to kill him. The group that I work for gives us as little information as is needed. I would have planned things a little differently had I known that he was FBI. I could have killed him in a more public area than his home. Of course I didn't know that his next door neighbor was his brother-in-law, who unfortunately is a state police captain.

After determining that there was no alarm system, my plan was to gain entry into his home around three AM while he was sleeping and disconnect the gas line leading from outside the house into his kitchen stove. The accumulation of gas inside the home would kill him in either one of two ways. He would die from either gas inhalation or from an explosion caused when he awoke and turned on a light or electrical appliance.

I easily entered the victim's house, disconnected the gas line and quietly left. I had parked a few blocks from his house and was walking away from his property when I heard: "Police. Stop. Raise your hands where I can see them." The rest is history.

That state cop arrested me on the spot. I learned later that he was on vacation and was leaving his home very early to go fishing when he spotted me walking across the victim's lawn. He kept asking me what I was doing and of course I refused to answer any of his questions. Soon more cops arrived and they placed me into a van and began driving me to the local police station. We were about two blocks away when we heard the noise of the explosion. As it turned out, I made a big mistake that night. A very thorough investigation revealed that I screwed up and left some fingerprints on the back door. No gloves. Stupid is as stupid does. The police would never have investigated the event if I had not been caught leaving the scene of the crime. It would have been treated as an unfortunate accident. My scheduled execution will not be an accident, and you can be sure of that. Goodbye everyone.

The Pact

By Angelina Singer

Anastasia opened her laptop to check for the latest barrage of emails from her highly unpleasant boss. She was working as an assistant in a law office, biding her time until something better came along. As the screen illuminated and came to life, she couldn't help but glance out at the bustling New York skyline—it seemed worlds away from the rolling, green Hollywood hills of her childhood.

Twenty emails? Really, Lucinda? I swear she's out to make my life miserable. Anastasia shook her head and then cursed under her breath, wishing desperately to escape her dingy office building and head outside under the crisp, clear, blue sky. *How things have changed... I used to think the entire world was an endless opportunity to make dreams come true. Now I'm starting to think that I couldn't have been further from the truth!*

Her phone buzzed loudly on her wooden desk, snapping her out of a silent reverie. "Yes, Ms. Orencia?" The feigned respect dripped from her lips like honey but congealed into sludge by the time it reached the receiver end of her cellphone. "Yes, I'll get right on that.... cream, sugar, no room.... But wait, wouldn't you need to leave room for the cream and sugar? Mhmm. Okay, yes. I'll figure out a way." Anastasia wasted no time in ending the call. Her resolve was weakening every hour from the wiles of that beast. How she wished to get away from it all, to a much simpler time.

Regardless of her unpleasant circumstances, she resolved herself to stay under the radar until the delicious moment when she had a new job lined up and she could finally drench that awful wench in her own putrid words. Until then, her lips were sealed.

Worried about being yelled at for taking too long, Anastasia began moving one stilettoed heel in front of the other as she entered the coffee shop.

"One *venti* iced coffee, with cream and sugar, please." And then Anastasia was on her way back to the office to deliver Cruella de Vil her caffeine.

Back at her desk, Anastasia decided to take a quick break and check Facebook as she usually did on the off moments when Lucinda didn't seem to need her *right away, o*r when she was too mentally drained to get any real work done. She opened the tab that was always stashed at the bottom of her desktop and checked the newsfeed. There appeared to be a solitary notification on her screen, a single red bubble above the friend request symbol. Anastasia clicked on it, and nearly stopped breathing. There, on her screen, was a friend request from a "Leonard Martin." *Leonard... Leo... MY Leo! How did he find me?* She immediately hit the "accept" button and sent him a message.

"Leo, is that really you?" The screen was still, until three little blinking dots appeared next to Leo's name, and Anastasia's heart filled with hope.

"Staci! I've been looking for you for a while now. How are you?"

"I'm okay, better now that I get to talk to you!"

"What have you been doing lately?"

"I'm an assistant in a law office in New York. Where are you?"

"I'm in New York, too! Well, for now. I've been touring with my band—we got a record deal about a year ago."

"No way! And how have I never seen you?"

"Not sure. But we should meet up. Are you free for dinner tonight?"

"Sure—how about 7:00 at Blue Lagoon?"

"Perfect! See you then, Leo!"

Anastasia clicked off her browser before her boss noticed that she was wasting time on social media. But she was unable to control the wide grin spreading over her face.

"Anastasia! What have you been doing? I asked you to file those documents twenty minutes ago!"

"I'm sorry, Ms. Orencia, I'll get right to it." Anastasia's sickeningly sweet replies never went unnoticed by her boss's ears, but the two of them shared a mutual understanding of a mutual distaste for one another. Civility was the one thing they *could* agree on.

Anastasia succumbed to the documents piled on her desk, but she couldn't stop thinking about Leo. For a quick moment, she clicked back onto Facebook just to see what he looked like these days. Based on his profile picture, her old childhood friend had traded the ripped jeans and band tee shirts for suave leather jackets and high-end guitars. Even his trademark shaggy brown hair was cut into a cleaner looking style, framing his chiseled jaw. He always *had* hated mainstream music, scoffing at the Hollywood sign as if he had a personal vendetta against it. But he didn't typically hold grudges, even when he could have. Like that one time that she *accidentally* pushed him off his skateboard when they were little and he broke his arm. Leo always had her back, regardless of what struggles the two went through. Like that one time she spilled soup on the mean girl at school and he offered to protect her until the whole thing blew over. They were tight, those two.

Anastasia remembered countless summers with Leo, going to the beach or sniffing out celebrities on Hollywood Boulevard. That is, until his dad got a job in Boston the summer after seventh grade, tearing Leo away from his friends and family in California to start a new life in Massachusetts, all the way across the country. The day he left, Staci hugged him in front of the moving trucks, and nearly didn't let go. With teary eyes, she waved good-bye. But with his impending move, the two had made what they thought to be a binding promise. Anastasia glanced down at the thin white line that spanned across her entire left palm and smiled. Sure, it hurt like hell at the time, but it was so worth it. She remembered that moment under her weeping willow tree like it was yesterday….

Leo carefully moved over to the branch that Staci was sitting on, and placed his arms around her small, frail frame. Her head naturally landed on his broadening shoulder, and they just sat there for a while, as the sun began its descent into obscurity.

"Leo?"

"Yeah?"

"We're thirteen."

"Yeah, I guess?"

"Yeah."

Leo began to fall, fast. He was tugged under the current of her emotions, her complex thoughts seeping into his own mind through a seemingly basic hug, an act merely meant as an attempt to calm the relentless demons inside Staci's head. "What if... I'm not good enough. What if... I never find anyone? What if..."

"Staci! What are you talking about? We're only thirteen... It'll happen when it's meant to happen. You wouldn't want to date anyone now, anyway. Thirteen is wicked young for that." Staci's face was covered with tears now, her face buried in the shoulder of Leo's often-washed tee shirt.

"I'm too timid to approach a guy... like ever. And I doubt any of them would like me..."

"I think you're pretty cool..."

"Yeah, but you don't count—you're my only friend... my best friend."

Leo was dumbfounded by the way she verbalized her attachment to him. It was completely out of the blue. He didn't necessarily realize how close they had become over the years. But then he came back to reality, and realized that her small body was tightly wrapped in his own—the two of them sitting there on the lowest branch of the weeping willow tree.

"Staci?"

"Yeah?"

"I have an idea."

"What's that?"

A devious smile crept over Leo's lips, a surefire sign of a crazy but awesome idea.

"So, what if I make a promise to you, and you make the same promise to me?"

Staci ceased crying for a moment, her tear-soaked face briefly separated from Leo's now-soggy shirt sleeve.

"What kind of a promise?"

Leo grinned.

"One that will ensure you won't be alone without anyone at thirty years old."

Staci's eyes lit up at that possibility, a chance to chase away her biggest fear as far away as the horizon line.

The sun was nearly below the Hollywood sign now, the rest of the sky answering back its daily swan song with a deep chorus of violet, orange, and red.

"If we are both completely alone at thirty years old... I'll take care of you."

Staci's eyebrows raised up with surprise. "Leo, what are you saying?"

Leo bit his lip, waiting for the right words to appear but half-wishing they wouldn't. "If we're both alone at thirty, I'll marry you, okay? There, I said it!"

Staci's face turned bright red, but Leo noticed a faint sign of relief emerge from the deepest core of her heart and then bubble up her pale, pure throat and into a tentative, unsure smile. I can't believe he just said that, Staci thought. What does this mean? Does this change anything now? I'm not ready for anything now...

"Really?"

"Yeah. I wouldn't... I wouldn't want to be alone either. But if either of us find someone else, then the deal is off, and I'll wish you the best life possible, even... without me in it."

Staci slowly nodded, but was still fighting a tiny bit of uncertainty gnawing at the back of her throat.

"But... nothing changes now, right? You're not going to... kiss me or anything, right?"

"Kiss you? Staci, I'm flattered but..."

She wasted no time punching him in the ribs this time.

"Leo, I'm being serious. I don't want anything to change, with this pact. Things will stay the same for now. Right?"

"Right. Nothing's different."

Staci breathed a sigh of relief, as if she was holding her breath the entire time.

"Okay, I agree. The deal is on. But can we make it official?"

Leo raised an eyebrow. "Well, you said you didn't want me to kiss you..."

Staci rolled her eyes. "No, of course not."

"Well... okay. I have another idea."

Leo carefully pulled a small pocketknife out of the pocket of his shorts.

"Okay, I saw this on TV once... if you're serious about this promise, then... let me slit your hand—"

"What? Why? Ouch. Won't that hurt?"

"Yeah, probably."

"You're insane!"

Staci turned away for a moment, looking off into the distance, and the rapidly darkening sky. "But I'll cut my hand too, and then... and then we'll join our bloody hands together and—"

Staci turned around to say what she knew he was thinking. "Share the same blood."

"Yeah. So can I?"

Leo motioned toward Staci's trembling left hand that was pressed tightly to her knee. Staci squirmed a little.

"You think, you really think that'll do it? That we'll remember? What if, what if we forget?"

Leo stared down at the knife in his hands for the first time since his impulsive suggestion, realizing the physical pain this would cause.

"Well, if it's meant to be, then we won't forget. It's just... a symbol of what we decided... if everything else in life changes, after I move away... at least this'll be the same. We'll always have each other, you know?"

Staci closed her eyes, took a deep breath, and then slowly nodded. In a small, uncertain voice, the word "okay" escaped through her lips, a nearly silent plea for a secured future, where at least one thing would stay the same. It was a small price to pay, really.

Then and there, as the sun finally reached its nadir, bathing their world in utter darkness, Leo gently lifted Staci's left hand off her knee, opened his pocketknife, and pressed the shiny silver blade to her pure white skin. The blade broke through her flesh, and called forth a crimson trickle which quickly became gushing. He cut her deeply, deeper than he meant to, marking her for life. She winced and cradled her surgically-opened left hand with her unharmed right hand, and waited for Leo to do the same. Carefully, but more swiftly to avoid unnecessary pain, Leo took the blade that was now bathed in Staci's blood, and broke his own virgin flesh as well. Against the logic of his first experience cutting Staci's hand, the blade cut him deeply as well, nearly with a mind of its own. Also wincing in pain, he brought the blade all the way across his left palm, bringing forth a veritable flood of his life-filled essence.

And then, as the dark night sky gave birth to the very first star, Staci reached out a very bloody hand to join with Leo's. Fighting through the stinging of broken flesh touching another opening, the two held their wounds together, allowing their blood to run together, pooling their rawest, most intimate substances together. Some even fell onto the roots of the weeping willow tree, marking its roots as the site of their binding ceremony. Allowing their blood to bathe their promise as a baptism brings new life through death, they merged into one being. One life force. One blood. One being. Forever entwined.

Anastasia never considered the possibility of the mark remaining, when at thirteen years old, she just tried to get it cleaned up and bandaged before her mother saw it and asked what happened. When weeks, then months, went by, Anastasia realized that she had chosen to mark herself for a long, long time. Or really, Leo had marked her. First her heart, then her hand. And now, even though they had been apart for seventeen years, she took comfort in knowing that they shared the same mark. It was a reminder of something that would hopefully not change. Even though things eventually did, the sentiment was a strong attachment to one another.

As the hours dragged on, Anastasia worked at her desk but her mind wandered toward Leo and her many memories of him. That time her grandma passed away and he showed up at her front door with a teddy bear and a card. Or another time when he had his heart broken by Amelia Brown and locked himself in his room for a week—Anastasia climbed in his window with fresh-baked cookies to cheer him up.

I wonder if he's dating anyone right now? Nah, that's silly—we're just friends. Always have been, always will be. Unless... I don't know. I wonder where he lives? I hope life has been good for him. I wish I was a part of it for the last seventeen years. Things changed even though we promised they wouldn't.

Anastasia finished the last of the filing and looked at her desktop clock. *Six o'clock. Time to clock out, finally!* She grabbed her purse and put her laptop in her case before turning off her desk lamp. "See you Monday, Ms. Orencia." Her boss offered a meager smile about as sincere as a blackjack dealer, and then returned to her own work.

Anastasia's stilettoed heels seemed to have an extra spring in their step, even after a long work day. She was about to be reunited with someone she'd always cared about, even if distance kept them apart. *Tonight, I'll wear this little white scar proudly.*

She returned to her small apartment to shower and change into something more comfortable than her pencil skirt and buttoned blouse. Anastasia chose her favorite purple sweater and dark-washed jeans. Taking one last look in the mirror before heading out, she wondered how much she had really changed since she was thirteen years old. *I wonder... I hope... I hope he still thinks that I'm worth his company. I really hope corporate work hasn't made me irrevocably dull.*

Yet another reason to hate her boss. Anastasia entertained the thought of being turned dull for just a moment before shaking her head and smiling. *Stop it, you're being silly. You're only as dull as you allow yourself to be.* With that, she headed out the door to meet her old friend from another lifetime.

Upon entering the restaurant, Anastasia scanned the dining room for an older version of a familiar face. Seeing no one that she recognized, she allowed herself to sit down alone at a table and waited for about ten minutes. *He probably stood me up. I bet he probably has a girlfriend and she didn't want him to see me, even as a friend, as I might be a threat. She probably has him watching Netflix at home right now, with a box of pizza on the coffee table. He'll probably never think of me again. He's too far gone... I was silly to get my hopes up.*

Mortified, Anastasia got up to leave with what was left of her dignity. Just as she was about to open the door, she nearly walked right into a tall, somewhat shaggy-haired figure wearing a leather jacket. Her heart stopped, her breath lodged in her chest.

"Hi, Staci."

***

Anastasia opened her mouth but no words would come.

"Leo, it's been… far too long." He smiled and gently took her hand.

"Agreed, but it's fabulous to see you." Anastasia felt his gaze travel from her face down her torso, as a smile pulled at the sides of his lips. "You look great." She blushed in response, trying to ignore the flutter in her chest.

"So you said you work right here in the city?"

Anastasia nodded. "Yep, but my boss makes it less glamorous, I can assure you of that."

His lips formed a soft "o" shape as she smiled sheepishly. "It's true—all I do is get her coffee and file her documents. What an utter waste of grad school. But enough about me, what are you up to?"

"Well, I'm working on an album with my band right now in the city, and we're hoping to go on tour next summer. This record deal changed everything for me—I finally feel like I have a direction for my life, and that it's all my choice, finally."

Anastasia nodded and thought back to when Leo was torn away from her so many years ago. It felt like the end of the world, and at the time, it kind of was. Because although Staci wouldn't admit it at the time, Leo *was her world, and she was his.*

Letters You Will Never Read

An excerpt

By Alycia Marie Shillan

When Calliope Jasper was nine, she made friends with the new girl in class, Jenny. Jenny was one of five kids, her father was a factory worker, and her mother a stay-at-home mom. Calliope had been fascinated by Jenny's family because it seemed rather perfect. Parents, siblings, and even a little beagle named Toledo. They were transplants from Ohio. The two little girls were inseparable for months, until suddenly Felicity forbade her granddaughter from playing at the other's house. They could only visit at school or at their home.

Jenny's mother was an alcoholic. Now, while it was explained to the little girl that the disease was not contagious, Felicity also pointed out that it was not the environment where children should reside. Overall, the situation got rather messy, but what Calliope recalled most vividly was how strongly her grandmother had addressed her concerns. Addiction, as this pertained to more than just liquor, was a battle fought every day. Jenny's mother could get the help she needed, but even sober, she'd never be cured. It was a journey down a difficult road that never ended. A spoonful of hard work, and a forklift of faith and grace were the only answer.

Strawberry-blond tresses a messy nest on top of her head and still attired in mixed-matched pajamas, an old faded robe, and froggy slippers after noon—why was this a memory the young woman could not somehow shake?

It was the steps. The ordered steps. Thirty-year sobriety didn't just happen; it was sobriety for one day, one hour, one minute, one second for 30 years. *God, Grant Me the Serenity* et al. It was praying for the strength for just the next moment.

Every time Calliope doubted she'd be able to continue to breathe, she prayed for that next inconceivable breath… and like manna from heaven, there it seemed to be.

There were so many people. Staring. Whispering together. Avoiding her. Attempting to talk to her. Where had they come from? When would they leave? … And if this was all some sort of bad dream—and of course, there was no way it wasn't—why hadn't she woken up by now?

Woken up… That morning, when she had woken up, she could see. Yes, her eye remained swollen, and yes, it had still been a funky shade of lilac. However, in those few blissful minutes inspecting her reflection, it could be described as nothing short of a miracle. One point on the Big Board for Sister Vera and her magic goop.

Weird. She'd been the first one up. That never happened. Ever. Grammy Filly never slept past seven. Even that time she had whooping cough. She'd been sorta gray, hackin' up a lung, spleen, and both kidneys, and didn't recognize anybody, but she'd been awake.

Ready to celebrate her good mood and given the rare opportunity to surprise her grandmother with a thoughtful gesture, Calliope had made a big breakfast: crepes, sausages, hash browns, and fruit, with a mug of her special chicory coffee. All placed on a heavy tray, with silk napkin and a stolen peony from the garden. She felt a little nervous, like when she was a little girl, bringing her grandmother breakfast in bed, hoping she wouldn't spill anything along the way.

Felicity had looked like an angel reclining in that armchair. Her gentle pretty face washed in the rays of morning sunshine casting in from the picture window. Gazing adoringly at her from the doorway, Calliope couldn't help admitting how nice it was to see. Those past few stressful days appeared to have melted away. Calliope suddenly hated herself for trying to wake her to enjoy the hot meal, … until she placed the tray on the bed, and touched Felicity's cheek.

That was when time had stopped. Funny thing is, it then both sped up to a frantic pace, and slowed down to almost a standstill. She couldn't remember who had called 911, her or Sean. He came, though. She must have called him because the ambulance would have drawn Charlotte to the house. She never would have forgiven herself if she had allowed Auntie Charli to see Gram this way. Phoebe hadn't come, though. Good. This wasn't the place for a little girl. She'd probably still been sleeping. No, she was another early riser. Just stayed with Neil, she guessed. Sean took care of it. They took Gram. Somewhere. Sean had promised she had never been left alone though. Sister Sarah was there with her. Then Sister Gwen. The Church Ladies would take turns for as long as would be necessary, they promised. Nothing for her to worry about.

But Calliope should have been there. It was Grammy Filly. It was her job to take care of Gram the way Gram had always taken care of her. She would have wanted her there.

No, no, she wouldn't. She had said so herself. They had talked about all this. Ad nauseum.

The bottom drawer of the hope chest. Notarized papers for her final rest, that and everything leading up to it for the next day or so. Calliope and Gram had signed them together. Her old attorney had retired a year or so back, but the new one was keeping her will at his office. He'd be in contact. This was just the immediate stuff. She hadn't wanted anyone to wonder what she wanted. She had made her wishes known, both documented on paper and to her granddaughter since the age of eighteen. Claimed that way it would all be a walk in the park for them.

Grammy Filly was obviously a lunatic!

Church service at Cornerstone Baptist with plenty of music. Cremation, no jewelry of any kind. Calliope would know where to spread her ashes, when the time was right. Sean had called Dr. Reginald to meet the ladies at Blankenship Funeral Home. He'd thought it would all be easier that way. He'd signed off on the transfer, of course, but the physician's presence was necessary before the facility could do anything to the body. Before they took the older woman, he'd made sure to offer Calliope plenty of time to spend with Felicity, but she had silently shaken her head no. Peeking over at the forgotten tray, she merely whispered, "She knows I know where she is now. We have all the time in the world to spend together talking." Sean understood, but sensed his best friend's grief might cause her to regret that decision one day.

With the diamond cross and chain laced across her fingers, she spun the gold band around her finger. She had never seen her grandmother without either. That was when she began to cry. She hadn't actually felt the tears. They were just there, sliding down her cheeks and landing on the cold hand she cradled, stroking the soft skin with her thumb. She'd have known these hands anywhere. They'd rubbed the side of her face when she'd awoken in the middle of the night with an excruciating earache. They'd slapped that same cheek, now belonging to a mouthy disrespectful teenager, who had more lip than was safe for a sixteen-year-old to share with the world… They'd spent a lifetime holding her hand, hugging her tight, and wiping away her tears. Similar tears to the ones falling. When a girl's heart is so shattered, there's no way to gather up all the pieces. The kind of sorrow where there would be no recovery.

Tapping in the distance drew her hollow blue eyes up toward the couple in the corner. Holly was the nervous type, and under real stress or trauma, she had a habit of tapping. Tapping her fingers against the table. Tapping her phone against her palm. Tapping anything she could find, to the tune of an irritating local jingle. This time, it was a plastic spoon along the top of her coffee cup. That was how they grieved in this state – somebody died, you brought danish from Perala's Bakery. Somebody died, you brought roses from Calhoun's Florist. Somebody died, you huddled in the corner with your green card fiancé, pretending to look comfortable, and tapping a plastic spoon against your Dunkin' Donuts coffee cup.

Gram would have hated the pastries, the roses, and the coffee, but she would have gotten a real kick out of Holly and Nikolas. She would have been the only one who spoke to them all afternoon, making a point of allowing everybody to see and hear every word they said. She typically never cared for idle town gossip, … which was precisely why and how she always gathered the juiciest tidbits to come back and share. Everyone talked to her — she just had one of those faces, ya know.

"Have you eaten anything today, honey?" Sister Rita inquired, bending down to meet Calliope's gaze, hands flat in her lap, and whispering her words as if she were speaking to a skittish alley cat. "I could make you a plate, if you'd like."

Calliope suddenly remembered the last thing she had eaten was the woman's coconut banana cupcakes the night before. They had been the only thing she had eaten all day yesterday. Well, them and a half of a Payday bar she'd found in her pocket. A lingering treat from her vending-machine road-trip dinner. No wonder she had awoken so famished.

"No, thank you," she murmured, the edge of her lips curling upwards. "I'm not really all that hungry right now. Maybe later."

Sister Rita stroked the back of Calliope's head. "I'll put a plate aside for you."

As the older woman wandered away toward where a smorgasbord of donated meals had been laid out along the dining room table, the redhead glanced in the opposite direction. It was amazing how torn she felt. She recognized how much they were all trying to help. They had loved her grandmother. So why couldn't any of them stop to think about what she truly needed right now? For them all to go away, and leave her alone. For today. For tomorrow. For the next week. For however long it took for this festering sting in the middle of her chest to fall asleep. Until she didn't need to focus on her next breath, until any of this started to seem real. Otherwise, all their best wishes, desserts, and cups of coffee were a waste to her.

Through the glass panels of French doors leading out to the patio, she could see Charlotte, sitting in a lounge chair in the corner, reading a letter. One of Gram's famous letters. The woman hated to text. Always said, if you had enough time to type out a message, you had enough time to dial her up and actually talk to her for real. It's not that she was technology-phobic; while she was working, she had learned every program given to her, but utilized simply out of necessity. The computer was not the enemy; the morons who used it to avoid human interaction were, though. She hated social media especially—beauty was rare, which was why those with the ugliest kids posted their photos most often, … and God seldom bestowed divine inspiration, and Satan sometimes caused us to think less of ourselves and others. The rest of the thoughts in our heads were due to random stupidity. Twitter proved that.

It was in letters that Grammy Filly always chose to correspond, if time permitted. Every birthday, Calliope purchased for her a purse of quality stationery from a small shop just outside Boston that had been probably standing since the days of Samuel Adams and Paul Revere. After a few years, she would joke that an updated iPhone would have cost less in the long run, but Felicity would hear none of it. She always argued, nobody could resist reading a handwritten letter. There was a mystery about it. There was something forbidden and confidential about it. There was something personal about it—it was addressed to someone. It was signed from someone. They were not disposable like digital characters and stupid emoji-figures. They took time to craft, and in the end, might be all we would really have left of a person.

Auntie Charli was crying. Laughing, but crying. Calliope wanted so desperately to look away, to protect such a private moment between the two women. After all, they had known each other almost twice as long as Calliope had known her grandmother. They had shared years and moments that were quite honestly none of Calliope's business. Yet, watching the older woman through the glass, sharing that last goodbye, was somehow therapeutic – Auntie Charli was the only other person who knew how she felt. What were they supposed to do now? How was life meant to move on without her? Who were they going to turn to now, with good news, jokes, or when they were simply pissed and wanted to rant to somebody. They'd of course have each other, but it wasn't the same. They were both too much alike in that way.

Flustered with emotion she wasn't crazy about sharing publicly, Calliope hesitantly peeked away, and rose clumsily to her feet from the chair. That was enough; it was time for her to wake up. This was the monster who was ready to grab you in the nightmare, just when you were wrenched safely into consciousness. When your eyes popped open, bouncing around the darkened bedroom, until you knew it was only a bad dream. That no matter what, he couldn't get to you. He couldn't hurt you. It was simply time, all right. And if this wasn't a dream, her exhaustion had just gotten the best of her, and she was hallucinating.

She would have known if she'd spent the last day she would get with Gram. She wouldn't have wasted it, bickering about Mark. Bitching about old hurts, stupid mistakes that couldn't be corrected overnight. She wouldn't have hidden out the entire day, until Gram had come looking for her. If that had been their last day together, she just would have known. They'd have cooked together, all her favorite recipes she'd never be able to replicate without the older woman. They'd have relaxed outside and gotten tipsy, Calliope listening to all the old stories she'd heard a million times before. Stories no one would ever tell again. The redhead would have made certain Grammy Filly understood how much she loved her, admired her, and needed her. She would have hugged her so tightly, refusing to ever let her go.

None of this could be real because Calliope would have known. She would have been ready to be left alone. Gram knew all that better than anyone. They would have said goodbye.

Castaway

By Jack Nolan

Rosa Elena Morales Hutchins had been on her side of the narrow bed for hours, awakened once by the frantic yapping of coyotes on the hunt, very nearby, and again by a motor that labored past, grinding down the uneven ruts of the packed caliche road, but not his, until at last she heard his pickup approach the trailer and die. After a long silence, the doors banged and his bulk rocked the trailer like a moored boat as he pulled himself in and squeezed down the hallway into the latrine. Rosa turned her face to the wall and listened to him piss unsteadily in the direction of the toilet. She forced herself to take deep, even breaths, filling herself with the stench of alcohol, cigarettes, and sweat as he stood over her, listening in the dark. He struggled with pulling off his pointed boots for a while before telling them to go "F" themselves and collapsing onto the bed fully dressed. Rosa slept.

She dreamt of the cool interior of a church, the air alive with sun stained by colored glass and flickering votive candles dancing through the haze of rich, sweet incense. And then she was in the orchards of her childhood, her *familia* working hard together, gathering apples under vast skies, her father's deep voice urging, "*¡Rosa! ¡Mas rápidamente!*" And they were in the vineyard, tearing soft bunches of grapes from the vines with gloved hands, and Rosa heard a crop duster overhead but could not see him in the clear skies above, though he circled closer and closer until he flew roaring over them, but still she could see nothing so said aloud, "*¿Porqué no puedo verle?*"

The clock was buried under her husband's blankets but outside, grayness had begun to mute stars on the edge of the desert sky. Rosa climbed over him carefully and felt her way down the black corridor to the pantry. Using the refrigerator light, she fumbled under the sink for a sponge, a bottle of cleanser, and rubber gloves. She knelt at the sill of the tiny latrine and patiently scrubbed her way by Braille to the point where she could squeeze herself into the reeking confines and latch the door gently behind her. She shut her eyes tight and switched on the fluorescent tubes. By degrees she was able to bear the white glare so she could finish washing urine from the floor and the toilet.

When the sponge and sink were rinsed, Rosa put her nightgown over the hook on the door and stepped into a lukewarm shower. The aluminum of the metal closet echoed her movements. Water thudded against the floor, which worried her, not because it was likely to arouse him but because the consequences, if it did, would be terrible.

In the cramped space, Rosa could see only the top half of herself when she wiped the mist from the mirror over the sink: the wide features, gingerbread hue, and dark eyes of her race were framed by the mirror. Tiny ears and shining hair that once cascaded to her hips but was now short, clipped straight at the base of her neck. As though deferential even to her own reflection, she glanced furtively at herself, at her breasts still perfectly round with acorn nipples. Bruises on her arms and ribs from the last time Desmond beat her were starting to fade.

Rosa stowed her uniform under a bench in the front so she could dress near the door, lace up her work boots, slide on a jacket, retrieve her lunch, and allow the door to click shut without waking him.

This was the good time. The edge of Tucson was four miles by car, but only three on the footpath that Rosa had helped to wear. She enjoyed her unhurried spiritual journey from the trailer to the church. Dawn lit the cloudless sky just enough to brighten the desert floor slightly between widespread palo verde, cholla, and towering saguaros as Rosa moved toward the faint outline of the Catalinas. Where the arroyo cut across her path, she followed its soft bed toward the notch of Reddington Pass. After a distance, she trudged up the far bank at the spot marked by a stand of saguaros, then along a narrow dirt road that threaded between houses to the first city street. She used a small flashlight from time to time but it was too late for sidewinders and too early for diamondbacks. She took great comfort from the desert and was at peace in the cool darkness.

Above the Rincon Mountains the sky was becoming pale blue, but the tall doors of the Church of the Assumption were not yet open. Father had grown unreliable in the years since Rosa had made this her parish. The rising sun pushed a cool breeze across the valley floor, so Rosa huddled in the half-shell of the Wishing Shrine nearby. A single candle flickered in a glass jar; wilted flowers lay at the feet of the Virgin, offerings from those who had come to remember El Tiradito. Two bronze plaques told the story of this shrine, built of stone by those who had known and mourned "The Castaway," as the plaque that was in English called him. He had fallen in love with the wrong woman and been killed, murdered by her husband with an axe, more than a century ago in this small village that had since become a large American city. The husband's revenge was understood, justified in the eyes of the Mexican villagers who established the shrine, and The Castaway was buried here, on sinner's ground, outside the consecrated churchyard. But the passion of the young man whose heart led him into sin was also understood and accepted by them, and so the shrine was maintained by those who had always understood and accepted these things, perhaps as a defense against the rational style of the invader.

Rosa felt she knew El Tiradito and the woman he loved, and the husband, and that she belonged to the family of those who came here to pray, light candles, and lay flowers across the small alabaster feet of Our Lady of Sorrows. She felt truly at home here, warmed by the candlelit half-shell of remembrance, nestled into the breast of those who had built it a century ago to comfort all who would follow in the community of sympathy. This crude mound of river rock and mortar decorated with trinkets of faith had no street value that required it to be locked against thieves, no value to those who walked by each day, pausing to view it as a quaint curio of the Mexican past, numb to the living experience it held for those like Rosa. She felt she could hear its rhythmic song, "*corazón...corazón ...corazón,*" echoing the spirit of life. She closed her eyes and saw the Sacred Heart held out to the blessed company of all faithful people, those who built the shrine and those who came to be transported by the power of it.

Rosa was startled from meditation by the squeaking of the church door. As she wandered toward the building and into view of the priest, she felt suddenly very odd, dressed in men's work clothes with heavy boots and a nametag that said "Hutchins," as though she wore a costume that hid her as a Mexican, a woman, a Catholic. She nodded in the direction of the priest, silent as the image of Mary, and she did not answer his mumbled greeting. She had prayed earnestly to forgive him in her heart, but these prayers, as many others, had not been answered. His words "duty as a wife...God's plan for each of us...obedience to His will not our own" disturbed her devotion with pangs of resentment and anger, so she went quickly to the side chapel of Our Lady and knelt. She folded a ten-dollar bill and stuffed it into the steel box where at least it would be safe from her husband and at most, a sign to God that she lay up her treasure where her heart was also. Then she lit a red votive light and began to breathe words of prayer into her crossed fingers while begging from her heart for guidance and for deliverance from her time of trial.

***

The bus arrived before Pima County Animal Control was open, but already vans and truckloads of muzzled greyhounds waited outside, innocent gladiators of the modern age who must die today because they had lost too many races. Rosa walked around to the cacophony of the kennel area and saw Lou, wearing his ear protection through his curly white hair. Rosa's face lit up with affection for her friend, but there was no point in trying to say anything over the tides of barking and howling that rolled through the cement cavern of the kennels. They were both taciturn by nature anyway, so even when outside, they spoke little. Rosa understood that Lou lived alone and preferred being at work to being at home, and he knew that she was married with no children and preferred not to talk about herself. Although in her manner she rarely looked directly at him or at anyone else, she was aware that he watched her, that he took comfort in being near her. She could not guess if he saw her as a daughter or as a young woman, but she relied on and needed his unspoken affection without wanting to know the nature of it. Rosa had worked here since high school and in those four years, Lou had become an important presence for her, though not one truly intimate word had ever passed between them.

As always, Lou had made coffee and brought in sweet rolls for them both. They sat on a bench outside the pandemonium of the kennel area and shared these while the desert sun drew the last coolness from the morning air. As if on cue, Lou stood, slid the headset from his neck up over his ears and pulled on thick leather gloves as the first greyhound was brought around. The choreography is established: trainers hand Rosa paperwork from the office, which she signs, returning the yellow copy. Then the spindly greyhound tiptoes anxiously forward on the stilts of its bony legs, its huge wet eyes darting nervously above its muzzle. Lou takes the short lead, brings the dog to the steel table and lifts it up. The greyhound is heavier than it looks, especially when rigid with fear, its tail between its legs, so Lou is careful to lift with a straight back. Rosa steps to the other side of the table and reaches under the dog, grabbing the paws on Lou's side and pulling them toward her. They gently lay the animal on its side, Lou bearing the weight, and place a towel over the hips while Rosa, wearing an apron but no gloves, embraces its head in her hands and murmurs to it in the soft lilt that mothers use with babies: "*Todo es bueno, pocito sin alma*, it's time to rest now. No more pain or fear. No more cold nights. No hunger or thirst. *Nunca más frío o caliente. No tienes hambre y miedo....*" And while she sings into its ears, with Lou pinning it to the table as a wrestler would an opponent, the animal falls very still, frightened but trusting in the gentleness of Rosa and in Lou's strength. It never sees and hardly feels the hypodermic Rosa expertly buries in an artery near the joint of its leg. Quickly she squeezes twenty milligrams of Xylazine into it while continuing to sing her words of comfort, Lou watching her, listening, inches away. Almost at once, the victim's eyes become serene, the body goes limp, and the utter indifference of death comes, although the animal is still conscious. Then Rosa replaces the syringe of Xylazine atop the needle with one of bright blue Pentobarbital while singing her English and Spanish song of farewell. Even before she removes the needle, the dog heaves one last sigh and becomes no longer a living thing. Rosa places her ear against the warm ribs to verify, never raising her eyes from her work to look at Lou. She then cleans the area and prepares new syringes while Lou ties a plastic bag around the body and carries it into the freezer room. The next animal is led forward and the next, throughout the morning.

Before noon, they had put to sleep 38 greyhounds which were hardly distinguishable from each other except for coloration. Seventeen domestic dogs were harder because each was unique. Rosa and Lou took time to play with the ones they had gotten to know during their 30-day holding period: energetic little Snow

White, matching sheepdogs Laurel and Hardy, gangly Woodrow Wilson, the terrier called Aleksandr Solzhenitsyn, and a dozen that had only numbers. Most had to endure having their fur shaved off the front leg for Rosa to find the artery, so most of them trembled with more fear than the greyhounds. Cats and other animals were done on alternate days, so Rosa and Lou sanitized the table area when they had finished the last dog.

After lunch, Lou filled a county truck with bags from the freezer room and made the trip to the landfill. Rosa slipped into a clean apron, rubber boots, and gloves and began disinfecting the empty cages and dishes of the recently departed. She liked her job and accepted the sad and difficult parts of it as she would have the hard part of any other job. Her faith assured her that it was not a sin to put down animals, which were living but had no souls, so her work did not involve sin. And she thought of ritual sacrifice as an ancient tradition of her people. It was just a difficult job in the world that, whoever did it, they would have to accept the hard part with the good part of it. Rosa loved to care for and minister to the little ones and, when the office said it was time, she put them to sleep with more tenderness by far than the man she had replaced, who had taught her the job. Her parents and her brothers were proud of Rosa, of her finishing high school, of her landing a good job with the county, of her marriage to a construction worker who, as she told them, made her happy, even though he was often out of work. They waited to hear that Rosa was pregnant still, though it had been four years so far.

On this day, however, a terrible sense of loss and anxiety was growing within her, as though she were being asked to work faster and faster by someone who was angry with her. The muscles in her back and legs grew tense as she carried buckets up and down past the cages of barking animals. Her hands began to shake inside her work gloves, until she was almost unable to control them. After an hour of struggling against these symptoms, but without a conscious thought, she placed a page of newspaper on the steel table, dropped four syringes of Xylazine and four of Pentobarbital from the locked cabinet into it, rolled the newspaper tightly and carried it to her locker, where she zipped the packet into a pocket of her jacket. It was as if she were watching someone else do it, from outside herself, but suddenly she felt better. Her hands became calm and her breathing returned to normal. She went back to her work unaware of any plan for the dangerous drugs in her jacket pocket, thinking about them only with a fleeting sense of reassurance, as though she had kept a promise she couldn't remember making.

At the end of the day, Lou called to her across the parking lot, “Don't you need your paycheck? I picked it up for you... here.” He stood with her at the bus stop, making a few comments about the office staff, waiting, really, just to see her off.

When the bus came into view, Rosa said, “I'm going away for a while...a few days...on a trip to see family. I won't be in Monday.”

Lou looked surprised and a little hurt that she hadn't said anything to him about this. “Have you given notice?” he asked. “I don't think the super knows about it.”

“Something just came up...but I wanted you to know.”

Lou’s eyes narrowed with genuine concern. He knew that her not getting authorization for leave meant something. “Look,” he muttered, “...it’s none of my business, but are you sure you’re...you know...all right?”

Rosa stepped away from the bus as it swung off the road and opened the door, not looking at him or answering.

“Rosa, let me drive you home...please,” he said.

“I’m okay...I’m okay, really,” Rosa told him, her jacket embraced in the folds of her arms.

“You’re sure?”

"Sure, Lou, it's family...you know..." and she looked at him and smiled warmly, hoping to convey the kindness she felt for him as well as to deceive him.

The last time she ever saw Lou, he was standing on the pavement watching the bus disappear around the curve on Silverbell Road.

She wanted desperately to enter the church, but that idea filled her with fear. She could not lie to God as she could to man, nor guarantee that He would not interfere with the path she was groping for in her heart. She knelt at the Shrine of El Tiradito outside the holy ground and said into her cupped hands, "Father, I know that sin is terrible in your eyes, but I cannot do what you ask me to. I have done everything I can do. Everything! I have prayed to Our Mother for help and guidance. But I am done. Please forgive me, Father...." She waited a long time, trying to control what she was feeling, but the passing traffic and the waning light of evening convinced her at last that she was abandoned. Rosa lit a candle for El Tiradito, who had died in sin because of his own frailty and passion but who was remembered by many with kindness now.

All the long way home, Rosa choked back a rising tide of overwhelming anger that clouded her mind and tore at her heart as if she were possessed by some strange thing outside herself. If it would be a sin to answer sin with sin, she thought, and then she and Desmond would both burn in hell for it. And Almighty God who had the power to help her now, if He did not, then so be it. The path she would take was clear now in her mind.

She stormed into the trailer and tore furiously at the work uniform, popping buttons and tearing the boots off half-unlaced, throwing it all out onto the dry grass outside. From the back closet she pulled a cellophane storage bag and ripped it violently away from the colorful dress her mother had made for her when she danced to the guitars, violins, and trumpets of her school's

Mexican dance group. When they found her, they would know who she had been — not a county employee with a serial number and a violent drunkard's last name — but Rosa Elena Morales, shrouded in bright colors, Mexicana.

In the darkened front room, she lit a candle on the table and unrolled the syringes. She crouched into her arms, holding the beads in her hands and counting out the Rosary as she whispered it into the flickering light. There would be no answer now, she knew, and no absolution afterwards because of her great sin. She stopped after a time, kissed her rosary and begged for forgiveness anyway. Then Rosa prepped a syringe of Pentobarbital and wrapped a nylon stocking tightly around her left bicep. She began to sing hoarsely, "*Todo es bueno, hija sin alma*, it's time to rest. No *more* pain and fear. No *more* cold nights...." but she was overcome and choked on the words. This so-familiar act was not working. Her hands shook in anger, her vision was hampered by tears in the candlelight, so that she poked and jabbed blindly into the crook of her elbow searching for the vein, until blood ran inside and outside her skin, making it impossible and Rosa stood up enraged and threw the syringe at the kitchen sink. Then the pain that she had not felt at all caught her by surprise and she wailed and wrapped her self-inflicted wound with the nylon to stop the bleeding. For the first time on this day, Rosa wept, allowing herself to feel the sadness of all she had lost.

It was during this crying that she resolved not to die alone.

The bar where he drank was on the Old Ajo Highway, not far from the trailer. Deliberate now, in possession of herself, Rosa wrapped the remaining shots in newspaper and stuffed them down the front of her dress. She put sandals on her feet and walked out to kill him.

He will be very drunk, staggering from the bar with the women he smells of, loud, happy. At first he will not recognize her in her dress, then he will make some phony excuses about his whore and he will insist on driving to prove he is not drunk. He will spin the tires climbing onto the highway, screaming at her, furious that she came to get him, an embarrassment in front of his friends, that she deserves exactly what she's going to get when he gets her home but.... he will have stopped for a red light by then and she will plunge 100 milligrams of Xylazine into his ribs, enough to stun him, then finish him with P.B. before the light turns green. She will have done a good thing for the world by taking away an abusive drunk who wants a slave he can beat but not a wife or children, and she will, calmly this time, sing herself to sleep.

Cars speed past on the Old Ajo Highway, lighting her way along the rough berm. Rocks get into her sandals but she doesn't stop. She is walking in a dream, wanting it all to be over, her left arm throbbing, blood running into her hand. "Okay," she tells the voice, the insistent, metallic voice of God asking her if she is all right. "Okay" is the only answer Rosa has the strength to give to this vast question. A deformed image of herself walking as a ghost appears before her and God asks, "What are you doing out here?"

Rosa turns into the brilliant white glory that has cast her shadow across the desert and is blinded. A shadow steps toward her through the wall of light and tells her, "You shouldn't be walking here at night. You could get hurt."

Rosa is not afraid of him, of the strange man walking toward her on the empty roadway, speaking to her in this familiar way.

"You got an I.D., ma'am?" he asks. "Do you *habla* any *Inglés*?" Cupping her eyes against the flood of light, Rosa sees his uniform now, but she does not answer. Over his shoulder he shouts, "Looks like we got a poster child for the fiesta." He reaches out and takes her wrist into his huge, warm hand, leading her firmly toward the globe of light surrounding the cruiser.

"She's illegal," he tells his partner. "No purse, no English, nothing. Tell Border Patrol to pick her up at the Kino E.R. Looks like some boy-friend cut her up."

To Rosa he says, "You're gonna get a free ride home, chiquita."

The word "home" nestles into Rosa's heart like a bird.

The Dot

By G.A. Miller

Spring of 1961 was an optimistic time. The youngest ever president was in office, and a general feeling of prosperity was in the air even for a single mother and her six-year-old son watching their black-and-white television as she read a book.

"All right Bobby, it's eight o'clock. Time for bed, buddy."

"Aw, Mom, do I *have* to?"

"School night, you know the rules. Turn off the TV and get ready, please."

Bobby paused, surprised. She'd never told him to turn off the TV before; he always just left the room to brush his teeth, and left the TV playing behind him.

He knew how, having seen her turn it off before. Turn the little dial, the one that makes it louder, until it clicks, so he walked to the set and turned it off.

The screen did an amazing thing. The top and bottom flew to the center in a white line, which then collapsed to a bright dot in the middle and began *shrinking*, as though it was moving, traveling toward the back of the set.

Bobby started to walk around behind the set, to see where the dot was going, when his mother called again. He turned and headed to the bathroom instead, his curiosity making him anything but tired. Did those pictures live in the back of the TV set, or did they go somewhere else?

"Let's go, brush those teeth and wash up and I'll tuck you in."

"Can I read for a little while?"

"Just for a little while," his mother smiled. "You need to be up early."

Bobby had been an early reader, and read whatever he could get his hands on, which fueled his highly active imagination. His mother encouraged his reading and would usually let him read for a while even after TV time was over.

He was reading one of the *Hardy Boys* books by Franklin W. Dixon and opened it eagerly to the bookmark when his mother tucked him in.

"Remember, not too long, okay?"

"Okay, Mom, I know."

She smiled, kissed his forehead, and left the room.

"Frank and Joe Hardy would know where that dot goes, I betcha," he whispered to himself after she left. He read until his eyes grew heavy, but that dot never left his mind even as he drifted off to sleep.

Bobby found himself walking through the apartment, darker than it had ever been before. There was light up ahead and he followed it into his living room where their TV was on, but the picture was bright, vivid color, not the fuzzy black and white it had always been. He instinctively realized this had to be a dream but gasped aloud when the man on the screen turned to face him and began talking to him.

"Well, hello there, Bobby. It's so nice to see you."

"H-hi," Bobby stammered. He'd never seen the man before and there was something unsettling about him. He looked very tall, all dressed in black, with a shiny bald head and hair on his chin. He was smiling, but it was a creepy smile, the kind of smile the monsters do just before they pounce on you.

"Would you like to come in and look around, Bobby?"

"You can't go into a TV, mister."

"Ah, but this is not the kind of TV you're used to, Bobby. This is a *magic* TV, do you see?" He waved his hand and the picture behind him changed, showing all of Bobby's favorite places, his favorite TV shows, everything so brilliant and crisp.

Bobby was frozen in place. He was amazed by what he was seeing, but there was something about that man….

The alarm clock in his mother's room started ringing and the man glared when he heard it, that creepy smile now an angry grimace. Bobby saw flashes of red in his eyes because the picture was so bright, so clear.

The man's arm extended right *through the glass*, reaching out for Bobby, and he felt a hand gripping and shaking his arm. His eyes flew open and he found himself back in his bed, his mother shaking his arm gently to wake him.

"Come on, kiddo, time to get up and get ready for school now."

He looked up at his mother and relaxed. She saw the relief in his eyes.

"You okay, kiddo? You look like you saw a ghost."

"Naw, maybe just a dream, Mom. I'm okay now."

He got out of bed, put on his robe and slippers and followed her toward the kitchen, casting a nervous glance into the living room. Their old TV sat on its stand, the rabbit ears fanned out on top just as he'd left them last night.

No magic TV, no scary man. He continued into the bathroom and then to his chair in the kitchen for his breakfast. He didn't have much of an appetite but didn't want his mother to worry about him.

He couldn't get that image out of his mind, the man reaching toward him, his hand actually coming through the glass screen like it wasn't even there. And since it was a dream, how did the man inside the TV hear the alarm going off?

The next few days passed uneventfully. Bobby's sleep was free of dreams about that man in the TV. His dreams now were the typical dreams that six-year-old boys enjoy, those of amusement parks, adventures with the heroes from their favorite shows and books, and such.

Life was back to normal. Well, almost normal.

He was still curious about that dot, but now considered it cautiously, fearing that the man from his dream might be connected to it in some way. He waited until Mrs. Staub, the Tupperware lady, was visiting in the kitchen with his mother and carefully looked at the back of the TV.

There was a box of some kind sticking out of the back cover. The cover was full of holes, but the box was solid, different from the cover, which added to the mystery.

Why does the cover need holes in it, anyway? he wondered, *is it so they can breathe in there?*

One thing was sure, though…there was no opening in that little box, so the dot had no way that he could see to leave the inside of the set.

With spring in full bloom, playing outside with his friends again gradually took over Bobby's thoughts and the dot was soon forgotten like his winter jacket in the back of the closet.

One Friday night after dinner, he was watching the news with his mother, knowing he'd laugh when the men said, "Good night, Chet" and "Good night, David" to each other at the end.

They were talking about a terrible fire in a big building and as they showed the reporter at the building, Bobby gaped at the screen, eyes wide.

"Oh my, what a terrible thing, Bobby. I feel so awful for those poor people." Bobby's mother thought he was reacting to the sight of the fire, but that wasn't it at all.

When they showed the reporter talking into the microphone, there was a crowd of people gathered behind him. In that crowd was the tall man from his dream, looking up at the building. As the reporter described the tragedy, the man looked right into the camera and smiled, that same creepy smile as before.

The worst part was that the man was in full color, even though everything else in the picture was the usual black and white…and his mother didn't seem to notice!

Oh, I'm still here, Bobby…I'm here, just waiting for you to come in, that predatory smile seemed to imply. Bobby instinctively knew that smile was just for him.

His mother noticed the look of terror in Bobby's eyes and walked over to the TV, turning the big dial on it.

"Let's see what else we can find, kiddo. Maybe 'Mister Ed,' if he's on... I think we've had enough news for one day," she said, but he wasn't listening. His mind went back with frightening clarity to that dream, especially where the man reached right through the glass for him just before she woke him up.

This time, though, he was wide awake and his mother was right there with him, somehow completely unaware of that man.

Bobby had never felt so alone and frightened in his life.

He slept badly that night, waking often, fearful of the dream coming back, possibly taking him away for good this time. He knew he had to do something but had no idea what.

He had to tell his mother everything. She'd know what to do. That decided, he slept for a while longer this time, no dreams interrupting his rest.

She made pancakes for breakfast. The sun was shining brightly outside, and there was a cool breeze flowing through the window screens. It should have been a perfect day, a storybook day, but Bobby cleared his throat and told his mother he had to tell her something.

She listened quietly as he described how he wondered about the dot on the TV, then the frightening dream he had that same night, and finally how he'd seen that man just the night before on the news.

She didn't respond, but he knew she hadn't seen that man at all. He could see it in her eyes.

Once he finished, she spoke in a calm, reassuring voice.

"Bobby, you know we sometimes have bad dreams. You've had them before and so have I. Everyone does, but they're just dreams and they can't harm us. I did not see the man you described on the news last night at all and I wonder if the fire was such a terrible thing to see that your mind brought back memories of your bad dream because of that. Do you think that might be it?"

"But, he looked so real and he stared right at me, just like in the dream!"

"Exactly. Just like in the dream. The memory of the dream. Tell me, is there a man like that in any of your books?"

"No, I don't think so."

"Well, it may have been in a TV show or a movie then, a bad man that left an impression on you. You have a very strong imagination, Bobby, you've always imagined places and people and adventures while you played. You do know that things like that dream can't happen in real life, don't you?"

"Yeah, I guess so," he replied, sounding doubtful.

"Here, help me clear the table. I'll wash the dishes, and then we'll do an experiment together, you and me."

"Experiment?"

"Yes. I'll show you what that dot really is, so you won't have anything to worry about any more. Once you understand it, I have a feeling that man won't appear in your dreams again."

"Okay, Mom." He smiled, feeling a ray of hope.

They cleaned the kitchen together and went into the living room. She turned on the lamp even though it was bright daylight outside.

"All right, kiddo, I want you to watch the bulb very carefully when I turn off the light, got it?"

"Sure, yeah." He stared intently at the bulb, and briefly saw the filament inside glow red when she turned it off.

"What did you see?"

"The wire inside was red for a minute, then it turned black."

"Exactly. It gets hot from the electricity and then it cools off, which is why it went from red to black. Our TV also uses electricity and that dot is the picture tube cooling off, just like the light bulb does, that's all."

"Really? It looks like it's moving to the back in there."

"That's called an optical illusion, Bobby. It seems to be moving because it's getting smaller and dimmer as it cools."

"Are you sure, Mom?"

"That's the next part of the experiment. I think it's going well so far, don't you?"

"Yeah, it's pretty neat." He was more relaxed now, happy he'd talked to her.

"Good, now wait until you see this. This is the big finale, as they say in *shew* business!" She tried her best to sound like Ed Sullivan and Bobby giggled.

She turned on the TV and when it finally warmed up, the morning cartoons were on. He'd forgotten all about it being Saturday, as worried as he was. She adjusted the rabbit ears until the picture looked about as good as it could and stood back.

"There. How does it look to you?"

"It looks good. That's Deputy Dawg!"

"Right. Okay, now the big finish. Are you ready?"

"Sure!"

"Good. I want you to gently put your hand on the screen, right in the middle."

"Like this?" he asked, placing his palm against the tube.

"Perfecto! Now, I'm going to turn the TV off and you'll see.... nothing! The tube will cool, that dot will get little, and that's absolutely all that happens."

"A-are you sure?" he asked, his voice trembling a bit, his hand moving off the screen.

"Yes, sweetie, I certainly wouldn't let anything bad happen to my guy. I only want you to see for yourself that you're safe and that dream was no more than just a bad dream."

"All right." His hand rested lightly on the tube as she rotated the volume knob and clicked the set off.

There was a bright flash of light that made her squeeze her eyes closed for just a fraction of a second and when she opened them, Bobby's robe and slippers were lying in a pile in front of the TV, but he was gone. The dot on the screen looked like it was moving to her now, drifting slowly into the distance as she pounded the sides of the cabinet and screamed at the top of her lungs.

"NoNoNoNo, Nooooooo! Bring him BACK, give me my BOBBY, bring him BACK, damn you!"

When the police arrived in response to the concerned calls from the other tenants in the building, they found her still screaming, still pounding the sides of the TV set, nearly knocking it off the aluminum stand. The rabbit ears were on the floor behind it, having fallen off from her incessant beating.

She refused to leave with them until they assured her one of the officers would wait at the TV for Bobby's return and then she finally relented, completely exhausted and out of her mind with fear.

Her last view of her apartment was that of Patrolman Joey Cannon, standing right next to her television set. Bobby's new framed school photo hung proudly on the wall behind him.

And his robe and slippers lay crumpled on the floor, like artifacts from a bygone time.

The Hat on the Bed

By Joanne Perella

I awoke to see the shadows of my four-poster bed in the dim light of the October dusk. My unfinished French homework spilled across the bed. A windy rain outside blew the branches against the windowpanes, casting a strange kaleidoscope of shadows and light across the walls. Across the room, the white cotton curtains billowed out in a rhythmic pattern as gusts of wind escaped from an open window. The scent of rain and autumn leaves mingled with the steam heat, making me feel at once both safely secure and strangely sad, lying in the dark alone.

All at once, the door pushed open and my mother burst into the room. She had a way of filling the room immediately with her presence, sweeping in suddenly, the scent of soap and cooking oil trailing behind her. Her apron was tied neatly around her waist, the creases still crisp from her iron. I never once remembered my mother tiptoeing anyplace. She was like a huge headlight appearing suddenly out of the darkness. I tried blinking her away but she was still there when I opened my eyes.

"Why are these windows open? Don't you realize everything will be soaked?" she exclaimed as she headed for the window. She shut it with one practiced hand, the other feeling the desk to see how much damage the rain had done. "Look at this, now your papers are ruined," she said, exasperated. I liked feeling the wind and the rain whirling around my little room, and now the sudden silence unsettled me. Her intrusion into my dream world made me feel incredibly annoyed.

She strode over to my bedside and snapped on the light, transforming the room into a bright and stark reality. I could see the dust accumulated on my bureau, the sheets wrapped around my blankets and my French homework scattered across my bed. The shadows on the wall disappeared; I could no longer see the streetlights or hear the gentle swish of tires on wet pavement. "Why are you lying in this darkness? How can you do your homework if you are straining your eyes like that?" my mother's voice continued despite the fact that she had gotten no response. Her questions rarely required an answer.

Nothing ever escaped my mother's scrutiny. Aside from a tube of Maybelline lipstick, she wore no makeup. My mom bathed with Ivory soap, smoothed Johnson's baby lotion on her arms and legs and dusted her body with Jean Nate. Her customary outfit was a gingham housedress with an apron tied primly behind her back.

Mom walked over to my bedside, smoothed the sheets and cleared herself a spot to sit. As she settled into a space close to me, I think she could sense my surprise. I had figured she was barging into my room to fuss over me in her usual manner, seeing that it was nearly suppertime and my homework should be done. I also expected a lecture about falling asleep in the late afternoon darkness. But I did not expect her to cozy up to me in this uncharacteristic manner. I immediately realized, with some foreboding, that she had something to say.

"Dad's downstairs and I told him the meatloaf would be ready in about a half hour," she began. I gulped and nodded. "I thought this would be a good opportunity to talk to you," she said brightly. Her forced gaiety was unsettling. I shifted uncomfortably in the small space on my bed and waited.

"Did you ever wonder where babies come from?" she blurted out with a weak smile. I was dumbstruck. Babies?! God help me.

Two months ago, I turned 12 and began my period the day after my birthday. Last week, I walked to Woolworth's and bought my first bra, which I kept hidden in my bottom drawer. I had begun shaving my legs furtively in the shower with a Lady Gillette razor I bought on the same trip.

Sex was something we never spoke of at home, but in school, my best friend Deb and I whispered about "loose" girls and the boys that pursued them. These girls, like Flora Caruso, were "easy" and wore lots of makeup, teased their hair high, smoked cigarettes in the girls' room and wore tight poorboy sweaters that strained against their ample breasts. I had not yet been kissed, but Deb and I speculated what went on in the back seat of the Mustangs we would see parked by the side of the road late at night on the top of Cherry Hill. We had pretty much figured out the details by now. Flora's cousin Judy had to be sent away to her "aunt's house in Michigan" last year and we all knew why. To me, boys were still creatures from another planet, but I nervously anticipated the change beginning in me. I dreaded the day I would be the one in the back seat of a car, while some sweaty boy fumbled to remove my clothing with unpracticed hands, all the while planting sloppy kisses on my virgin lips. I knew it would be a truly wretched experience.

I looked at my mom in horror and managed to nod in agreement. I couldn't imagine what was to come out of her mouth next. But I felt a little thrill of excitement, anticipating that I might actually see another, more human side of my mother for a change.

"Do you remember a few months ago, you remarked that Julie Whitcomb was getting really fat? Do you know why?" My mother's voice seemed to rise and quicken. I looked at her, speechless. "Because she was pregnant, that's why!" she burst out, obviously pleased with herself. "And do you remember that last month, she showed us her new baby? Well, that's because she delivered the baby! It was in her stomach and just grew and grew from a tiny seed to a newborn. This is what happens: When it is ready, it slides right out of the woman's body! That's what happened when I had you!" My mother's face was flushed now, and her eyes shone. She seemed oblivious to my reaction of total shock. I sat frozen on my bed, fearing more, wishing desperately that this would soon be over.

"So how do you think the baby gets in the mommy's tummy?" My mother's final question hung in the air. She sat back slightly, pausing for a moment, a little smug. I felt sick to my stomach but was I relieved she could not read my mind. There was no way I was going to answer this last question, even though I could have given her several different answers, complete with graphic details.

Months ago, Deb and I were picking out books for our summer reading at the Mt. Pleasant branch library. We came across a dusty, obscure book on a forgotten shelf near the periodicals. The book was called *The Hat on the Bed*, but I never could figure out why. Like most pornography, it had no real plot, but there was chapter after chapter detailing the sexual exploits of a dirty old man in some sleazy hotel. To our innocent eyes, it was like a treasure, filled with lots and lots of lurid descriptions of every possible position, played out in perfect detail. Every chapter delighted us with tales of lusty ladies whose clothes never stayed on for very long. We devoured this book and managed to renew it all summer, trading it back and forth, and hiding it under our mattresses.

I waited for my mother to finish, knowing it would not take long. "Well, I'll tell you," my mother's voice lowered in a conspiratorial manner. "When God decides that a woman and a man are ready to have a baby, after they have prayed enough for one, he plants a little seed in the mommy's tummy and it grows into a baby! Isn't that wonderful? Isn't it just a true miracle? Aren't you glad you finally know?" My mother's beaming face had broken into a light sweat.

She stood suddenly, smoothed her apron and headed for the door. "The meatloaf should be just about done, why don't you clean up and come down for supper?" she said. The door slammed shut behind her.

I could hear my mother humming as she padded down the stairs, already absorbed in her meatloaf dinner. She had mentally checked off this unpleasant task, and she was satisfied she had accomplished it successfully. She never even noticed that I had not uttered a single word.

A Crown of Diamonds

By Barbara Ann Whitman

At the edge of the woods, there lived a family of oak trees. The smallest wished to someday grow taller than all of the other trees in the forest. She dreamed of stretching her arms so high that a bluebird might nest there in springtime. She would wear a bonnet bursting with buds and sprouting new leaves. She would stand proud when the baby birds learned to fly. One by one, they would leave the nest and spread their tiny wings for the very first time, landing on her lower branches and singing their song.

When the summer sun became very warm, she'd wear a floppy, green, leafy hat! She would give shade to the velvety moss and colorful wildflowers that grew in the soil beneath her. A swing made of wood and rope would hang from her thickest branch. Children would laugh and play there until their parents called them home for dinner.

In autumn, her hair would be a fiery wreath of red and gold. The breeze would gently lift her leaves and they'd float down to the ground, where she'd wear them like a fancy petticoat. She would scatter acorns around on the grass below, where small animals would collect them when the weather turned cold and the snow began to fall.

The season she loved most of all was winter. At night, the skies were dark and the air was clear. One of her favorite things to do was to look up and wave her little branches at the man in the moon, who shone brightly above the earth.

One night, she looked up at her mother, who towered above her. "Mama," she said, "I wish that I could wear the stars in my hair, like you!"

"Be patient, my child. First, you must grow strong and tall in my shadow. It took me many years to reach this height. Someday, you will have stars sprinkled in your hair, just like me."

Beside her mother, her grandmother stood. She was the tallest in all the forest and her powerful roots spread far, in every direction. She had so many bright shiny stars in her hair—even more than the little oak's mother!

"Grandmother," she said, "I wish that I could wear a crown of diamonds in my hair, just like you."

"Someday, you will," her grandmother answered. "But I have lived a hundred years. Every day, I stretched my arms up to the heavens, so that I might grow stronger. Sometimes, the wind blew so hard that I twisted this way and that. I dug my roots deeper into the earth and held on. One time, the snow was so heavy that I bent all the way to the ground. I was afraid I would break in half."

"What happened?" the little tree asked.

"The sun came out and it warmed me. Soon, the snow melted and the birds returned. I stretched my arms again, reaching for the sky. My branches grew sturdy again and lush with new leaves. By the time summer arrived, I was taller and mightier than ever before."

The little oak sighed. "Growing up is hard. And a lot of work."

Her grandmother smiled. "Sometimes, but most of the time, it happens while you're not paying attention. When you're busy playing and learning, you are always growing. You might feel small, but your dreams are not! They are grand! They are amazing, just like you. Someday, they will all come true. Then you, too, will wear a crown of diamonds in your hair."

The Interview

By Bob Sherman

I don't know why I allowed myself to be taken in by someone I hardly knew, a man I had met only three times. It's not as if I had been a stray dog wandering homeless on the streets. But there he came and there he was, and cute I might add; all smiles and sweet talk about caring for my every need, a warm bed, meals, and the physical comforts of indoor living, because he had a good job, nice apartment, and believed we had enough in common to make it work. *Exactly what did we have in common*? I wondered. Men, I know, look at you and see what they want to see. If they believe you will be to their advantage, they develop a plan, shallow or complicated, deep or simple, then set the hook and reel you in if you don't mind the metaphor. My schooling's not formal, as you know.

The first week was touch and go, if you understand my point, until we settled into a first acquaintance, get-to-know-you-level relationship with trust and understanding hovering somewhere over a distant horizon. I spent most of my time watching and listening to learn where he wanted me to be in his apartment and what he expected. I suppose this happens in every relationship, but not all live-in invitations come about so quickly, and while I was grateful for the offer, a certain amount of stress came with accepting the proposition.

I think you knew, as would any reporter doing their homework before an interview, that I came from the streets. In fact, I suspect this matter of homelessness, as you call it, drove you to do this story about me. Our numbers have increased as you know, but we're seldom seen, camouflaged by our ragged environment or man's blind eye. Where did you say this story would be published?

By the way, what you call homelessness, we call living on the street. The street is our home and some of the time it's not all bad; and when you grow up on the street you think little of it, which must be true for most everyone growing up anywhere. Sure, I wished for a better deal than the one I got, that's our nature as I am sure it is yours, but comparisons were circumscribed by our immediate and confining location. So, while I may decry living downtown along restaurant row when someone describes the benefits available on the east side, I take respite and some pleasure in knowing that at least I don't live along the waterfront by the docks where life can be punishing and frequently short-lived.

As for me, I lived alone with my mother. Of course, there were brothers and sisters, but they had gone their separate ways and our father was never around. Well, yes, he was around. Mom pointed him out to me, but he spent no time with us, and I'm not sure I would have benefited from his company. He was an older male and I, a young female. There was nothing for us to talk about or do together.

By the way, this description of my past, this background information as you call it, is only provided for your perspective, not to seek, or arouse condolence or commiseration, for I was fine where I was with no complaints right up to the day I left.

So, then began the next phase of my life: meeting this fellow who took interest enough to look me up on the street more than once and enough to invite me to live with him in his apartment. I'm not so naive to think this was the result of my resplendent personality, which, cloaked beneath the characteristics of my lifestyle, he received barely a glimpse. However, I am, as they say, pleasant to look at, and, under more accommodating circumstances, would turn a few heads, which, by the way, once I am brought up to snuff by the graciousness of my benefactor, could easily happen, in which case I may just move up the ladder. That's what we all do, isn't it? My point is, and he admits it himself, that after you have checked me out, it is my face that holds your attention, and once you look into my eyes, I'll be a month in your memory. I was blessed with a package of impressive genes, that's the truth. But, here's the conundrum.

As appreciative as I am, we are not at all alike, which, I understand, is to be expected in these circumstances, but even at the most basic level we lead separate lives. The most obvious difference for me is our sleeping patterns. He sleeps straight through the night, which is not my nature. I spend the hours after midnight nosing around his apartment and looking out the window to kill time, just watching, wondering what it might be like back on the street. Then, of course, during the day when he is wide awake, I find myself taking naps to make up for my nighttime lapse of continuity.

Oh, and I eat the same way. That is, he has three meals a day, which I never had and am not convinced is necessary. I eat when I'm hungry and that could be any time of day or night, and my meals are unaccompanied by the trappings of ritual, that is, ordering out or spending an hour in the kitchen preparing food in I couldn't tell you how many ways, setting the table, sitting, serving, eating, talking; you know all of this better than I. Give me something simple. I eat a little and am on my way.

Of course, I've only been here two weeks, so it may be too early to wrap up my conclusions, though I am suspect of what will become of this disjointed affair. It may come down to living with each other's expectations, finding a level of tolerable comfort, ignoring what bothers us, being true to our nature and holding on to our inner values, or this whole adventure may unravel like a ball of twine. But, what do I know, I'm just a cat.

Take it to Her Grave

By Kathy Clark

It all started when Mary Ellen was six years old. She and her family traveled to Texas that summer of '64, a few months after her mother's favorite president was assassinated. Pictures of President Kennedy were plastered all over her mother's living room walls as he was an Irishman like her so, perhaps, this was going to be a historical trip.

They stayed with her parents' friends: a man, a woman, and a teenage girl of about seventeen. She was tall and blonde like Mary Ellen's mother but spoke with a southern drawl. Being six and free from suspicion, Mary Ellen found that it was not a big deal to stay with friends and family and she never imagined that the teenage girl she met that summer would come back to haunt her later on in life.

***

Mary Ellen Lansing grew up in the sixties with a father, a mother, and James, her older brother by two years. She went to school, came home, did homework, ate supper, and went to bed at the end of the day like everyone else did in her neighborhood.

When she was ten years old, she overheard an adult conversation between her mother and father. A conversation that she wished her ears never had access to.

She heard her father's footsteps make their way to the kitchen door. This was a constant reminder that her mother was home. And when she did arrive home, he would often tease her and tell her that it was high time she started dinner. But the kitchen's fragrance of potatoes, carrots, and pork chops simmering atop the stove could not be hidden. Slender and standing just five-foot-seven, Leo was not a big man but he was a humorous one and Flora loved that about him. She told Leo she had a good check-up and was glad to be home. Flora feared doctors would find something wrong with her. But they never did.

Flora, who resembled the 1920s figure skater Sonja Henie, was the picture of health. She was a thick-set woman of five-foot-six with shoulder-length blonde, wavy hair, and her eyes were as deep blue as the ocean. Her skin didn't have one wrinkle, which complimented her peaches and cream complexion. Flora was a looker. She could and would turn any man's head. Even with all her mother's beauty, nothing could have prepared Mary Ellen for what she was about to learn.

With her bedroom door ajar, she replaced her homework for their conversation. She walked soundlessly and leaned closer to the opening of her door. Whispering parents are always attractive to kids.

Leo asked Flora how her visit went and Mary Ellen could see her father's smile through the slight crack her door had created. Her mother said that no one tells me what to do. Flora's weight never bothered him. Leo loved big women. The doctor told her that even though she was tall, she still shouldn't be as heavy as she was. Then she whispered that the doctor didn't know she had had four children.

Mary Ellen remained behind the door paralyzed. Her mouth dropped open. Her stomach tightened. She wanted to vomit. Her tears dropped on the hand she used to cover her mouth. She tried not to sniffle or blow her nose as that would have brought attention to her and the conversation would have ended. She didn't know what to do, so she used her shirt sleeve to wipe her tears and nose, as well as the drool that came from the corners of her mouth. She continued to listen but stopped when she was called to dinner. For a moment, she felt rescued from that awful feeling, but only for a moment. With dry eyes, nose, and mouth, she went to the dinner table and hoped that no one would notice her shocked expression. No one did.

Flora was a great cook and housekeeper, but where were those other two kids? What happened to them? This was way too much for Mary Ellen to handle. She wanted to demand an explanation, but she continued on with dinner and regular conversation and never said a word about what she had heard, not even to her brother James.

Was Mary Ellen in a dream? Her mother was Irish Catholic and they don't abandon their children or have children without being married. Her mother drilled that into her head often.

"You get married first, Mary Ellen," she'd say, "and then you have children. Your children come first, even before your husband."

Flora made no secret of her rigid judgment of anyone who fell from grace.

***

Going through snapshots for a school project about Kennedy's assassination in Texas released past memories of that summer trip of '64. Mary Ellen came across a few photos of that teenage girl and Flora. She sat at the edge of her bed and puzzlement overwhelmed her. Was that teenage girl she met years before one of the two kids that were missing from her home? Maybe! But where was the other kid? Was it a boy or a girl? She struggled to think back in time, a time even before she was six, possibly three. Then, she jumped up from her bed with a gasp of breath. Yes! She remembered when she met an even younger boy than the teenage girl, yet still older than James, but his face was fuzzy. Were they the two missing from her life, her home, her heart?

***

As Mary Ellen grew older, bickering and drinking between Leo and Flora took over as the years passed by. Mary Ellen often played referee as she wedged herself between them, so much so that she even advised them to divorce and then maybe there would be some peace in their unsettled house they called home. There was only so much the human heart and conscious could carry before it exploded. But putting your cards on the table, airing dirty laundry, or going for counseling was unheard of in most families of the sixties.

Mary Ellen tried to move on, and for the most part she did. At eighteen, her high school graduation was the only thing on her mind. She held her parents dear to her heart, but she was tired of being the grownup. It was her time, not theirs, and that left her no time to bother with their poor choices.

James disconnected from his family's discontent. He joined the Army and made a new life for himself without any knowledge of what Mary Ellen had heard when she was ten. She never knew those other two kids and she didn't want to know them–or did she? She was graduating from high school, something that neither of her parents had accomplished. That was all she cared about, and again she buried those thoughts deeper, but never to the point that she had forgotten.

***

Leo had been dead for 18 years, and Mary Ellen had to move Flora into a nursing home to help better care for her as she slipped into a deep depression, or what the medical professionals called dementia. Both acted the same and because she knew of her mother's past, depression seemed like a more logical diagnosis.

With the alienation of three of her four children, Mary Ellen was left to care for her mother on her own.

She'd say good morning and place her mother's favorites, a cup of black coffee and a Bavarian crème doughnut, on the end table beside her bed. A new tradition began between them. Flora would smile and ask how the family was and Mary Ellen would tell her the family was good. She wanted to make her mother feel happy, accepted, and loved, something Flora lacked in her past before Leo.

Flora would tell her daughter that she would like to go sit outside to have her treat, even if the weather wasn't good, and with the aid of a walker and some assistance from Mary Ellen, they'd sit at a table located near the huge windows that brought the outdoors in. This encouraged Flora to smile to think she was outdoors.

Flora started to forget her daughter's name every now and again as she dropped the Mary and called her Ellen. Her mother's repetitiveness and forgetfulness were more obvious each day but she still recognized her daughter – most of the time.

Flora continued to ask how the family was and Mary Ellen would respond that they were good. Mary Ellen knew that she would ask again in her next breath.

"She doesn't participate in any of our activities. She never wants to leave her room except for mealtime. Only when you come she leaves her room. You're all she talks about," said a robust caretaker.

Mary Ellen informed the caretaker that her mother was over 80 years old and coffee time with her was her only activity. It wasn't anyone's fault that she didn't participate. That was just the way she was. Mary Ellen was always nice to the caretakers, as her mother could be stubborn and could make their job difficult at times. But she knew her mother's past ate at her and all she could do was to be there for her.

Flora would ask her daughter for the umpteenth time how the family was, and Mary Ellen would run her hand over her face, impatient and exhausted from the repetitiveness. She'd sigh and respond that they were fine–again–and Flora would smile.

All Flora wanted was to visit with her daughter. And when the visit came to an end, Mary Ellen told her mother she loved her and gave her a substantial hug on her way out the door. Her weighted, tired mind saddened that the person she called Mom denied her other offspring. Was it a messy divorce or a child out of wedlock? Maybe! Only one person had the answers and she wasn't talking.

***

Dan and Mary Ellen have been married for over twenty years and have two grown sons. Dan had taken an interest in his ancestry and dabbled in Ancestry.com. Mary Ellen knew that he could help her attain information about her family.

She could hear her own heartbeat when she approached and told him the story. Then she asked, "Can you help me find my sister? I think she's the teenage girl we visited in 1964."

"Well, what's her name? I need a name," Dan said.

"And I know there's a boy too," she continued. "I think I know his first name but not the last."

Dan never judged people, so it would be easy to get his help. He said, "Without a last name it may be difficult to find the boy but give me the girl's name anyway."

"Her name's Rebecca Holmes from San Antonio, Texas," Mary Ellen said. "Do you think you can find her?"

"It may be difficult to find her if she married and changed her name, and the boy, probably not without a last name to go on," Dan said.

Dan entered her name and came up with quite a few Rebecca Holmes. He began with the ones closest to what her age would be today. She was born in 1947 and knowing this would cancel out many by the same name.

They contacted only the ones who came close to her name, age, and state where Mary Ellen had last seen her but no one responded. It boiled down to one lady who had similar facial features Mary Ellen had compared from an old photo she found after she moved Flora to a nursing facility. After Mary Ellen messaged her over the course of a year, she thought it best to stop before she was accused of harassment. The burying of the lost siblings was the only thing she could do, and again she suppressed the notion of ever finding them.

***

Mary Ellen's friends traveled from time to time and posted photos on Facebook for all to see. Their photos from San Antonio stirred past memories and she decided to take another chance to find Rebecca herself. Since she and her husband had exhausted the Facebook realm, Mary Ellen typed her name in the search engine on her computer homepage and a page came up with a link to a Rebecca Holmes Beaumont in San Antonio, Texas. She clicked on it and there was Rebecca's high school photo and it matched up to the photo she had from their 1964 vacation.

She heard the back door open and knew it would be Dan. Mary Ellen flew off the recliner and met him in the kitchen.

"I found her! I found Rebecca and I have her address. I am going to write to her tonight!" She waved the little piece of paper in front of his face like a child who had received her first A.

He asked, "Are you sure it's her?"

"I'm sure," she said. "And Rebecca being eleven years older than me, she'll know who I am."

Mary Ellen wondered why Rebecca never looked for her. They did visit her in 1964, so her letter shouldn't have been too much of a shock and she needed to know what happened. She shrugged her shoulders and began to write:

> *Dear Rebecca,*
>
> *My name is Mary Ellen Edwards. I am formerly Mary Ellen Lansing. I am in search of my sister who shares your name. My mother's name is Flora Lansing. I believe her to have had another daughter around 1947. I have been searching for a while. If you can give me any information on this matter I would greatly appreciate it. Please respond either way.*
>
> *Sincerely,*
> *Mary Ellen Edwards*

"Can you mail it for me?" she asked.

Dan obliged, knowing full well how important the letter was to his wife. Mary Ellen sat with her feet up that night, pleased that the letter would be on its way. She knew she had found her sister Rebecca.

***

Later that evening, she looked at Dan for reassurance and said, "It shouldn't take long for her to answer me. We're both adults now and have nothing to lose."

Dan remarked, "*If* she answers you. It's been fifty years. There's been no connection with her and your mother. And there's a reason for that, one that you may never know. Your mother will take it to her grave."

Dan couldn't understand how Mary Ellen's father had put up with the charades and asked, "What was your father's part in this?"

"I don't know," she said. "I'm hoping Rebecca, if she's the right one, will shed some light on this whole fiasco."

Within a week, a letter arrived from Texas. Mary Ellen's hands shook with excitement and fear. She opened the letter with Dan by her side. Her stomach tightened as she slipped it from its envelope. Tears dropped one by one as she read:

> *I am the sister you have been searching for. Flora was married to my father for five years, and I am the product of their marriage. Flora was young and did not want any children, and I'm surprised that she bore three more after me...*

She told of another older brother, Steven, and how Flora never took him home from the hospital. She wrote that Flora's mother never forgave her for the way she treated the two of them and how they were raised by other family members. She told Mary Ellen that Steven would contact her soon and within that same week he wrote:

> *Where have you been the last fifty years? I'm glad you looked me and Rebecca up and I don't want to alarm you but, although Rebecca and I share the same last name, I was born out of wedlock and I never knew who my father was. Maybe you can find out for me without Flora knowing that we've talked. I was raised by our mother's family and I long to know who my father is...*

And Steven continued that it would serve no purpose to be angry for choices Flora made back then. He never knew her. He told Mary Ellen that he would be happy if the two of them could meet and have that long overdue coffee. She wrote to Steven and let him know that she would try to find out who his father was and what had happened. She knew it would be a long shot to drag that kind of information out of her mother. She let Steven know that she wouldn't ask right out because she had tried that before and it made Flora anxious. She didn't want her mother to cry or feel inferior for the choices she had made, and without knowing the real reasons why she made them would be cruel on Mary Ellen's part to hound a woman with no desire or perhaps no memory to tell all. Flora had had enough. Mary Ellen had the answers about her missing siblings. Mary Ellen believed that what was done was done, and she ceased asking questions.

***

Although Steven's father was never disclosed and Rebecca's connection to Mary Ellen weakened as time went by, their new-found relationship continued and Flora did take her secrets to the grave, just as Dan had said she would.

From time to time, Flora had blurted out her famous adage, "Children pay the price for their parents' mistakes."

Now Mary Ellen knew what her mother meant.

Sometimes Being Honest Is Just Being Stupid

By Marty Pena

Does anyone really want to hear the truth?

"Honey, does this outfit make my butt look too big?"

Most husbands know the universal, correct, and safest reply to one's wife's question is,

"Yes, dear."

But he was only half listening and the auto-response mode backfired. Why had he opened his big mouth? However, on closer inspection, it really was a matter of too much butt and not enough material. Besides, the slacks were school bus yellow, and her snarky friends would be sure to make that connection when they got the rear view of the red patch pockets on her rump.

What did this designer have against mature women? he thought.

She would be mortified. He could not let that happen. He chose to take his bullet now rather than later. Later would surely be an all-night, wine-fueled firestorm to contend with. He could not let her go into that den of vipers she called friends. They were the mean girls from high school days and they hadn't changed a bit.

Now she was rummaging through her closet, throwing outfits across the bed.

"Here's another one ready for Goodwill. Honestly, I have nothing to wear," she snapped.

"Oh, there must be something in there, sweetie," he cooed, trying to appease her. "How about the blue one? You know blue is your color. You look beautiful in blue."

"It's TOO BAGGY!" she moaned.

He bit his tongue and thought to himself, *I'm no fashion expert, but baggy seems the way to go since middle-age spread has set in.*

She was sobbing now, standing there in her slip and staring at the blue dress.

"I think I wore this the last time I went out with the girls."

"Surely they won't remember, will they?"

"OF COURSE THEY WILL!"

Of course, he agreed to himself. *Elephants never forget.*

"I really need to update my wardrobe."

He could tell already, this was going to cost him some big bucks. He sighed, flicked his newspaper and settled back in his armchair. *I wonder what time the game is on?*

She wiggled into the blue dress, mumbling to herself. She checked her makeup.

"Oh my God! I look like a raccoon! Why did you make me cry?"

Wait! What? He looked over the top of his glasses. *How did I do that? Can she read my thoughts?*

She repaired her mascara and stormed out.

"Have a good time. You look lovely, dear," he shouted after her.

No one wants to hear the truth.

The Butterfly Effect

By David Boiani

The giant oak tree towered over the deserted county road with its canopy of branches and leaves shading the blacktop. It was a bright and crisp autumn day with a few white, fluffy clouds occasionally bringing shade to the countryside below. A sporadic flurry of breezes caused the long strands of grass on the side of the road to shimmer. One solitary rogue gust caused an acorn to detach from its branch and fall onto the middle of the road below. That gust and that lone acorn would cause the lives of three people to be changed forever.

***

A young raccoon wandered away from his den, located in a hollowed-out oak tree. He was the largest and bravest of the kit, and those attributes caused him to be the most difficult to track. Mother was down by the stream searching for food, so he ventured out in the other direction to explore. If his mother knew what he was up to, there would be hell to pay.

He climbed up the steep hill which was covered in shade from a canopy of oak and pine trees. When he finally reached the top of the hill, he eagerly glanced across the horizon and noticed something he had never seen before. There was what seemed to be an endless, hard black surface that stretched out in both directions.

He waddled closer to inspect this new discovery. As he reached the surface, he stuck his paw onto it and felt the rock-hard composition. It had absolutely no give to it, unlike the ground around the den and stream. Suddenly, something fell from above, landing only a few feet away in the center of the strange surface. He crawled over and curiously picked up the small object.

Wait, he has seen these before! It was an acorn, which Mother brought home frequently to eat. He cracked the hard outer shell open and picked out some of the delicious inner meat and shoved it into his mouth. An intense rumble and vibration shook the ground. He looked up just in time to see a huge monster heading straight at his little body. He froze in fear and braced for the impact.

***

Steven Taylor turned onto Route 101 in a rush, his mind racing even faster than his sports car. His wife Katie had just gone into labor, two weeks early. Steven was away on business, planning to arrive home on the weekend until the panicked phone call came. He had an hour's drive ahead of him on 101, then another thirty minutes west to the hospital. A couple of months ago they learned that the baby, their first, was a girl. Steven's mind wandered to his daughter as he drove down the long and winding country road…

There he stands in the delivery room at the foot of Katie's bed. His daughter cries as the nurse cleans her and then places the baby in his arms. He feels an extraordinary, unfamiliar emotion when he looks at the baby's little face and thinks: Andrea, my daughter.

On a perfect autumn morning, the black Mustang continued down the road as bright sunshine cascaded down on the countryside. His mind focused on another time in the future…

It's Andrea's first day of school. Steven parks the car in the lot and escorts his daughter to the front entrance.

"But Daddy, what if I get scared? What if I miss you and Mommy?"

Steven drops down on one knee to look into Andrea's eyes.

"Pumpkin, take this and keep it in your pocket. If you get scared, just take it out and look at it. You'll know we're with you, always. Remember, we both love you very much."

Andrea looks down at a picture of their family, smiles, and puts it in her pocket. Steven watches as his little girl walks away from him and into her own life for the first time. He knows in his heart there will be many more experiences like this in the years ahead.

The wind kicked up as Steven called his mother.

"Hello?"

"Hi, Mom. How is she?"

"It's getting close, Steve. Are you on your way?"

"Yes. I'll be there in an hour."

"Please hurry, honey. She's coming quickly."

Steve hung up and took the Mustang around a sharp bend. The road straightened, and his thoughts wandered once again…

He sits in a large college arena as his daughter's name is called.

"Congratulations to our valedictorian — Andrea Taylor!"

She is handed her diploma to a standing ovation. Tears trickle down Steven's face. He wipes them away and cheers for his daughter.

Steve pressed the gas pedal as he tried to make up for lost time. The feeling of anticipation was overwhelming. The wind was blowing through the car, giving him a pure, exhilarating sensation, almost as if nature was cleansing his soul, getting him ready for the next chapter in his life…

He stands with his daughter in front of an altar and a priest. She is the most beautiful woman he has ever seen. He hands her off to a handsome man with a kind face who loves her unconditionally. The bride and groom both say, "I do," and the priest pronounces the couple husband and wife. Steven smiles, realizing he gave his own flesh and blood a life that includes love, success, and hope.

Suddenly Steven was jarred out of his daydream by something in the middle of the road. He jerked the wheel to the right and lost control of the vehicle as the little raccoon ran to safety. The Mustang careened over the side of the road, down a steep hill, and directly into a large pine tree. Steven Taylor died on impact.

***

Andrea Taylor entered the world in a rush exactly two hours after her father's death. Just before dusk, the family was informed of the tragedy. An inquisitive policeman noticed a destructive path through the shrubbery leading down the steep hill to Steven's car. Katie was heartbroken. Steven's passing sent her spiraling into a depression that would last for many years and cause a chain of events that would alter the course of Andrea's life forever.

***

Five years later…

"Andrea, get dressed. I know you're scared, but everyone goes to school. You can't be late the first day of your first year!"

"But Mommy, what if I miss you?" Andrea said as tears fell down her little cheeks.

"You'll get over it; we all do. Now get in the car."

Katie pulled up to the front of the school and dropped Andrea off. She didn't walk her daughter inside; she didn't talk to her and hand her a picture of their loving family. Katie was still in a deep depression over the loss of her husband. She loved her daughter dearly, but, no longer possessed the ability to display her love freely. She had lost her job and was living off her husband's life insurance policy. Katie started drinking in moderation at first, then excessively over the years, starting the binges earlier and earlier in the days. Andrea spent her first day of school scared and withdrawn. She would become an introvert without the confidence required to socialize in a healthy manner. That afternoon, when her mother picked her up, Andrea told her everything went well, and she enjoyed school. Even at five years old, she knew telling her mother the truth wouldn't help Andrea solve her problems.

***

Seven years later…

Katie walked into the junior high school and headed for the parent-teacher lounge. Mrs. Jackson, Andrea's teacher, had called for a conference to discuss Andrea's schoolwork and attitude. The two women shake hands and sit down across from each other.

"Nice to see you again, Mrs. Taylor. Glad you could make it."

"Likewise. Now what's the issue with my daughter?"

"Andrea is a very bright girl, but she seems withdrawn and despondent. With a bit of effort, she could be a special student. As a teacher, it breaks my heart to see intelligence and talent wasted and I feel that way about your daughter."

"Has she done something to disrupt your class, Mrs. Jackson?"

"Well, no, but that's the worst part. If she was disruptive, at least I could get through to her, talk to her; maybe we could work it out. However, she is unapproachable. When I try to push her, she just pulls back further inside herself. I think your daughter suffers from depression."

"Well, Mrs. Jackson, thank you for your diagnosis. I didn't realize teachers doubled as psychiatrists these days."

"Mrs. Taylor, I'm trying to help. I care about your daughter… and you."

"With all due respect, try losing your husband an hour before you give birth to your child. Try missing him every day. Try feeling the pain of watching your daughter grow up without her father, knowing our perfect family had been destroyed. When you've gone through all that, then come back and see me and maybe I will listen to you."

"Katie, your daughter needs help, before it's too late."

"We're fine," Katie said and stood so suddenly the chair scraped back. "Teach her math, science, history. Do your job and don't worry about what isn't your concern. Good day."

Mrs. Jackson watched Katie walk out, feeling defeated and helpless, knowing exactly where her intelligent, but wayward, student was heading.

***

Two years later…

Andrea skipped school to hang out with her only friends Paula, Thomas, and Gary. Gary's parents were out of town and he scored some weed, vodka, and cocaine. Gary sat on the couch and lit up a joint.

"Andrea, come sit next to me while I set up a line."

Andrea walked over and sat next to Gary. He handed her the blunt. She inhaled the smoke, sat back, and relaxed.

"Wow, feels great."

"First time?" Paula asked.

"Yes, never tried coke, either."

"Well, now you have," Gary said as he held up a little mirror containing the line of white powder for her to inhale. Andrea felt the nearly instant jolt of dopamine and collapsed back on the couch to the laughter of her friends. Andrea spent the rest of the day in a drug and alcohol-induced high. She forgot school and her mother, wondered what her father was like and whether he would have loved her. She lost her virginity that day to a young man who didn't care about her or the responsibilities that came with having sexual intercourse. Andrea walked into her house at 11:00 that night to find her mother passed out on the sofa with an empty bottle of vodka on her lap, not having once wondered where her fourteen-year-old daughter was.

***

Two months later…

Andrea said a prayer to no one as she waited for the little stick to share its secret. She didn't believe in God, so she really had no clue why she would implore for help from a higher power.

Just another reason to be a disbeliever, she thought as the pregnancy test reads: POSITIVE.

I'm pregnant, two months shy of my fifteenth birthday. I don't believe this. What am I going to do? She lay in bed that evening and cried herself to sleep, a horrifying fear running through her.

She bunked school the next day and spent most of it walking around the park, digesting her predicament and trying to figure out how to handle it. She would tell her mother. She knew she had to, because she couldn't manage it on her own. She walked in that afternoon and sat beside her mother on the couch. There was an empty bottle of wine on the coffee table next to a half-filled glass.

"Mom, we need to talk."

"Oh, no." Her mother knew as soon as Andrea opened her mouth. "How do you know?"

"Home test. What the fuck, Andrea? You're fourteen! Who?"

"My friend, Gary. He doesn't know. No one knows."

"Don't tell anyone. You're going to abort it."

"What if I want it?"

"Andrea, we are not having this discussion. I'll make a few calls and set up an appointment. Don't tell Gary. We don't need him wanting to keep it and complicating the situation."

Andrea sat there and looked at her mother.

How could she be so cold? How could she just give up on life the way she has? Why didn't her mother love her?

Andrea got up and without a word, left Katie alone with her wine.

The following week, Andrea returned home from her appointment. She was sore, exhausted, and heartbroken. She crawled in her bed and lay on her stomach with her face buried in her pillow and cried all night. She craved peaceful sleep, but none came.

***

Three years later…

Andrea dropped out of school. She became hooked on cocaine and landed a part-time job waitressing in a low-end restaurant, which didn't garner nearly enough money to support her addiction. She started turning tricks for older men who paid her well, and soon quit her job. She hated herself and her life. She was humiliated by the woman she had become and she lived just to feed her habit. The sweet, successful woman that Steven Taylor had dreamed about was a forgotten memory.

Andrea walked into her house, having made enough that day to cover her needs for the upcoming weekend. She immediately noticed her mother. Katie was collapsed on the floor with her hand still grasping a broken glass. Vodka puddled next to her. On the coffee table were three empty bottles.

Andrea hurried over to her mother's lifeless body.

"Mom, wake up! Mom!" There was no response. Her mother had drunk herself to death.

Andrea sat down on the floor with her head in her hands and wept. She wept for her mother, for herself — for everything they had lost in life. When there were no more tears to give, she stood up and headed to the basement.

She knew what she had to do.

***

Three days later…

She was found by a policeman in the basement, hanging from the light fixture. Andrea Taylor left the earth four months short of her eighteenth birthday. She died the same day as her mother. A funeral was held for them three days later. Very few people came.

***

Steven Taylor drove his Mustang down the long, winding country road. He turned to his wife in the passenger seat and smiled. Katie, the only woman he had ever loved, smiled back and grabbed his hand. Behind Katie sat five-year-old Andrea, the same age she was on that first day of school, so long ago. She was innocent, beautiful, and loved dearly by her parents. As the car approached the spot of the terrible accident that took Steven's life, Andrea noticed a small animal on the side of the road.

"Look! Mommy, Daddy, it's a baby raccoon!"

"Wow, look at that, sweetie," Katie agreed, amused.

As the family traveled happily together on that endless vacant country highway, Steven turned his hand over. "Look what I have for you, Pumpkin. An acorn, freshly dropped from that tree we just passed."

He handed his daughter the acorn and drove into eternity with his loving family by his side.

The Difficulty of Navigating a Corn Maze on Halloween

By R.N. Chevalier

A brisk breeze blows the tops of the cornstalks slightly to the north. Spotlights at the two front corners of the huge maze illuminate people in a long line waiting for their turn to try to make their way through.

Midway in the line is Donna, a hot, five-foot-tall firecracker. With her is her best friend Gail, a Puerto Rican bombshell. Next to them is Laurie, their equally attractive blonde friend who believes herself a debutante. Rounding out the quartet is Jay, the resident computer geek and the only man in the group.

The line moves along at a good pace and everyone is having a great time. A sudden burst of arctic air whips through the field. Several people zip their jackets. The rest don't even notice. Lights flicker as the generator sputters. The line of people continues to move at a moderate pace.

Donna looks around at the folks who have come for a shared experience. There are your typical families, enjoying the bonding experience. There are groups of young people, mostly twos and threes, both boys and girls, enjoying the maze as well as possibly hooking up for more private fun later.

And there are couples, alone and in pairs. There are groups of older women buying fresh fruits and vegetables while gossiping about neighbors and family, as their husbands wait impatiently at the barn entrance. Donna notices one man in particular. He is in his late sixties and seems oddly out of place but she can't figure why.

"Hey," Donna says to Gail. "Wasn't that strange old man here last year?"

"Yeah," Gail answers. "And the year before as well." After a few seconds of thought, her attention returns to the reason she is at the corn maze, to have fun with her friends.

As the four approach the man at the podium with money in hand, a bolt of lightning illuminates the night sky, bathing the corn maze in an eerie blue haze-like light. They pay the man and enter.

They make their way in about ten yards when the trail splits in two directions.

"Which way should we go?" Donna asks.

"That way," Laurie replies, pointing to the left.

"Good idea," Jay cuts in. "You and Donna go that way and Gail and I will go the other way."

"We'll meet at the exit," Gail concludes. The four split up.

Laurie and Donna go off to the left as Gail and Jay head to the right. The two women get several yards down the path and follow the left turn. A few yards more leads them to a right U-turn. They stumble into a chamber ten feet square. Vines from assorted shrubbery make up a roof, causing darkness to envelope the inner three quarters of the space.

There is a pole in the center of the chamber holding a lantern. Faintly illuminated against the back wall are two doors. To either side of the pole are small plaques. Each of the plaques contains a riddle. The left plaque reads:

When day is night
Sunrise, twilight

The number of cities
Destroyed by atomic emission is?

"What the hell does that mean?" Laurie asks.

"Two," Donna answers.

"What?" Laurie's eyes are wide.

"Hiroshima and Nagasaki," Donna replies. "The cities destroyed by atomic bombs."

"Oh, yeah," Laurie says as they move on to the right plaque.

Three are,
Yet are not
How many represent
The number in the present

"That's easy," Laurie tells Donna with a smile. "It's one."

"How?" Donna asks.

"Me, myself and I," Laurie explains. "In the present it's I, one."

"So, what kind of sense does that make?" Donna asks. "The first answer is two. The second answer is one. There are two doors, one and two. Can they both be the right answer?"

She is answered by a bell's ding seemingly from nowhere and the two doors open, exposing darkness on both sides. Laurie enters the door on the right while Donna enters the one on the left. The doors close behind the women, plunging them both into lightless voids.

Jay and Gail make their way in ten yards before the corridor turns right, then immediately begins a zigzag pattern that confuses them. The path turns straight and becomes a four-way intersection. They go right.

The path takes an immediate right and continues before turning right once more, dead-ending five feet in.

"This looks like as good a place as any," Jay says.

"For what?" Gail asks, flashing a grin. He grabs her upper arms firmly and pulls her close, slamming his lips into hers.

Neither one will remember how long they were kissing when they were interrupted by two five-year-olds giggling. They separate, both embarrassed, as the kids run away. The two leave the niche and head back to the intersection.

Jay and Gail go straight across and spend the next two hours exploring the ten openings in the center of the maze. They find that every opening circles back to another of the openings. The eighth opening they go through leads them down a long, twisting path.

They walk on for ten minutes in near total darkness and find the path turns to the left.

They are now in total darkness as they inch along the corridor. Jay's hands are extended in front of him as he tries to feel for the wall. Suddenly his hands find smooth, soft orbs.

"Hey," an unknown female voice says loudly. From the darkness an object makes contact with Jay's face and a fleshy slap sound is heard. "Those are mine!"

"Oww!" Jay shouts. Gail activates the flashlight app in her cell phone and aims the light toward the sounds. The beam finds Jay gently rubbing his cheek. Under his hand there is a large welt forming, a welt in the shape of a hand. Standing in front of him is the owner of the strange voice, facing Jay and gently caressing her left breast. Gail laughs. Jay offers his sincere apologies.

Without warning, the wall in front of Gail and Jay parts and a blinding light engulfs them all. When their eyes adjust, the six people see another corridor leading to the exit twenty feet away.

Just as Donna's eyes adjust to the darkness she sees a pinpoint of light in front of her. It looks like it is a mile away yet she is mesmerized by its crystal-like brilliance. The diameter of the beam starts to expand and the shimmering, inner facets reflect light coming from an unknown source in multicolored rays of intense color.

The beams of light dance around the room in a flood of colors. In an instant the colors become a blinding white light so brilliant that Donna can no longer differentiate between the floor, walls, and ceiling.

In another instant the white light flashes away and Donna is standing in an empty field nearly a hundred feet from the entrance to the maze. It is now early afternoon and she sees that she is the only one around.

"What the hell?" she says aloud. She starts walking to the maze.

"Laurie!" Donna screams loudly. She waits for an answer.

"Gail! Jay!" She gets to the entrance and looks inside.

"Laurie!"

In the darkness of her small chamber, Laurie can hear the faint sound of Donna screaming her name. She giggles, thinking Donna is lost within the mile square wall of stalks. She makes her way forward. The darkness seems to thicken around her. Apprehension overwhelms her as claustrophobic blackness envelops her.

"Donna, where the hell are you?" she screams. Silence is her reply. The darkness squeezes in around her. It is so black it seems like light itself has vanished from reality.

"Donna," she screams again. "Where are you?"

Gail and Jay exit the maze with the other four people they encountered. They stop as soon as they clear the stalks, expecting to find Donna and Laurie waiting, annoyed that it took them so long. The two are nowhere to be found.

"Do you remember us?" Gail asks the attendant at the entrance.

"Yeah," the attendant answers. "I remember you."

"Did our other friends come out?"

"What other friends?"

Gail looks at the attendant strangely, then goes back to Jay.

"What'd he say?" Jay asks.

"He remembers me but not Donna or Laurie."

"He was probably too busy staring at your ass to notice anything else."

"I think he was too stoned." The two laugh.

Gail takes out her cell phone and calls Donna's number. The phone rings… and rings and rings. After fifteen rings she hangs up.

"That's strange," she tells Jay. "It didn't even go to voicemail."

An hour passes and the crowd is down to a handful of people. Gail goes back to the attendant with Jay in tow.

"Hey, dude," Gail says. "Our two friends haven't come out yet and we're getting concerned. Can you send someone in to find them?"

"What friends are you talking about?" he asks her.

"We came in here with two friends," Jay says.

"No, you didn't," the attendant replies.

"Yes we did," Gail says loudly, getting the attention of passersby.

"No," he insists with a chuckle of disbelief. "The two of you went in alone."

"How can you say that?"

"Because you did."

At that moment, the owner of the farm, alerted by several patrons, comes walking over.

"What's going on here?" he asks.

"Our two friends are lost somewhere in there and he won't do anything about it," Gail says.

"What about it, Mr. Vickers?" the boss asks.

"Like I've been telling them, sir, they went in alone, no friends, just the two of them."

"How is it you remember them in particular?" The boss's question makes the young attendant uncomfortable. He pauses.

"Spit it out, Mr. Vickers." Several long seconds pass.

"You may fire me," Vickers explains. "But I was staring at her ass. It's impossible not to stare at her ass. I watched her go all the way in. I remember him and I would have remembered their friends."

When the darkness fades and her eyes adjust, Laurie finds herself a few feet in front of a rock wall several hundred feet high.

She looks around in confusion as she glimpses something that makes her knees weak and stomach turn. Hanging in the night sky just to the right of the moon is a second moon, much smaller but definitely in orbit.

"What the hell am I going to do now?" she asks herself out loud as she looks around, surveying the alien landscape.

"Ah, damn," she mutters. She starts walking away from the cliff wall towards a dark silhouette in the distance.

Donna walks toward the barn-like building where, when she went into the maze, several vendors were selling produce. She enters the building to find an empty room. All the bins and wagons are empty and there are no signs that anyone had ever been there in a very long time.

"Hello," she shouts as she walks to the back of the building. She gets silence for an answer. It takes another two minutes until she gets to the door leading to the offices.

"Is there anyone here?" she shouts into the offices and still gets no response. She makes her way through the maze of hallways and offices. At the end of the hall she finds an exit door. She goes through and is blinded and disoriented by a brilliant light engulfing the room.

She walks blindly forward with her arms extended in front of her, feeling for obstructions. After inching along, her hands stop at a wall. She side-steps to the left, feeling the wall for a door. It takes her a few minutes but she finally finds a doorknob and exits the room.

Her eyes adjust and she finds herself on a path in a light patch of woods. A glade several yards ahead shimmers in the sunshine. She approaches the clearing with caution when her ears catch the distant sound of a whistle.

She takes cover behind a large tree as the whistling grows louder. Around the bend in the path a young woman comes walking toward the glade. She is taller than Donna, with long blonde hair.

The woman is wearing bell-bottom jeans covered with floral designs. A home-made vest covers a bright yellow tee shirt. Her hair is held in place by a headband with the same floral patterns as her jeans. Donna can see a sadness in her eyes.

"Hello," Donna says to the young woman, who screams out in surprise.

"You scared the crap out of me," she tells Donna.

"Sorry, I didn't mean it. My name is Donna."

"I'm Robyn."

"Robyn," Donna starts on a more serious note. "I'm confused. Where am I?"

"I don't understand," Robyn answers.

"An hour ago I went into a corn maze with three friends. I went into a room and there was a freaky light and then I was outside of the maze. It was daytime and no one else was around. I went into a building and there was another light, then I was here. Where is here?"

"I went into the maze, too. I got to the doors with the riddles. My boyfriend, Mark, went in one door and I went in the other. I ended up here alone."

"I don't remember seeing you in line and with that outfit. I'd have remembered."

"We were in a group with eight other people. We had a portable radio with an eight-track player playing the new Doors album. I could hear the music playing for a little while when I first got here but it's been quiet for a while now."

"The Doors haven't had a new CD out in twenty plus years," Donna tells her.

"You're tripping," Robyn replies. "This one just came out two weeks ago."

"Now *you're* tripping," Donna answers. "Jim Morrison died in like nineteen seventy-two. There's been nothing new since then, so which one are you talking about?"

"It's called *Waiting for The Sun*," she replies.

"*Waiting for The Sun* came out in nineteen sixty-eight," Donna says.

"Yeah," Robyn says. "Two weeks ago."

Donna staggers back against the tree as what Robyn says sinks in.

"Robyn," Donna says numbly. "What year is it?"

"Nineteen sixty-eight," she answers and sees Donna get pale. "What's wrong?"

"I went into the corn maze in two thousand and sixteen," Donna replies and now Robyn's face goes pale.

"There has to be some logical explanation," Donna says.

"Yeah," Robyn retorts. "A horrible nightmare… or maybe I took some bad acid and this is just a bad trip."

"It's not a nightmare or bad acid," Donna says.

"What else can it be?" she asks, tears flowing. Donna grabs her gently by the shoulders and looks at her eye to eye.

"Listen," Donna begins. "My husband is a huge science fiction nut. He likes all those TV shows and movies. I see some of them from time to time and they talk about shit like this."

"There's nothing on TV that can explain what's going on," Robyn says.

"Not in nineteen sixty-eight, but in two thousand sixteen there is much more known about phenomena like this, and some movies and TV shows try to teach that science through their story-lines."

"Sounds like an awesome time," Robyn says.

"It is, in most respects." Donna tells her. "I only wish I had paid more attention to the science behind the plots."

"What?"

"I just need some time to try to think about what the hell happened to us."

"Listen, pal," Gail says. "I'm flattered that your guy here was checking me out, but my chicas are lost, so we are going back in there to look for them. That's not a problem with you, is it?" Several seconds pass.

"Listen, lady," the boss says. "You and your friend can go back in and look for your other friends but you need to keep your voice down."

"She can't help it," Jay tells the boss. "She always talks that loud."

"I see," the boss says. "Please try to turn it down a notch… so the other patrons can enjoy themselves."

"Okay," Gail says. "Thanks. We'll let you know when we find them." Gail and Jay re-enter the maze.

"Which way did they go?" Gail asks.

"They went to the left," Jay answers.

"I remember that. It's after that that concerns me."

"We'll figure it out," Jay responds.

The two make their way around the twists and turns that lead them to a dead end. They backtrack and find the route that leads to the U-turn and the pole with the riddles. They figure out the answers and are ready to enter the two rooms.

"Which one do you think they went into?" Jay asks.

"Knowing them, they each went their own way."

"Then we should do the same thing."

"Oh, hell no. We go in together."

"Then pick a door."

"The left," she answers, and the two enter the door on the left.

The door closes behind Gail and Jay and darkness envelops the two. Both feel a shudder of apprehension. They see the pin-point of light and watch as the crystal-like brilliance overtakes them. When the brightness fades and their eyes adjust, the two find themselves just outside of the maze in the middle of the afternoon.

"What the hell?" an astonished Gail says.

"I have no clue," Jay says. It takes them several minutes to absorb the full scope of what happened.

"Let's see if there is anyone around here," Jay suggests and Gail agrees.

The two walk around the huge barn but don't find anyone. They walk around the outside of the maze. An hour passes and they find nothing, no person, no animal, no bird, or even insect.

"The only place left is the barn," Jay says.

"Then let's get out of the sun and search it," Gail suggests. They enter the structure and begin walking to the left side, where they start searching along a long wall, looking behind and around everything in their path in hopes of finding a clue about what's going on.

Not finding anything, they start searching back up to where they came in a systematic search so as not to miss any possible clues. They start their next pass to the back of the barn. Getting to the back, they discover the door leading to the offices.

"Shall we go inside?" Jay asks.

"Well, duh," Gail mocks. "There's nowhere else to go." The two enter cautiously and slowly make their way through two short halls and three offices.

"Donna, Laurie," Gail shouts into the empty rooms.

"Let's keep going," Jay says.

"This is pissing me off, Jay."

"What? The fact that no one is around? Or maybe that it's daytime now? Or that we can't find Donna and Laurie?"

"Yes," she replies. "All of it."

"I know and I don't mind saying I'm scared yet amazed."

"I'm scared too but more pissed. None of this makes any sense."

"It does somewhere," Jay tells her. "Let's keep moving."

They continue down the short halls. As they pass through each office they take the time to search each drawer in each desk and cabinet. All they find are the normal documents needed to run a farm. They reach the end of the hall and find the exit door.

"Hey, I gotta pee," Gail tells Jay. "The bathroom is two doors down so I'll meet you outside. She starts walking back as Jay opens the door. The room slowly fills with brilliant white light. Gail turns to see Jay walking toward the threshold.

"Jay!" Gail screams in terror as she moves closer to him. She feels the light drawing her in. She grabs onto a door frame with one hand and Jay's shirt with her other.

"Jay!" she screams again. "Snap out of it!" He shakes his head after hearing her screams and grabs onto the doorframe, inches from the blinding oblivion.

"I hear you," he replies, as he fights his way back into the corridor.

A brilliant sphere of light grabs the attention of both Donna and Robyn.

"What the hell is that?" Robyn asks, as the sound of rushing air gets progressively louder as the sphere grows brighter.

"That's how I got here!" Donna shouts. "Come on." She gets up and heads toward the sphere, Robyn in tow. As they approach the sphere, Donna makes out the faint image of a rectangle, standing on the short end.

They get closer and the two see a fainter outline within the rectangle. As the seconds tick by, the image becomes more focused. It is the image of a person, standing in a doorway.

"Jay!" Donna hears a voice coming from inside the sphere.

"Jay!" Donna shouts back. "Those are my friends," she tells Robyn.

"Donna?" She hears Jay's voice shout.

"Yes, it's me."

"Come closer," Jay shouts. "Grab my hand."

Donna starts moving toward the light, grabbing Robyn's hand as she goes.

She moves in close and stretches out her hand, feeling resistance from the light. She pushes through, still gripping Robyn's hand, her fingertips just inches away from Jay's.

"Jay, Donna!" Laurie's familiar voice screams above the rushing air, coming from the light, thick with terror and confusion. Both Donna and Jay see the faint silhouette of Laurie standing in the light beside them, her outstretched hand searching for them.

The three hands find each other in the brilliant light, their fingers locking together. Working in unison the four force past the bizarre forces and they all stagger back into the corridor. Gail lets go of Jay's shirt as he falls back and slams the door when the four are clear. The four stand and the friends, long separated, unite in a group hug.

"This is my new friend, Robyn," Donna tells her three friends.

"Hello," she says and the three reciprocate.

"Now here's where it gets weird," Donna begins.

"Weirder than this?" Jay interrupts.

"What can be weirder than this?" Laurie adds.

"Robyn went into the maze in nineteen sixty-eight," she answers.

"You had to ask," Gail chimes in.

"Now I'm freaking out," Laurie says.

"Now I know why I don't remember you in line," Jay says to Robyn.

"Donna," Gail begins. "What would your husband think is going on? He's into this weird-ass crap."

"I'm not sure," Donna admits. "I know we have a temporal paradox and I think we may be experiencing altered reality or different dimensions."

"I don't believe this," Laurie says, her voice showing signs of emotional strain.

"Hey, all that Star Trek crap that I'm forced to see rubs off. I do understand some of that science crap. There has to be some kind of machine around here that creates the vortexes that we've been going through."

"I don't believe this," Laurie repeats.

"Then how do you explain what's happening?" Donna asks her.

"I was just in a corn maze, then somewhere that had two moons, two moons!" Laurie's voice sounds more panicked. "Now I'm here with you guys again and with a sixty-year-old teenager, no less."

"Laurie," Gail interjects. "We'll figure something out."

"I'm fine," Laurie reassures the group. "I'm just wrapping my head around all of this." She stands up and takes a deep breath. "Let's find whatever is causing this and go home." Everyone agrees.

They make their way back through the maze of offices. They search every drawer and cabinet once more now that they have some idea of what to look for. Making their way back to the huge interior of the main barn they are still without clues.

The group spreads out and they thoroughly search the barn in three sweeps. They search every nook and box and crate and wagon and come up with nothing.

Gathering at the large door that they entered, the group moves to the outside. The maze is to the left and parking lot to the right. They all walk to the center of the parking area and survey their surroundings.

"Gail and I already searched the back side of the barn and we circled the maze," Jay tells the group.

"We didn't see anything like what we're looking for," Gail adds.

"I went straight into the barn," Donna says.

"I've never been here," Laurie says.

"Neither have I," Robyn shares.

"Then there is only one place it can be," Donna says after a few minutes of quiet contemplation. "Somewhere in there," she continues, pointing at the maze.

"Gail and I made it through the first time and didn't see anything out of place," Jay tells them.

"But the path we found didn't come anywhere near covering the whole maze," Gail says.

"Then we've got to go back in," Laurie says. Everyone agrees.

"But now we have the upper hand," Robyn follows. "We know what we're looking for and we know where not to go." They enter the maze.

The group follows the path first taken by Gail and Jay. They avoid the path to the doors as well as the dead-end the pair found earlier. They approach the end of the corridor and must go left or right.

"We need to split up," Jay says. "We can cover more ground."

"No, no, no," Donna replies.

"Why not?" Laurie asks.

"In every movie ever made, when the group has to split up, something bad happens," she explains.

"But that's in the movies."

"Do you really want to risk that?" The group goes quiet for several seconds. "Neither do I. Let's stick together and get out of here together."

"Which way looks like it goes toward the center?" Donna asks.

"The left," Robyn says after a few seconds.

"Why left?" Jay asks.

"When we came out of the barn I noted the orientation of the maze to the sun," she explains. "Taking into account the directions we've turned we are in the left, rear section. If we go right, we'll go in a circle or dead end so… left."

"Left it is," Gail says.

"You really kept track of all that in your head?" Jay asks her as they start walking. "Or are you just winging it?"

"Yes, I really kept track of all that in my head."

"No shit? How can you do that?"

"No shit. How come you can't?" She inches ahead of him.

"Ouch," Gail says with a laugh. "That had to hurt."

They get to a turn which becomes a zigzagging corridor, and eventually a four-way intersection.

"What now?" Laurie asks. All eyes focus on Robyn, who is looking around carefully.

"Either straight or left," she answers.

"Let's try going straight," Donna suggests.

"We have to mark the direction we're going," Gail says.

"Make an arrow with some stalks," Laurie recommends.

"Good idea." They grab stalks and build an arrow pointing in the direction they are going.

They head down the corridor and find themselves at another intersection.

"Now where?" Gail asks.

"Straight," Robyn answers.

"How do you know this time?" Jay asks her.

"Look," she tells him as she points to the ground around the corner to the right. On the ground is an arrow made of corn stalks.

The five head straight through the intersection. They turn left and are faced with a corridor nearly half a mile long. They can tell that the corridor turns left at the end.

When they get to the corridor they choose to explore it first but not before placing another stalk arrow on the trail. They head down the corridor and find themselves in a ten-foot-square courtyard with four benches in a square in the middle.

"Thank God," Donna says as she walks to a bench and sits. The others follow suit.

"You know what this means, don't you?" Laurie asks.

"Yeah," Jay answers. "We went the wrong way."

"Yep," Laurie confirms. "We went the wrong way."

The five intrepid explorers begin their trek back to the stalk arrow. Once they arrive they turn left and make their way along the half-mile stretch, making a left at the end.

"This is getting annoying," Donna says as they trudge along.

"Yeah," Robyn agrees. "But it's necessary." They reach the end and turn left.

Ahead of them is a corridor that opens to another quad. Along the wall opposite the entrance stand five metallic rectangular panels four feet wide by seven feet tall. The panels are spaced about a foot apart.

On the panels are a series of glyphs taking up half the surface area. There are fifteen glyphs on each panel. In front of each panel is a bench suitable for two people. They all sit. The air of disappointment hangs heavy around the group.

"Another dead end," Jay says disparagingly.

"No, it's not," Donna corrects him.

"What do you mean?"

"Remember the doors with the riddles?"

"Yeah."

"Why have these picture panels? We've run into all kinds of dead ends. Only one, other than here, that had something to look at. The riddles opened the doors. There has to be a meaning for those symbols."

"More Star Trek crap?" Laurie asks.

"Nope," Donna answers. "Ancient aliens crap. Russ loved that stuff, too."

"What does that mean?" Robyn asks.

"It means that the panels are here for a reason and the symbols tell us why. We just have to solve the riddle."

"Somehow that makes sense," Gail says as she looks up to the sky. "Thanks, Russ," she shouts. "Let's figure this out, shall we?"

They sit down, each focusing on a different panel. Time passes quietly.

An hour passes to no avail. Donna finally gets up to stretch her legs and suddenly stops in her tracks. Several glyphs on the center panel catch her eye.

She gets close to the panel to study them closer.

She sees a symbol of a three-dimensional box. The notches on the front of the box make it look like a crude picture of a computer. Another symbol is a spiral with lines radiating outward from the outer edge of the spiral. The other symbol is a face with an elongated skull and oversized eyes. The box and spiral are displayed side by side while the face sits above them in the center.

She leans forward, gently tracing the outline of the face with her finger. Gail stands and bumps into her, forcing Donna to press against the metallic surface for balance. When she does the symbol depresses then stops with a clicking sound.

Donna pushes on the spiral symbol, which she believes is a representation of the sphere of brilliant light. This symbol also recesses into the panel and clicks into place. When she presses the third symbol it clicks into place and the three images begin to glow, faintly at first but growing steadily brighter. After a few seconds the entire panel begins to shimmer and disappear, revealing a hidden entryway through the corn stalks.

"I found something," Donna says in astonishment. Everyone looks up. They cautiously enter the opening to find themselves in a room with walls, a floor, and ceiling.

They continue in to find a large computer terminal interface. Behind the interface are two rows of glowing cylinders five feet in diameter and eight feet tall. The rows go back for nearly a quarter of a mile.

"This must be what we're looking for," Gail announces.

"Does anyone know how this thing works?" Donna asks.

"I thought you would know," Laurie says.

"It was sheer luck that I even had an idea of what to look for," Donna admits. "As to working it, don't look at me, Jay is the IT guy. He knows his way around computers. If anyone can figure it out, he can."

"I can try," Jay says as he approaches the interface. He slowly examines the console, then he keys in some commands. An overhead view of the maze appears on the display screen. He keys in several more commands and a light blinks on the display.

"If I'm reading these controls right, I've locked a location for the sphere to form," Jay tells them. "Now I'm trying to set a timer." He keys in more commands. A symbol appears in the upper right corner of the display screen along with a corresponding tone. Every second the symbol and tone change.

"I think I've got a timer going," he says.

"How long do we have?" Robyn asks.

"Less than a minute," he answers.

"Where do we have to go?" Laurie asks.

"The end of the corridor and around the corner," he replies.

"Well I suggest we get there," Gail adds.

They make it around the corner and see nothing but two quiet stretches of corn stalks. The air around them is peaceful and still. The seconds tick by slowly, making time feel like it's standing still.

"Hey, Jay," Gail says.

"Yes, Gail."

"Why isn't anything happening?"

"I don't know, Gail. I said a minute. For all I know it could be an hour or even a day, I just don't…" He is cut off by the sudden sound of rushing air as the familiar sphere of brilliant light appears in front of them.

"There you go, Gail," he shouts above the sound.

"Thank you, Jay," she replies as she jumps into the light. Everyone else follows close behind, Jay going through last.

The five friends go from brilliant light to pitch darkness in the blink of an eye. Several seconds into the darkness, doors open to reveal the exit of the corn maze.

The group, along with about ten other people, exits the maze twenty feet from where they had entered. The line of people waiting to get in is still past the young man collecting money at the podium.

"Holy crap!" the money collector shouts in disbelief as the five walk by.

"What's wrong with you?" Gail asks.

"You four just went in, like, ten minutes ago. I've never seen anyone make it through that fast. But I don't remember her." He points to Robyn.

"We're back where we started," Donna says and the four join in a group hug. Sadness sweeps across Robyn's face.

"What's wrong, Robyn?" Donna asks.

"If we're back to when you went in that puts me fifty years out of time."

"We'll help you," Donna tells her. "We're all here for you." The four agree.

"You have an opportunity never afforded anyone else," Laurie tells her. "You have moved up fifty years into the future. There is so much awesome stuff you get to learn about."

"Excuse me." A voice from outside the tight circle of friends interrupts. They turn to see the older man Donna noticed as they went into the maze. His gaze is focused on Robyn.

"Robyn," he says. "It is you. My god, it is you."

"Mark," she replies. "Is that you?"

"Yes, my love, it's me. I've come here every year for the last forty-eight years waiting for you to come out, to come back to me."

"I think I'll be all right now," Robyn tells Donna and the rest of her new friends. "I've got the four of you and Mark. I know I'll be all right."

"Call me," Donna says to Robyn, who is walking away with Mark.

"Tomorrow," she replies with a smile.

Stuffy

By Leo C. Frisk, Jr.

A small, stuffed white bear brings you this bedtime story of friendship and love whether you are 6 or 60.

He tells you of his adventure to your house, and the joy he finds in your heart.

He is not only a bedtime bear, but he can also be a friend who waits for you to come home from school, or work, or play. Now sit back, read, enjoy, and remember; you can be Farthi (Gail), but the bear is Stuffy. Now, I lay here in my bed, my soft pillow beneath my head with Stuffy here beside me to keep me company. Here in the darkness of my room, I have crawled between the sheets and a warm blanket. I am lying on my back, staring up at the ceiling, into the darkness. I am a little afraid, but then I remember Stuffy is here beside me, protecting me, loving me, keeping me safe from harm. I reach over and wrap my arm around him and pull him close to my side. I hug him and squeeze him tight but not too tight. I wouldn't want to squeeze the stuffing out of him, you understand. Then, I close my eyes, but the sleep doesn't come. Nothing happens.

I don't understand what is going on. I took my bath. I said my prayers, and it is late. So why am I just lying here, me and Stuffy. I tum my head and ask, "Hey Stuffy, why are we still awake?"

Then to my amazement, he answers. "Because, Farthi, we are not sleeping."

I couldn't believe my ears. Stuffy, my small white bear filled with stuffing and made out of cloth, was talking to me. I rubbed my eyes just to make sure I was still awake, and not asleep and dreaming.

Then, with both my hands gently holding Stuffy, I raised him up above my head and stared straight into his round black eyes.

I held him up there for what seemed like a very long time. It was very dark in my bedroom, but his eyes were so shiny, I could see them through the darkness.

"Okay, my little bear. Am I dreaming, or did you really say that to me?"

Stuffy began to move. First he wiggled his little feet back and forth and then his tiny arms moved up and down. Then, oh my goodness, he began to laugh.

"Ha ha, hee hee, ha ha! I'm a silly little bear with a funny little voice living here in this funny, little place," Stuffy giggled.

"Wow!" I shouted out loud.

I got so excited, I let go of him and he fell down upon my nose and rolled down onto my belly. I quickly reached down and picked him back up.

"Are you all right? Are you okay?" I asked.

Then I carefully lifted him back up over my head, and stared back into his eyes. I waited for his response, but there was nothing, nothing at all! There was no 'Ouch, why did you do that?' No 'That hurt, you know!' No 'Boy, oh boy, are you clumsy.' There was nothing, nothing at all.

Tears welled up in my eyes. A small teardrop slid down my cheek, and settled in the corner of my mouth. Then, there was another teardrop, but this time it fell onto my face. It splashed, a very tiny splash that it splashed upon my nose.

"Hey, now where did that come from," I asked out loud.

"It came from me!"

It was Stuffy, and he was talking to me again! Oh, I was so happy to hear his voice, I almost dropped him again. But this time I held on tighter than ever before.

"Hey, are you trying to see what color my stuffing is?"

"Oops, I'm sorry," I told him. "It's just, well, I didn't want to drop you again."

"Oh, that was nothing. It didn't hurt me, not one tiny little bit. I'm a bear, you know. I'm a pretty tough critter."

"I know," I told him. "But there was a teardrop that fell from your eye, and I thought that when I dropped you, you may have been hurt by the fall."

"Nope, I didn't get hurt. I thought I had hurt your nose when I fell on it, and you were crying, so I cried too."

I laughed. I laughed so hard my arms and hands shook, and poor Stuffy shook, too.

"Hey, ey ey ey, stop pa pa, shaking me pa pa, please!"

"You sounded so funny, I had to laugh. I'm sorry about the shaking."

"Hey, you are a stuffed bear, and stuffed bears are not supposed to be able to talk, so how is it you can?"

"I am not just any stuffed bear. I was sent here with a lot of love to comfort you when you are sad, to make you laugh when you are down, and just to be here whenever you might need a friend. You know, someone to talk with whenever you can't sleep. So, here I am. Okay, now, close your eyes and I will tell you the entire story of how I was made, where I came from, and how I got here."

***

"I come from a place very far away from here. Very, very, very far away. Are you asleep, yet?"

I had closed my eyes to listen to Stuffy. Now, I opened one eye and peeked at him.

"Nope, not yet," I whispered.

"I was just joking," Stuffy laughed. "Phew, I guess I should continue."

And, he did. "The place was a huge building called a factory. Inside this factory were lots and lots of women. They all sat on these tiny chairs in front of these machines called sewing machines. The women took small pieces of cloth and placed the cloth beneath the sewing machine, and zip zip, stitch stitch, they sewed the cloth together into the shape of an animal, which in my case, as you can tell, was a bear. They sewed the animal almost all of the way, leaving only a little bit of a hole on the back side where the stuffing was stuffed through. Then the final stitches were sewn, and a bear was born. Me!"

Farthi opened her eyes again. "Wow! That must have hurt having all of those stitches going up and down your back like that!"

Phew, this is going to be a long night, Stuffy thought to himself.

"Close your eyes now," Stuffy told Farthi. And Farthi did. "Hmm, okay, now where was I, oh yes, I remember. When that woman had finished sewing the stuffing in me, I was stuffed into a box with all kinds of other animals. There were elephants, monkeys, and giraffes, but I was the only bear. I was so lonely squeezed in there with all of those other kinds of animals. I felt so out of place. I mean, after all, they could talk to one another and understand what each of them was saying, but there were no other bears. I was afraid that if I were to say something they would not understand, or even worse, misunderstand and then be angry with me and squash me like they did that bug."

"Bug, what bug!" This time Farthi had both eyes open and was not doing what she was supposed to be doing, falling asleep.

"Hey," Stuffy growled in a soft growling voice. "You are supposed to be falling asleep, not asking questions."

"I'm sorry," Farthi told him. "I will close my eyes again and try and go to sleep, but you have to promise if I miss any of this story that you will tell it to me again another night."

"I promise. Now, go to sleep."

Stuffy waited for Farthi to close her eyes and then he continued with his story. "Some kind of a bug had crawled into the box with all of us animals, and when it made a strange noise, Tony the elephant stomped on it and with a loud creepy noise the bug went flat. It never moved, again. It was a horrible sight and that is why I kept as quiet as I possibly could."

After that thing with the bug, Stuffy continued. "The box began to move in all different directions. First, it went up, and then it went down. All of us animals bounced up and down with it. Oh, it was horrible! One minute, I was the one getting squashed. The next minute, I was the one doing the squashing. Then finally the box slammed down and stopped moving. It was a long time before the box moved again and this time it did the exact same thing. First, it went up, and then it went down, bang! It is a good thing us stuffed animals don't have to go to the bathroom otherwise that would have scared the ... well, you know, stuffing right out of me."

Stuffy stopped for a second to check on Farthi, but for only a second and then he continued his story. "It seemed like a long time had passed, since I had been squashed into this box, but then it happened. There was a loud ripping sound! Then there was light, and one at a time the animals began to disappear. First, all of the elephants were gone, then the monkeys. Before I knew it, I was the only one left in the box. I had felt terrible before being with all of those strange animals, but now, I felt even worse being all alone. That was the first time I realized just how bad it must be to be all alone. A lot of time went by and still I was all by myself sitting there in that big empty box. Well, almost empty, because I was still there inside it. But then a large hand reached in and grabbed me by the throat and yanked me out from the bottom of the box. It hurt, but I refused to say anything. I was really scared! Then, I was shoved onto this tiny space on a shelf high above the floor. I looked all around, and there were lots of animals on the shelf with me. There were even some other bears. Oh, now I was excited. "Hey," I shouted to a black bear that was sitting just a few feet from me. "What's your name?" I asked. He didn't answer. Hmm, he must be sleeping, I thought. I was kind of tired myself after that nerve-wracking experience, so I closed my eyes and fell asleep, fast asleep.

Stuffy had lowered his voice with each sentence of his story, and he was now pretty sure that Farthi had fallen asleep, so he stopped talking and waited.

Stuffy didn't have to wait for very long, because Farthi's arms fell to her side, and Stuffy fell with them. He bounced off of her belly, and tumbled down onto the bed beside her.

Ouch, ow, my nose! I wonder what happened?

Stuffy was lying on his back, staring up at the ceiling, wondering not only what had happened, but what was going to happen to him next?

***

The night slowly slipped into morning and the bedroom grew brighter and brighter. Stuffy was still lying on his back when Farthi awoke from a good night's sleep.

Farthi turned her head and looked over to where Stuffy was supposed to be sleeping, but he wasn't there.

"Oh no, where is Stuffy!" Farthi exclaimed. She sat straight up in her bed and that was when she noticed Stuffy was lying in the middle of her bed. "Stuffy, what are you doing over there? Hey, wait a minute, I remember now. You were telling me the story of how you came here from a place far, far away and, oh my gosh, I must have fallen asleep, and dropped you. Oh my. You did exactly what you were trying to do, put me to sleep. Oh, I can't wait until tonight when you can finish the story," Farthi said to Stuffy as she picked him up and placed him back on his pillow.

Farthi got up, got dressed, and left the bedroom. She was in a hurry for the day to go by and for the night to come, so she could get undressed, climb into bed, and listen to Stuffy tell her the rest of his story. She felt like a silly little girl, but she wasn't, she was a happy big girl.

Farthi hurried home from school that day and the first thing she did was to run into her bedroom and make sure that Stuffy was still there, and he was. He was sitting up on top of the pillow, right where she had left him. His round black eyes were shining as brightly as ever. "Phew, it is so good to see you," she told him. "I will be back later when it gets dark, so don't you go anywhere, okay? I will be back, I promise."

Farthi was feeling better now that she had checked on her new friend. She stopped for a quick drink of water, then went outside to see some of her other, human, friends.

Farthi had gone out in her backyard to talk with her friends, and all the while she was talking with them she never once mentioned Stuffy. She was afraid that they would laugh at her. She was afraid they would not believe her, and they would make fun of her, so Stuffy was going to be her very own secret friend.

The afternoon went by quickly, and when Farthi came in for supper, the first thing she did was check on Stuffy. Yup, he was still there. Farthi washed up, sat down, and after eating all of her supper, she went into her room and did some work on her computer. Then, it was time to get ready for bed.

It was the very first time Farthi was in a hurry to go to bed. Tonight, getting ready for bed was going to be fun. She quickly washed, put on her pajamas, and even kissed her brother good night. Then, she raced into her bedroom, and jumped in between the sheets and the blanket. "Okay, okay, I'm here, and I am ready," she said out loud.

It wasn't long before the darkness of the night filled the bedroom. Farthi reached over and pulled Stuffy over to her and then she lifted him up into the air. His eyes shone through the darkness just like they had the night before.

Just then, she heard, "Are we going to have to go through this again?" It was Stuffy.

"Yes, oh yes!" Farthi shouted. "Please tell me the rest of the story."

Stuffy sighed, but then he took a deep breath and tried to remember where he had left off. "Okay, now I remember," he said. "I was sitting on a shelf, when I was dropped onto your belly."

"I don't remember dropping you," Farthi told him. "But I do remember you were sitting on a shelf, and the other bears wouldn't talk to you."

"Hey, you have a good memory," Stuffy told her. "Okay, let me see. Okay, here we go. I was sitting on that shelf, getting more and more depressed, because not one of those bears would even say hello to me. It was as if they couldn't talk, or something. Well, I didn't let that stop me. I kept trying and trying, but then something strange happened. A man came by and took one of the elephants off the shelf, and it never came back. Oh my goodness, I thought. Now, I know why they don't want to talk. They are afraid if they do, that man will come by and take them to well, who knows where, and do who knows what to them."

Farthi's eyes were closing, but very slowly, as Stuffy continued. "I stood on that shelf staring out into that place wondering just where could I be, when another man came walking by. He stopped, walked back toward me, and raised his arm.

His hand wrapped itself around me, and then he very gently picked me up and looked me over from head to tail. He stared into my eyes for a couple of minutes, and then he put me back on the shelf. Then after only a few seconds, he picked me back up and placed me into a huge wire cage. It was a frightening experience! I didn't know what was happening!"

Just then, a worried look appeared on Farthi's face. Stuffy stopped talking, and stared down at Farthi.

"Don't stop, don't stop!" Farthi told him.

"But, you looked so worried," Stuffy replied.

"Oh, I'm okay," she said. "What happened next?"

"Well, I went for one heck of a ride. I passed all kinds of things that were sitting on shelves. Then the wire cage stopped, and the man picked me up and put me on this neat ride. I sat on this thing and it moved me all by itself. Then a really pretty lady picked me up and looked at me. But, then a bad thing happened. She dropped me, and I fell into this scary place. It was dark, and it felt like I was hanging upside down. Then, I started moving and swinging all around. Oh, it was not good."

Stuffy had stopped talking so he could catch his breath, and at the same time check on Farthi. Farthi's eyes were almost shut, and her arms were beginning to move downward. Oh, I hope she doesn't drop me again like she did last night, Stuffy thought. Just then, one of Farthi's eyes opened.

"I'm not finished. I'm just catching my breath," Stuffy told her. "Okay now, where was I? Oh yes, in that miserable place where it was dark and constantly moving and swinging all around. Well, after a while that thing stopped moving and before I knew it I was sitting on a table. The man had taken me out from that place, and put me on a table. I watched him as he walked around the table, opened a drawer, and took out a pair of scissors. I knew what they were for, from my younger days at the factory. Oh no, I thought. He is going to take me apart, and I will lose all of my stuffing! I will be no more! I will be a coaster, or even worse, a dish rag!

"The man put the scissors down on the table and went into the other room. He came back with a large box, and some wrapping paper. The man then sat down at the table, and stared at me, and then he began talking to me.

"Hey little fellow, my name is Chuck. I am going to send you to a special person, because this special person is having trouble sleeping. I know if you are there with her, you can fill her imagination with happiness. Then, she will be able to close her eyes, and all of the stories of all of the animals will fill her dreams, and she will sleep all through the night. She will listen in her sleep to their laughter, and share in their joy, knowing she is not alone. Now, do you think you can do that for me?

"I shook my head yes, but I don't think he noticed, because he was too busy getting the paper ready. The man then picked me up, and placed me inside the box. He did it very carefully and gently. I wasn't squashed or nothing. As a matter of fact, it was kind of comfortable. It did get dark when he closed the top, but I knew that I was headed somewhere special, so I didn't mind.

"Then the day came when I arrived here at your house and you opened the box, and smiled from ear to ear. I knew from that moment that you were that special person he was telling me about, and I knew that the day would come, or I should say the night would come when I would tell you this story and it would put you to sleep, fast asleep."

Bang, bounce! Farthi's arms had fallen by her side, and Stuffy had once again bounced off from her belly and onto the bed.

"I wonder if she is going to want me to tell her a story every night?" Stuffy said in a low voice, as he lay on the bed. "If I do, and she does, I think I will ask her if we could do it in a different position. Like maybe with me sitting on her belly. At least that way I wouldn't have so far to fall. Hee hee hee!" Stuffy giggled.

"Hmm, I wonder if I should tell her she snores. No, better not. Well, good night Farthi. Sweet dreams. I love you."

Nonfiction

Hawkeye and the Boxcar

By K. Eric Crook

This was getting dangerous, very dangerous. I was inside a boxcar, up to my eyeballs in pool furniture, beach umbrellas, outdoor grills, chaise lounges, and picnic tables. There were actually two boxcars side by side. Not the kind of retail stuff you rent at Home Depot. No, these were heavy-duty corrugated steel units designed to be transported on a flatbed or a rail car. The heavy metal handles on the massive double doors far behind me were each at least a yard long. These units come in standard sizes, fifty-four or sixty feet. I was hoping for the former but I suspected they were of the latter; I was halfway in – the point of no return.

So why did I choose one car over the other when they were both crammed to the brim with the same random assortment of pool party paraphernalia? Far ahead of me in the right-hand corner of this boxcar I could hear the strained, desperate, plaintive meowing of Hawkeye. I was on the ultimate mission of mercy for my trapped kitty. The Hawk had been pushing the envelope a lot lately. His newest thing was to scamper up the pile of firewood I had stacked along the side of the house. All too often I would come home from work and see him perched on the roof above the front steps. I was living in a three-story house on Mattituck Inlet. The house had three detached roofs straddling a large second-story dormer. Hawkeye had somehow figured out how to get from the woodpile to the right-hand roof and then jump from roof to roof to roof at will. I never could decide if he was just showing off or he found it to be a more challenging pastime than chasing squirrels and rabbits.

Either way, it is a well-established principle that cats are far better at ascending than descending. I could have called the local fire department, Lord knows they love saving cats on a sunny day, but I came up with a more immediate, homegrown solution: I brought my ironing board upstairs, stuck it out the window and held it in place against the roof. Hawkeye stared at it a long time. He stared at me, too. Minutes passed. He let out a very suspicious, questioning meow and then gently put his paw on the ironing board. I put my hand on the board and thumped it a few times to prove to this doubting Thomas that the damn thing was solid. My shoulders were getting tired from holding it in place so I yelled out a few demonstrative invectives in what would have to pass as encouragement. Finally, Hawkeye leapt onto the ironing board, plowed across it, then scampered over my head and exited the scene via my neck and back. Before I even had time to pull the board in or tend to my bloody scratches, he was down in the kitchen looking for something to eat.

But let me give credit where credit is due. Several years earlier, I separated from my ex-wife on the first of February. I found an apartment within a gorgeous French provincial waterfront home for an astonishingly cheap rent because it was tied up in an estate settlement. When I first visited the place with a realtor, I saw three deer browsing in the back yard - so I took the place on the spot. After months of counseling and negotiation, it became obvious to me that twenty-seven years of unresolved grievances was too high a mountain to climb. So after a month of living in secrecy, I walked into my manager's office at Merrill Lynch, closed the door, and brought him up to speed. I recall him responding that I must be an amazing poker player because he never saw it coming. Office gossip being what it is, within a half hour the entire office was in the know. One of our sales assistants made a terse observation, "You know, I never liked her." In the end, I suppose I didn't either.

One of my co-workers, Jeff Worthington, offered a more helpful comment. He said, "You need to get a cat." I've always liked Jeff, he was a good guy, and it also turned out that he was the financial advisor for the nearby Riverhead animal shelter. Like any responsible financial advisor, he was always looking out for his client's best interests. But I had to admit that he was right and I am forever grateful for his advice. That very afternoon I followed a winding road off into the middle of nowhere and ended up at the door of the animal shelter. I asked to look at the cats; there were a lot of them. Enough to break your heart many times over. I couldn't choose by just looking at them so I started asking questions about how all these poor felines came to be homeless. Well, it turned out there was one cat who was a recent arrival. He'd been through a tough time and he was taking it out on his brethren. It seemed that he had been dropped off at the front door of this place one evening in a small box taped shut with masking tape and left that way all night. I asked to take a look at him. He was being kept in another room that was relatively spacious, loaded with the not-so-friendly cats.

I went in with the attendant to check him out. There in the middle of the room was this imposing creature with shoulders like a linebacker. He stared at me, his eyes shone yellow and gold like the eyes of a bird of prey. When I came close to him he arched his back and snarled. Then, totally out of the blue, he rolled onto his back and invited me to rub his belly. I swear he was daring me to try. His claws belonged on something much bigger than a cat. As I took up his challenge and rubbed his fur, I looked closely at his coat. It would best be described as petting vanilla-fudge ice cream. Not the cheap stuff, something like Breyers, with a distinctive swirl and a well-struck balance between the vanilla and the fudge. And then there were his boots, which were as white as snow, and the tip of his nose which looked like it had just been dipped in white paint. So I paid the forty bucks and took him home. They made me use a kitty carrier; I never used it again. After that, if he wanted to go for a ride he would have to learn to sit in a seat like the rest of us.

But I digress, so where were we? Oh yes, he hadn't budged from the corner of the boxcar and I was straddling a stack of chaise lounges, five chairs high, and peering through the dim light cast through the open doorway. I had last broken my tibia when I was eleven. It had really been Brian Baird's fault. We were playing football in my back yard on a summer's day. I was rolling out to my left when Brian blitzed from the blind side and jumped on my back. I stumbled forward several steps and caught my left leg in a small gully. Crack! You could hear it for miles. Doctor Chambers called it a spider fracture because the joint was blown out like the legs of a spider. That's what you get for playing football out of season. But where would I be now if I went tumbling off this accursed lawn furniture and broke something? The tibia again? Or maybe just a femur? In all probability the crew that had loaded up this boxcar had already closed up the marina and left. Gone for the season, gone until spring. I was only a few hundred yards away from home and here I would die. The police would answer a missing person's alert in a couple days and eventually discover my putrid remains in a storage unit full of poorly stacked chairs, side tables, outdoor grills, and even Styrofoam noodles. And was this all deliberate? Had those marina workers known that the Hawk had jumped inside while they were loading it up? What callous evil lurks in the hearts of men? Would these guys be extradited to stand trial for being accessories to my demise? Maybe I'd be fortunate and receive a devastating puncture wound and go quickly into that good night. Was saving my cat from just as gruesome a fate worth risking my neck?

I spent a long moment contemplating this dilemma while perched on the stack of furniture. Finally Hawkeye pierced the silence with a long heartbreaking meow that was laden with fear and hope. *So why have you stopped? Aren't you coming to save me?* Well, he's been a better companion for the last five years than my ex-wife had ever been, so I slid off the chairs and carefully edged toward him in the darkness.

You can't make this stuff up. The next hazard was a bulwark of outdoor grills packed tight from wall to wall. I couldn't fit under them because the propane hookups were in the way. At least the propane tanks themselves were elsewhere. So dying in a fiery explosion was not a possibility. I didn't like the way they were packed. (I didn't like the way any of this was packed, but then I guess you've figured that out by now.) There was no room to get between them and they seemed too unsteady to traverse along the sides of their frames. Gymnastics had never been my strong suit, but that now seemed to be the only choice. I mounted the first grill gingerly, held the metal lid by its handle and reached through the darkness to the next in line. Then I threw my hips over and vaulted onto the next unit. And the next, and the next. Well, wouldn't you know it? These pool workers had left cheap aluminum lawn chairs on top of some of the grills. Unfolded. My legs plowed into one of them between the third and fourth vault, with a noisy, painful crash. Hawkeye howled, I cursed profusely. I hadn't even seen it coming. I reached for the chair, folded it up, and threw it against the wall. I found another, then I found several more. I ended up having to fold the lot of them in order to clear my path. Finally, bruised but not beaten, I proceeded to cross the frontier between the outdoor grills and the land of glass tables.

Here was the thing of it. Beyond the tables I could just make out the back wall of the boxcar. So I called out to the Hawk, but he replied, *No way, you come and get me*. So I submerged; I crawled under the first table and slinked between the table legs. I absolutely didn't want to mess with the glass table tops. Besides, inverted tables sat on top of each of these three round tables. The only room to move was underneath. I edged along quickly and came to my kitty cowering in the corner. I grabbed him by the scruff of the neck and held him tight. I was as happy to see him and hoped he was to see me. But of course, I couldn't see him nor he I; this corner of the boxcar was pitch black. I caught my breath and thought about the next Herculean task. I wanted to explain to him what was ahead, but how do you tell a cat that there is a light at the end of the tunnel? And you should just go for it? There was no other solution. I had to do the whole thing in reverse carrying a husky cat with claws like an ocelot. We started our journey home.

The first piece was deceptively easy. We snaked back through the land of impassable tables with the big guy nestled to my chest. Then I started to climb back onto the outdoor grills and he would have none of it. He pulled away from me and scampered back into the corner. Well, I had been at this for over an hour and my patience was worn severely thin. I crawled back to the corner, grabbed him bodily, and quickly brought us back through the glass tables. But he really had a point about the grills; I couldn't vault a five-foot-long metal grill with a cat in my hands. So I went low once again. I located the wing nuts that hold the propane tank bracket in place and turned them with my thumb and forefinger. Once it came loose I threw it aside and slithered on my back with the cat huddled against my chest through to the next grill. I continued this arduous process until it was something that might euphemistically be called progress.

In fact, I would opine that the best way to remove a kitty from a boxcar full of pool party paraphernalia is to stay low, endure the bruises and scratches you receive from the furniture and the cat, and curse with reckless abandon. You can take that to the bank, you can even quote me on it. After some sweaty minutes of struggle in the dark we got back to the halfway point. But now the options were fewer. There were spots where we had to go high and straddle those chaise lounges that were certain to find their way onto my coroner's report. (Cause of death: Blunt trauma inflicted by lawn furniture.) And then Hawkeye got loose again! I was working my way over the pile and he bolted. I moved fast and grabbed him before he fled in full retreat. Good God, we had less than a third to go and he was ready to put me through this misery again.

I held him against me and stood full up. There ahead was finally a visible patch of moonlight emanating from the doorway. I showed it to him. He recognized the implications immediately. I could feel his muscles boil up in my arms. I put him down between the jumble of chairs, side tables, and pool toys and he disappeared in a flash. I worked my way slowly through the last fifteen feet of the boxcar. I was recalling an old photo I had once seen of the inside of King Tutankhamen's tomb when it had first been discovered. I was struck by how sloppily the priests and tomb guards had filled his tomb with the artifacts for his journey into the afterlife. I wondered if their ancestors were now gainfully employed loading boxcars with lawn chairs. At least I was relieved that this boxcar would not become Hawkeye's final resting place. Nor mine.

When I finally got back to the house Hawkeye was sitting on the front steps, wondering where the hell his dinner was.

We had plenty of adventures over the years, but the escape from the boxcar stands above all else. Before I finally made the transition from Long Island to Rhode Island, I first moved from Mattituck Inlet to a retirement village in Southold. There, Hawkeye made it his business to keep his feline brethren in line. Not to mention there were frequent squabbles with rabbits, squirrels, raccoons, and once even a very nasty fisher cat. For several years I maintained a pied-à-terre in Calverton while I gradually set up shop in Providence. The Hawk had the run of the place for weeks at a time. He even convinced my landlord Tony that he was supposed to be fed twice a day. In fact, it was Tony who did some research online one day and called to inform me that my cat was definitely a Maine Coon. This was something of a revelation; the Hawk had always been reticent about discussing his ancestry.

Then he became a traveler. We rode a ferry together and went on a three-hour trip to his new home in Riverside, Rhode Island. He pointedly refused the kitty carrier and he would have driven if I'd let him have the keys. He had to settle for riding in my lap and counting cars. I think he might have been looking for unusual license plates.

When he had used up all of his nine lives I gave Hawkeye a proper burial. I picked out a quiet corner of the yard a week or so beforehand and waited. We took him to the vet that Saturday just to confirm what we already knew. He was an old kitty now, at least sixteen by all accounts. He was down to six pounds; I could remember holding him on the scale and seeing him weigh in at twenty-six easy. Where once he had looked like a linebacker, then trimmed down to free safety – in the end he was like a frail, aged farmer sitting on his front porch in a rocking chair, recounting the seasons. He died in his sleep on the new living room rug. It was the first day of spring, but the ground was still frozen too hard to dig a grave. A few weeks later, after a lot of rain and a thaw, I dug a deep hole in a spot in the corner of the yard and made him a tomb of red bricks. Joanne and I buried my old friend together. It wasn't quite as dramatic as an ancient Egyptian tomb, but we planted a garden around him of purple catmint and Tiger lilies. He deserved no less.

A Storyteller's Inspiration

By A. Keith Carreiro

For almost as long as I can remember, I wanted to be a writer. I wrote mostly adventure stories when I was a boy. They were inspired by many sources that I was blessed to have around me. Also, several individuals in my family were spellbinding in their powers of storytelling. Music was ever present. While I played the piano at the age of four, and then completely fell under the spell of playing the classical guitar starting at the age of six, I just was fascinated by the music I heard in stories.

It was the power of stories and the manner in which they were told that fastened such a strong grip on my imagination. I then became addicted to them. I discovered that I could not get enough of what they offered me. Whenever I did not have a book in my hands, and there were adults around, I plagued them with the old and constant refrain of "Tell me a story."

Lacking adults to share their stories with me, I would make up all kinds of plots, settings, conflicts, and characters that I could think of conjuring into existence.

I read every book in the children's section of my town library and every book I could get my hands on in the library available to me in every school I attended. I would sit in the back of the classroom, have my textbook on the desk in front of me, and have a favored book on my lap as well. This literary stealth approach soon ended when my teachers became alert to it. I ended up in the front row.

Reading became something more than a passion; it became an avalanche of acquisition. I felt it as a powerful melody I could not get enough of, and thus I consumed as much of it as I could possibly obtain. The children's fables I read morphed into a fascination of Greek, Roman, and Viking mythologies. As I was a child of the 50s, westerns firmly gripped my attention as well as mysteries and thrillers.

I was stunned when I went to see my first movie—"Bambi." Another avenue of storytelling opened. And then, of course, television came into its own and I could not get enough of all the shows offered for children and even some for adults, such as "I Love Lucy," "The Jackie Gleason Show," "Ford Theatre," "The Ed Sullivan Show," "Dragnet," "Alfred Hitchcock Presents," and "Gunsmoke."

I became fascinated with war stories. As a child of World War II parents whose members in my immediate family were all involved in the war, and served in the Army, Navy, and Coast Guard, I yearned to know more about what they went through and experienced. I felt misplaced being a child of the fifties, and wished that I could have grown up alongside my parents' generation. Raised by men and women of World War II. I was, and still am, in awe of them. I am amazed at what they experienced, and what terrible sacrifices they made to wage war abroad and at home, as well as the grievous times in which they lived. I feel a deep debt is owed to them as a result of what they faced, lost, accomplished, and won.

I devoured everything I could read about the Second World War. Learning about its historical connections to the previous two generations, I learned more about my grandparents' era and what their lives were like in the world they experienced. I learned more about The Lost Generation (1890–1915) as well as The Interbellum Generation (1901–1913).

My historical interest shifted to the American Civil War. I read everything about it that I could get my hands on, which in this case were two school libraries, as well as what books were on hold concerning the Civil War in the Swansea Public Library. The work of narrative historian Bruce Catton (1899–1978) stunned me in its depiction of the era, the people who inhabited it, and the terrible experience of war on individuals, families, states, and on all Americans alike. I eventually read all of his books, especially being fascinated with his trilogy work, *Army of the Potomac* (1951–1953) [known also as *Bruce Catton's Civil War* (1988)], and *Centennial of the Civil War* (1961–1965). Eventually, my reading of history expanded to the American Revolution, World War I, and the Spanish–American War (1898), and I went on to read more about the rise of empires and the wars fought by them.

As I have said above, but will say again, I was humbled by the World War II veterans around me. The ones I knew best would visit my grandmother (*vavo*) and grandfather (*vavu*), who were my father's parents. They had a farm in Swansea, although it was in decline when I was young. Sometimes these veterans would help out doing chores there or getting ready for a feast, in which case they would go through extensive work in readying the meat that was to be served. As we had an active pig farm, men and women would participate in this activity by culling the pigs out that were desired, butchering them, and cooking them. This usually took a whole weekend to do. Nothing was wasted. Throughout such events, stories poured forth abundantly. I heard about what life was like in the Azores. Sad songs of the islands were sung (*fado*), ballads really; yet, they were counterpoised by improvisational songs that teased and provoked laughter by insulting one another (*desafio*).

After a while, when the first blush of drinking homemade wine had settled into them, the veterans began telling their war stories to one another, particularly when preparations for slaughtering the pigs, geese, and chickens were started. They became progressively more graphic throughout as the animals were either killed, bled out, or assiduously prepared for the table.

Several of the men did not participate in any of these grisly tasks. They were what they called at the time shell-shocked or had soldier's heart. Today, we know this condition as combat-related post-traumatic stress disorder. Those around them kept an eye out on these individuals, being sure that they were doing okay. All of the men mostly had served together in Europe. One, in particular, suffered from severe body tremors. He scared the absolute hell out of me. They would speak in low tones, sometimes drifting into whispers. Their Portuguese was flavored by their Azorean roots and culture. American slang sometimes accompanied their recalling some very harrowing times as well as experiencing the frustrations of command decisions, the foibles of men and machines and the horror of what they could not forget remembering.

At one point in time, the man suffering from battle fatigue approached me. In Portuguese, he said to me, "I know that I scare you. I don't mean to. It hurts me to see your fear."

He knelt down by my side and placed a shaking hand on my head. He explained to me what happened to him one night during the war when the men with him were hit for the fifth time by several hours of intense artillery fire. Big, swollen tears fell from his eyes. I lost the sense of the words he was sharing with me, and felt and heard the pain radiating off him instead. As the tears fell from my eyes, I watched him go back in time and saw someone transfixed in another moment in his life and into another world. When he finished talking with me, I gave him a hug. For some reason, empathy I think, and the way the other adults seem to revere him, I never was afraid of him anymore after that.

This experience brought an avid desire in me to learn more about what occurred to my parents' generation. My reading expanded into other areas of writing and I began to read stories written by those who had witnessed combat. The works of John Steinbeck (1902–1968), Ernest Hemingway (1899–1961), and J. D. Salinger (1919–2010) became important to my reading interests. I also read the Great War poets, such as Siegfried Sassoon (1886–

1967), Wilfred Owen (1893–1918), and Robert Graves (1895–1985).

However, of all of these storytellers who so firmly had captured and riveted my attention upon them, those in the movies equally affected me, perhaps even superseded them. Westerns, thrillers, science fiction, and adventures stories had me addicted to them. Then I saw "Quo Vadis," "The Robe," "The Ten Commandments," "Ben-Hur," and "The Greatest Story Ever Told." I watched them over and over as many times as I was able to see them at the theaters or mostly when they aired on television.

The emotions felt from watching these movies had a deeply cathartic effect upon me that I did not have from any other literary or cinematic genre. The closest feelings were from science fiction and fantasy. I eagerly sought out and read works by Mary Shelley (1797–1851), Jules Verne (1828–1905), Aldous Huxley (1894–1963), George Orwell (1903–1950), Robert A. Heinlein (1907–1988), Arthur C. Clarke (1917–2008), Ray Bradbury (1920–2012), and Frank Herbert (1920–1986).

Yet, the works of J. R. R. Tolkien and C. S. Lewis immensely ratcheted up my esteem for their writing and what they were accomplishing in their literary achievements. I started wondering if I could do something in a similar vein. Their sense of mythmaking was breathtaking.

Wouldn't it be cool if I could do something like what they did!

Consequently, over the last half century, I have read as much science fiction and fantasy writing as I could consume. Tolkien and Lewis remain paramount in my admiration. During this time, I attempted, over and over again, to write something that I could say was well-conceived and written in a manner similar to their accomplished style.

Almost a dozen tries at doing so during this time proved ineffective. I would write 30 to 60 pages and then reach a full halt.

Nothing else happened. The muse fell silent. Perhaps it even snickered at me as well. I gave up and turned to writing poetry, which I had started in high school. Poetry, although elusive, still was available to me in its inspiration and fulfillment in creating.

From the time I was a young boy, I wanted to create an epic story. This quest was accompanied by the weapons of being a voracious reader. As a former public school teacher, tenured university faculty member, and now a part-time adjunct professor at Bristol Community College and Bridgewater State University, I also read books and scholarly research for academic purposes. However, the kind of reading and writing that I want and need to have is for pleasure. For fulfilling the soul. For purposes of wonder. To be lost in the middle of a grand narrative saga. I am adrift without such a good book to read during the week. I make the time to burrow into one on a daily, usually nightly, basis.

Mesmerized by storytellers as I have explained here, I am also fascinated by their capacity to summon together a yarn or a tale and to share it with those around them. Thus, the yearning to be able to participate in such an exquisite adventure remained a distant realization. I was plagued with not being able to complete a story idea that sprang to mind. Attempting to do so would screech into a grinding silence. I had no place to go with the plot, the characters, the setting, and all of the other literary elements of what I was hoping to put together and depict on paper, or computer screen. The attempts fell apart and stuttered into entropy.

In the early 1980s, I briefly was a part-time newspaper reporter and photographer for the Lewiston, Maine *Sun Journal*, a daily newspaper whose reporters covered western Maine. I loved writing for this paper and wondered then why I could not write a fictional story on a sustained basis.

To avoid this feeling of looming and complete writing failure, I started reading those storytellers who deeply influenced me during the first five months of 2014. As I read their respective work, I tried to keep an eye on the craft of their writing while I was in the midst of enjoying what they had conceived.

I noticed that each one has a powerful sense of presence. Their copy (i.e., their use of prose, or wording), their sentence structure, their phrasing, and their sense of cadence in the delivery of what they are saying, all are a joy to receive. While each author has a unique literary style and voice, I noticed how they bring out excitement and avid interest on the part of their readers, especially in what they have to say to them. I saw how the desire to keep turning their storybook pages was equivalent to my being captured by the stories they were sharing with me.

I need to do the same thing, I told myself over and over again.

I kept that thought close to my heart. It became inscribed deeply into my mind and imagination.

No matter what idea I end up writing, I want my readers turning page after page that I write in order for them to see what happens next in the unfolding of my story.

That sentiment became a prayer. An invocation. An eleison.

I started to glimpse the outlines of an idea for a story, but it was too illusory; it was only a brief, fleeting thought that I could not yet firmly grasp and bring into sharper resolution.

I wanted the spell of listening to stories to inundate me with the equal power of composing them as well. I needed the cachet, the ability, even the self–permission, to write such an unfettered thought experiment that became *the Penitent* and the beginning trilogy of a planned nine book series called *The Immortality Wars*.

During the first five months of 2014, I revisited all of the poetry I'd written and could retrieve in my home and compiled it together in my living room. Turning to poetry was an alternative path to writing prose fiction. I was turning 66 that year. A clock had started on my understanding that the time for me to write a novel was ticking away in shorter duration than ever before in my life. Finished and unfinished poems were scattered on old typewritten papers and handwritten in pencil or pen on the back of envelopes, napkins, and other scraps of paper that had been available to me when such ideas and/or lines of verse came to light in my mind. I reedited the finished poetry, brought the disparate lines of verse into finished poems, and stored them in several files in my desktop and laptop computers.

I felt that I had accomplished a daunting and Herculean task.

At the beginning of May of that year, I read a book written by Neal Bascomb entitled *Hunting Eichmann: How a Band of Survivors and a Young Spy Agency Chased Down the World's Most Notorious Nazi*. Musing over it for the remainder of the month, I believed that I could write something that honored my parents' generation, especially in terms of describing what they were fighting against on the European front. As I just had accomplished something I had never done before with my poetry, I thought that writing an epic poem was within my grasp.

From Bascomb's novel, I took a statement uttered by Heinrich Himmler (1900–1945) in reference to contacting Adolf Eichmann (1906–1962) to help in orchestrating the Holocaust called the "Final Solution to the Jewish Question." I titled the poem, "Send down the Master in Person." The poem was originally conceived and written on May 11, 2014, which also happened to be the same month and day when Eichmann was captured in Argentina by the Mossad in 1960.

I spent the first half of May working on this poem. I carefully kept track of the research and used it as my writing notes and references that I added as a postscript at the end of the poem. This was a strategy I had just used for updating and redoing all of my poetry. I thought that this method was a good annotative approach, and it might be helpful if a prospective reader had this information available to him or her in learning more about the background of each poem.

I had never attempted to write a poem quite like this one. It is dark, haunted and filled with utter dismay that such willful slaughter and torture occurred through the hands of a modern day culture. I will never be able to understand what was so grotesquely unleashed on those caught and helplessly trapped in the concentration camps. However, what I can see is that evil itself openly and contemptuously flouted its power in front of the world's eyes. The sprawling war that enveloped the globe between allied and axis forces was not one fought between contending mortals and nations, but one in which horrific ideas and deeply misguided principles morphed themselves onto hell itself.

Such wartime evidence of this kind goes far beyond the realm of men and women and leads to another dimension in its entirety where war of a similar kind is waged as well. It spilled over into our world, corroding and poisoning our sense of reality, justice and moral behavior. Regarding such evidence of war and the calamity it brings down on all, it does not matter whether or not one is a believer, unbeliever, or someone caught between both points of view. The genocide alone conducted during that time, particularly on the scale practiced during the 1930s and 40s in Europe, in the former Soviet Union, in Asia and in the nations and islands of the Pacific Ocean, is evidence enough of the corruption in the human spirit of the utmost sinister and degrading kind.

I believe we live in a world today that is directly shaped by the events my parents witnessed firsthand. I do not think that the brutal demons of war raging in the heart of humanity were utterly vanquished. They still are present today and gather their forces together for another great conflagration. Its fires are being fanned even now as I type these words on my computer keyboard.

After all, despite the argument being voiced here, doesn't history simply repeat itself? Haven't we, at least, seen that human beings do not learn by their mistakes and lies? Such is the ground for much speculation about not just the present, but of the future, too. What is in store for my children, their children and beyond?

Heading toward the end of May of that year, I felt a closure and satisfaction of reaching the goal I had set myself on the eve of 2014. The resolution to update and gather together all of my poems in one collection was realized. I felt strongly enough to tackle the questions raised in the above paragraphs.

Instead of writing another poem, or even a cycle of them, I thought that I could better address these concerns in prose form. I had only the tingling of an idea. Yet, this matter was of vital importance to me. At this point in time it remained an unrealized quest. I felt that I was at the moment of inception. There was a poetic tension that became as a bowstring being pulled slowly and steadily back. There was still no arrow nocked on the string, but one soon was about to be placed there metaphorically.

With this germination in motion, I happened to read Ray Kurzweil's book, *The Singularity is Near: When Humans Transcend Biology*. I read it through completely three times in five days. Complementary to peering alongside Kurzweil's glimpse into the future, I turned my attention towards our national founders and read biographies on George Washington (1732–1799), John Adams (1735–1826), and Thomas Jefferson (1743–1826).

I started thinking about the course of history, its trajectory and its destination. I gathered together more sources, and eagerly read more historical material along with what certain other futurists were saying about civilization's fate.

A thought experiment began to crystallize in my mind. However, I felt that I needed to concentrate on some old writing heroes of mine. I turned to the literature of J. R. R. Tolkien (1892–1973), and C. S. Lewis (1898–1963), first. Then I embraced those of the Brothers Grimm (1785/1786–1859/1863), George MacDonald (1824–1905), General Lew Wallace (1827–1905), Lloyd C. Douglas (1877–1951), T. S. White (1906–1964), Stephen R. Donaldson (1947–), Terry Goodkind (1948–), and Frank E. Peretti (1951–).

These creative artists are as rare jewels so delightfully found in the wilderness of imagination that are brought back its sundry places and placed together in a prized place of view. Assembled in such array, they formed an implicit illumination waiting to be moved by the hand of inspiration, by the sweat of dreams and by the birth of wonder. They awaited the touch of a prescient or farseeing storyteller, one who could stare into the future, peer into the past and write as if both were in the present . . .

The Author's Rhode Island Connection: Lonsdale Sports Arena

By W. Gauvin Barber

Sixty years ago, racing history was made in the smallest state, Rhode Island, at the Lonsdale Sports Arena. A relatively short-lived, but high banked racing surface approximately one third of a mile oval track was completed on the outskirts of the Blackstone River, a short distance from the capital of Providence. The date was October 26, 1947, and it proved to be a very important date in racing history.

The late Bill Tuthill, the man who promoted it, believed that it was the most significant stock car race that was ever completed. A young radio station guy from Providence got the call for a hefty $25 a week and to later move on to national fame. The young rookie was Chris Schenkel and the *Providence Journal* newspaper did not hurt its chances in advertising, attracting a loyal fan base from the get-go.

The story goes that Bill Tuthill was a big midget racing guy, and saw the handwriting on the wall that big money was taking over his favorite sport. His big gamble was seeing if full-size start harvest could make the transition to the high-banked oval track. They were already running on dirt tracks in the South, and if he could get them to run on his high banks, he might just be able to fill the 34,000 seats and the Lonsdale Sports Arena was the place to do it.

Written accounts state that Rhode Island native Sammy Packard was to become the first entry. When it became apparent that Sammy was the only entry, panic set in. Bill Tuthill made a phone call to a man named "Big" Bill France to get involved and make the race part of the National Championship Stock Car circuit. The common name that we all recognize today is NAS-CAR, which began in 1959.

Buddy Schuman, the current king of the day on asphalt, signed on second and soon all the other national names followed. Rhode Island was going to be on the racing map and 9,000 awestruck race fans paid the high price of $1.20 per ticket to witness this racing event.

Legendary Fonty Flock, Red Byron, 1949 champion, and even Junior Samples made the trip up the coast from the deep South. Tommy Bradshaw, Tommy Coates, and even Pepper Cunningham were all New Jersey drivers; it also lured the top flagman, Johnny Brunner, to take control of the race flag colors.

Red Byron was awarded the pole with a very fast time of 18.5 seconds on the Saturday part of the show. Junior Samples and Pepper Cunningham could not finish any higher and had to settle for a tie at 19.1 seconds of the second fastest in the qualifying heat races. The heat races were worth the price of the admission, the race fans were overheard saying. Buddy Schuman finished sideways over Red Byron in the first heat. The car count was huge and Junior Samples and Pepper Cunningham also won the heat races. A man named "Pickles" Bickehaupt shocked the racing establishment when he won a very heated consolation race from the best of the rest.

Long Islander Billy Frick won the New England Championship race. Fonty Flock jumped out to win an early lead in his division and never gave it up in the 30-lap headliner. He pocketed an enormous amount for the day: $625 in cash, no checks, from the record $3,500 purse. He also accumulated a lot of momentum toward the 1947 NCSCC Championship. Schuman, Samples, Byron, and Bradshaw followed him across the finish line for the checkered flag.

Bull Tuthill also claimed that he got short-changed on the paid attendance figures; no one has come forward with the actual huge crowd count total that swelled in attendance with the hunger for stock car racing on the high banks in Cumberland, Rhode Island.

The track operated from 1947 until 1956, but commercial building so close to the famous Blackstone River in Cumberland proved to be its demise. In 1956, the Blackstone overflowed its banks, carrying away much of the backstretch; the third turn was also gone. The race track was never rebuilt. The Wall Stadium, which is banked 30° on the corners and 16° on the straightaway in New Jersey is patterned after the Lonsdale Sports Arena. The racetrack site is now a large shopping plaza with a supermarket as its anchor. If you look close at the property surrounding the plaza, you can still see traces of the historical Lonsdale Sports Arena. Big Bill France and Bill Tuthill split the alleged $1,100 profit.

In the Rhode Island early years, as many as nine locations had a legitimate automobile race area and the most famous were Tiverton, Rhode Island and the Kingston, Rhode Island fairgrounds. Narragansett Raceway also posted automobile races in this timeframe. On an end note, Rhode Island to this day is the only state in the country without an automobile race track.

Source material provided by author, pit crew member, Providence Journal microfilm, conversation with R.A. Silva, and Wikipedia.

Terra Extra Firma: Hiking the Great American Strip Mall

By Peter Mandel

The last uncharted frontier? It isn't the North Pole, I decide. It is the terrain that is right under my nose.

Man has conquered Everest. Pinned it to the point where its trails are as crowded as avenues. And adventurers have gotten into city cracks and crevices, crawling around in tunnels and free-climbing even new, smooth skyscrapers from the sidewalk to the roof.

The last uncharted frontier? It isn't the North Pole, I decide, or any secret corner of Manhattan. It is the terrain that is right under my nose. Early one Sunday I decide that I must be the first: the world's first pedestrian to hike the suburban strip mall and come back alive.

It so happens I know just the place. Warwick, Rhode Island's Route 2. Where everyone in the state drives and shops. And where nobody—ever—walks.

It's got weedy, crumbling strip, monumental covered malls, and big box stores sprouting out of unmeasured acres of asphalt. There are even a couple of hills to trudge up—that is, if I don't get nailed by a truck in the first 15 seconds of my hike.

Gear check: Hiking boots with Vibram soles that should be tough enough for cement curbs but flexible for traction in mulch. My Brookstone "Night Walker" pedometer for counting mileage. An optic-red knapsack for visibility in eight lanes of angry traffic. And a brand-new "Write in the Rain" notepad since it's starting to drizzle.

Am I really going through with this? demands my worried wife. "Why?" she insists. "Why would you do it?"

"Well," I say. "because it's there."

I park my car in the lot behind an Olive Garden, just west of the Warwick Mall. After using the restaurant's bathroom, I'm off past the Showcase Cinemas next door. Now playing: "Peter Rabbit." But I've no time for a matinee. I am hiking south along Route 2's razor-thin sidewalk, fighting blasts of wind as north-bound cars and trucks roar past.

Under a highway overpass, traffic sounds explode like shots from a gun. I pick up my pace until I reach the competing Rhode Island Mall. Though I've driven between these two malls dozens of times, I've somehow never noticed the gurgling river that divides them. But here it is, as plain as the Hudson to a hiker. I make a note to look up its name.

A few minutes later, when I snag the corner of my sock against a dwarf-sized cedar outside Wendy's, I decide to switch to the southbound side of the road. There is, of course, no crosswalk for pedestrians. I've got to try and time the next pack of cars and make a run for it.

I get to the median, but it is spitting rain now, and I get soaked by a wave from a Ford F-Series pickup. I see the pickup guy grinning back at me, pumping his fist. Drowning a hiker, I think. That's got to be worth bonus points on this road.

The median is kind of pretty even in the rain, with patches of puffy dandelions and some type of purple flower that looks like lavender, but can't be. Not here. Not growing wild.

I sprint again and make it safely across to somebody's "Palm and Tarot Readings" with a neon sign shaped like a hand. I am anxious to find out the fate of my hike. But — it is hard to interpret this omen — there is no one home when I knock.

As a hiker in a land that is sculpted for cars, I keep discovering that my path is broken up with jutting clumps of bushes and busted lampposts that have been bent over in collisions or beaten into the ground.

'Isn't this a great day to buy fresh flowers?' suggests a sign for Ka-Bloom. But I say no. It's still spraying rain. And now I know that I can pick the blossoms I need for free from the Route 2 median.

At this point, I am maybe halfway to my goal. And I am thirsty. One thing about hiking a strip mall: you don't need a canteen. I stride up to the drive-thru at a Chock Full O' Nuts and, ignoring the look from the attendant, order a large iced coffee to go. "You have to be kidding," she says. "Can I have that black, with sugar?" I reply.

After a honk from a Chrysler on my tail, I move on, slurping my drink past Walt's Roast Beef and a Boston Paintball Supply. I've made it to a line of stores at the top of a ramp and some stacked-up boulders. I decide the boulders might be interesting to climb.

My boots are slipping, and when I step on a Cadbury wrapper, I am sliding backward. Finally, a hold—industrial-sized weeds, tough roots. The summit: Staples, Chili's, an American flag.

There is more of my hike ahead. The patch of cattails I stomp over in front of Sports Authority. The cluster of big box giants—Sam's Club, Best Buy — that I manage to weave through. But somehow scaling this cliff of boulders makes the whole, strange hike worthwhile.

From the upper lot, I am the king of Route 2. I can trace my pilgrimage from the Showcase all the way to my goal just a short distance ahead: The Li'l Rhody Ice Cream Shack. Minutes later, I am reaching the sidewalk-less crest of a hill.

I check my pedometer: My hike has covered exactly 3.1 miles. I have discovered a river between malls (which, I learn later, is the Pawtuxet). I've conquered plains of mulch and dangerous forests thick with prickles. I've crossed a median in a storm. I've climbed a cliff.

And I am going to celebrate with a cone. A double.

The soft-serve vanilla slides down and I slump onto the cement to rest. I'm thinking about sleep. About traffic-less quiet. And then I see it, something fat and orange billowing above a used-car lot just up the road. It's an inflatable gorilla. A gorilla with a message: Great deals? Low rates? I can't be sure.

I finish my cone, stand up, dust off. Must push on.

This mall's got more to explore.

Connie

By Sam Kafrissen

That spring was a long time ago. Almost forty years now. It was before the young president was shot and before the Vietnam war took my brother and my patriotism away. In some respects it was the last twilight of my innocent youth. By the next fall I would be off to high school and my thoughts would soon turn to college and leaving our little town for the larger world. Once I left for good I would return only occasionally to visit with my parents and old friends. In time those visits would become less and less frequent. When my parents retired to a warmer clime I seldom went back at all. But I still often think of that time and of a girl named Connie.

We were still a family then. My father had a small store where my mother also worked when she wasn't chauffeuring us to little league games, music lessons, and scout meetings. After school my brother and I helped out in the store for a little spending money. My father thought it would teach us the value of hard work and thriftiness. Later my older brother Dan became too busy with his friends and cars to pay much attention to me. By his senior year at high school our house was littered with brochures from different branches of the armed forces.

Earlier Dan had thought about going to one of the service academies, but his lack of academic success put that opportunity out of reach. So for him it would be the regular army after graduation. When he left for boot camp that fall, I had our bedroom all to myself for the first time. It felt both liberating and lonely. It remained my room until I left for college three years later. After that my mother turned it into a rather impersonal guest room where I could stay when I was home for the holidays. Dan returned once a year when on leave, but he was now the property of Uncle Sam and Uncle Sam would never completely give him back. But in the warm, wonderful spring of my fifteenth year none of that had meaning for me yet.

It seemed like I'd known Connie for some time. We'd been in a couple of classes together, so she wasn't really a stranger, though when you're fifteen all girls are strangers. Our romance just sort of happened. One day we were casual acquaintances trading stupid jokes about teachers and the next we were boyfriend and girlfriend. In time we were a couple, or as we said back then, we were 'going steady.' I scarcely remember how it began. Probably one friend of mine told a friend of Connie's that I liked her and a reciprocal message worked its way back through the junior high grapevine. That was how all-important messages got conveyed when we were young. I don't know how or why I fell in love with her. Maybe it was because I was fifteen and I wanted to be in love and she looked especially good that spring.

We met every day after school and I walked her home. I can't recall anything we ever talked about though I remember well how I felt on those lazy afternoons as if they were yesterday. Connie wasn't much of a student, so it was always my books that I was carrying on our strolls. I didn't know that our relationship wouldn't last, because to us the future was just some vague idea lurking over the horizon. We didn't have a physical relationship to speak of. Hormones and sexual yearning hadn't quite become part of our makeup yet. We'd hold hands and sometimes I would put my arm across her shoulder and she would let me leave it there. We'd hug awkwardly and kiss tentatively, but without much passion. We were just happy being together and knowing that it was spring and we were young.

Connie didn't have a father. It was only she, her mother, and her brother. I never asked what happened to him and she never told me. Still, it was weird for someone not to have a father.

Everybody had one, though they might not be much to speak of. Some of my friends' fathers drank too much, took out the strap too often, and even cuffed their mothers around once in a while, but at least they were there. My best friend's father was just a hairy presence sitting at the kitchen table in his undershirt with a bottle of Schlitz in front of him. One kid's father even ran off for a weekend with another woman, then slunk back home the following Monday, hung-over and repentant.

Although Connie didn't have a father, I was secretly relieved, especially since her mother liked me so much. There was no man there to pass judgment on who his daughter was spending so much time with. We were Jewish, though non-practicing, and that made me different from her family. I didn't go to confession on Saturday as Connie did, or Mass on Sunday. Still, her mother treated me like family and fed me as if she were expecting a famine. I took pride in the fact that she always introduced me to her neighbors as "Connie's boyfriend."

On Friday nights all the kids went to the Knights of Columbus dances. Of course, Connie and I never went together. She and her girlfriends arrived in a car driven by one of the mothers, while the boys always walked to the hall. We would say a casual hello to one another outside and nothing else would pass between us until we were inside and the lights were turned down low. In those moments, the tiny hall became our Shangri-la. We danced the fast dances and the line dances—the stroll was big that year, but it was the slow dances I remember best. Whenever I hear songs like "Tears on My Pillow," "In the Still of the Night," or "You're a Thousand Miles Away," I'm transported back to those nights in the K of C hall. Throughout the evening the nuns circulated around the floor, parting couples who were dancing too close, cautioning them to "leave room for the Holy Ghost." When the song "Goodnight My Love," came on we knew it was last call before the dance was over and the harsh bright lights were turned on.

Afterwards, we separated again. Someone's mother picked up the girls and the boys left on foot. Then we'd all end up at Martucci's, a local Italian restaurant. Connie sat in one booth with her girlfriends and I sat in another with the guys. We ate French fries with vinegar on them and drink cokes from tall glasses with lots of ice. The boys called attention to themselves by acting stupid and making funny noises. Meanwhile the girls giggled and talked about us behind their hands. Connie and I stole smiles at one another and then try to hide, for fear of being teased by our friends.

On Saturdays we often went bowling. Although the group was always large, Connie and I made sure we bowled on the same alley. When the weather was warm she wore shorts, dark wool socks, and sneakers. I loved the way her smooth adolescent legs looked. When it was my turn to roll, I threw the ball as hard as I could to show Connie what a man I was. When others were up, I kept score and Connie sat next to me, sometimes resting her hand gently on my shoulder. I was so pleased at moments like that just to be her guy.

As spring wore on and the days grew longer our walks became more meandering and less purposeful. Sometimes we wandered by the baseball field to watch the school team play. Other times we ended up by the pond where we could hear the frogs make their mating noises. If no one else was around I might steal an occasional kiss. When it was still light after dinner we met up again and walked into town to get an ice cream cone. We wandered around until dark holding hands and trying not to think about summer vacation. I'd be going off to camp that summer to be a junior counselor while Connie would be left hanging around town taking care of her brother and picking up odd jobs babysitting. I'd been a camper at a YMCA camp for years and had always looked forward to going each summer. But this year it was the furthest thing from my mind. I just couldn't imagine being away from Connie for two months.

In late June, our ninth-grade class held its end-of-the-year dance, the biggest event of our junior-high careers. I had visions of Connie and me all dressed up in the middle of the dance floor snuggling close to each other and moving slowly to the same wonderful tunes we danced to at the K of C. hall. My English and science teachers were to be chaperones. My mother said she would drive us and I envisioned her exchanging pleasantries with Connie's mother while Connie put the final touches on her hair. I pictured them taking pictures of us with their Brownie Hawkeye cameras, to preserve our relationship forever.

In the end, things didn't work out as I envisioned them. Sometimes life just throws you an unexpected curveball. A week before the dance, Connie had one of her friends tell me that Connie wanted to break up with me and go to the dance with someone else. I was confused and devastated. Apparently, she'd recently spent some time with another guy she decided she liked better than me. He was a couple of years older and, as it turned out, had no desire to go to some junior high dance with her. As for me, I could feel the best spring of my life slipping away. For the first time I found myself feeling pain because of a girl. I didn't understand how the person I loved so much could like someone else more—someone who obviously didn't care about her like I did. Her friends told me that Connie had already bought a dress, a dress that would now hang in her closet unused.

Three days before the dance I screwed up my courage and called Connie's mother. I wanted her to make Connie go to the dance with me. What I really wanted was for her to make Connie love me again. In those days we still thought our mothers could work their magic powers to make things right. Her mother was as disappointed as I was. She said she'd tried to change Connie's mind but had failed. The next day I cornered Connie in the cafeteria, hoping to convince her to go to the dance with me. I put great store in the fact that she'd already bought a dress and that we shouldn't miss the big dance just because we weren't going steady anymore. She called me that night to say she would go even though nothing had changed between us—we were still broken up. I held out hope that once she heard the old songs her feelings would change.

The night I once believed would be the best night of my young life turned out to be pretty humiliating. Connie insisted that her mother drive and that no pictures be taken of us together. She allowed her mother to take pictures of her in her new dress though; even then, she refused to smile for the camera. At the dance Connie was cold and distant. She spent a good part of the evening dancing with other boys and generally ignoring me. I walked around our gaily-decorated cafeteria feeling sick and empty. I had trouble breathing and it wasn't because of the unfamiliar tie around my neck or the stale smell of cafeteria food that still hung in the air. I felt that everyone was looking at me and that they could see how much I hurt inside. A few people asked if Connie and I were back together. I answered vaguely with words like "I don't know," and "maybe." But deep inside I knew we were finished.

After the dance we all went out to eat, but by then I was no longer a part of Connie's world. She spent most of her time gossiping with her friends and making trips back and forth with them to the ladies' room. For all practical purposes, I'd become a non-person to her.

Within a week, school was out and I was off to camp for the summer. I had a fling with a female counselor two years older than I, who introduced me to the early stages of sex. From then on every relationship I'd have would have a sexual component to it. In some cases, it might be the only component, though an important one nevertheless.

In the fall, my brother left for the army and I went on to high school. I'd occasionally see Connie in the corridor or the lunchroom. At first we just nodded to each other. Later we were able to exchange small talk. She and I no longer traveled in the same circles, so there was little left that we had in common except for that spring, which was rapidly receding into history. Connie was one of the girls who was channeled into the general track and would most likely go to work or marry right after high school. In our brief conversations neither of us ever mentioned our junior high romance.

I soon discovered I had a love of learning and that academics engaged me in a way they never had before. I was smart, ambitious, and popular. I played several sports, was on the student council, and made the honor roll. In time I came to love high school and all its trappings. During senior year I purposely applied to colleges far from home as I could already feel my mind moving beyond our little town and its provincial ways.

I went to college halfway across the country, I carried a picket sign, and I traveled the world and hardly ever looked back. Women came and went. Some relationships were serious while others seemed less so after they were over. Eventually I met the woman who would become my wife; we had some crazy times together and then settled down to raise a family.

One time in college while reading Hemingway's *A Farewell to Arms*, my favorite book when I was twenty, I came across a passage that talks about how the world hurts everyone and how we become stronger in those places where we've been hurt. It made me think of Connie and how she was the first person to truly break my heart. I knew that I would never hurt again as I did that spring when love and all that went with it was so very new to me.

Over the years I heard she married a nice guy from our graduating class. They had two kids and later divorced. I've seen Connie at reunions and one time I actually told her how much she'd hurt me back then. I tried to say it in a way that indicated it all seemed very silly now when in fact it wasn't. She had taught me something so very important about emotions and I believe I became a better person for it. I learned that a life without deep feelings, even painful ones, is a life not worth living. We are both middle-aged now with children far older than we were back then. Still, there is a part of me that will never forget those lazy spring evenings when we sat together, watched the last rays of the sun disappear, and tried ever so hard not to think about the future.

Under Her Protective Mantle

By Paul and Heather Caranci

The sun had not yet illuminated the landscape of the fifteen small landmasses that comprised the Northern Mariana Islands. Through the post-midnight darkness, several men of the United States Navy hurried about preparing their Boeing B-29 aircraft for takeoff. World War II had been raging for almost five years and this was, to most of the crew, just another exercise of the long, traumatic war effort.

Tinian Island, the largest of the string of islands secured by the invasion of Saipan on June 15, 1944, provided a strategic location from which to launch an attack, as it was located only 1,500 miles south of Tokyo, Japan. Now a commonwealth of the United States, the island was home to a US naval base and airfield hurriedly constructed by the SeaBees. Within two months of securing the island, this group of naval construction battalions had already completed six runways of what was soon to become the largest airbase in the world. They also built an administration building, oil storage facilities, barracks, weapons depots, bomb loading pits, an air-conditioned bomb assembly building, and docks substantial enough to accommodate large warships. In late July one such ship, the USS Indianapolis, had delivered its payload to the island. This was now being carefully packed onto the aircraft. Assembled by a group of men under the command of Phillip Morrison, the "Little Boy," a new type of bomb able to instantly deliver utter destruction, contained American hopes of ending the devastation caused by World War II. Throughout the period of preparedness, United States President Harry S. Truman called upon Japan's Emperor Michinomiya Hirohito to surrender, but his calls were ignored, and the war continued.

Now, the twelve-man crew of the Enola Gay, the chosen name of the B-29 super fortress charged with delivering the payload to Hiroshima, were safely aboard. The bomb was secure and flight commander Paul W. Tibbets and his co-pilot Major Robert Lewis taxied over to Runway Able, prepared for takeoff. It was just after two o'clock in the morning on August 6, 1945 and the flight to Hiroshima, Japan was expected to take about six hours.

August 6 is also the day that the Catholic Church celebrates the Feast of the Transfiguration. The New Testament of the Bible explains this event, telling how Jesus of Nazareth climbed the mountain from which he was transfigured in the presence of Peter, John, and James, three of his beloved apostles. Matthew 17:2 describes how *"his face shone like the sun, and his garments became as white as light."* In Hiroshima, however, the Transfiguration would not be paramount on the minds of most of the Catholic population.

The sun shone brightly over the blue skies of Hiroshima that morning. The city was home to about 350,000 people, some of whom prepared breakfast while others hurried off to work and school. At about seven o'clock in the morning the air raid alarm sounded. It sounded pretty much every day in the city, so few paid much attention to it. Ironically, at about eight o'clock, just as the Enola Gay approached, the all-clear was sounded and those who may have been momentarily inconvenienced by the alarm carried on with their morning rituals as usual. Only fifteen minutes later, at eight fifteen in the morning, the first atomic bomb ever used in war was dropped in Japan on the city of Hiroshima.

The blast wave was felt as far away as thirty-seven miles. Seventy percent of the city's buildings were destroyed and seven percent of the remaining buildings were severely damaged. Although no official figure exists, it is estimated that between 80,000 to 140,000 people, mostly civilians, were killed by the blast, many of them instantly. The hundreds of fires ignited by the thermal pulse combined to produce a firestorm that incinerated everything within 4.4 miles of ground zero. Incredibly, only 1.2 miles away from ground zero, eight German Jesuit priests staggered out of their home.[1] Theirs was one of the few buildings still standing in the area. The priests themselves sustained only relatively minor injuries. The eight Jesuits not only survived the blast but went on to live healthy lives for many years. None of the eight suffered any ill effects of radiation exposure.

Science cannot explain what happened, as these events seem to defy all laws of physics. Secular scientists are dumbfounded by the priests' unfettered survival. Though they searched for an explanation, to this day, none has been offered. The eight Jesuits, however, never doubted what happened that day. "We believe that we survived because we were living the message of Fatima. We lived and prayed the Rosary daily in that house."[2]

Dr. Stephen Rinehart, a spokesman for the U.S. Department of Defense, explained, "A quick calculation says that at one kilometer the bulk temperature was in excess of 20,000 to 30,000 degrees F, and the blast wave would have hit at sonic velocity with pressures on buildings greater than 600 PSI. If the Jesuits, at one kilometer from the geometric epicenter, were outside the atomic bomb's 'plasma,' their residence should still have been utterly destroyed. Un-reinforced masonry or brick walls, representative of commercial construction, are destroyed at 3 PSI, which will also cause ear damage and burst windows. At 10 PSI, a human being will experience severe lung and heart damage, burst eardrums, and at 20 PSI limbs can be blown off. All the cotton clothing would be on fire at 350 degrees Fahrenheit, and your lungs would be inoperative within a minute of breathing even one lungful of air at these

---

[1] Dr. Stephen Rinehart of the United States Department of Defense, an international expert in the field of atomic blasts, estimates that at one kilometer from ground zero, the bulk temperature was in excess of 20,000 to 30,000 degrees Fahrenheit.

[2] TFP.org, The Amazing Story of the Hiroshima Eight. 2008. p. 3.

temperatures. No way could any human have survived, nor should anything have been left standing at one kilometer. At ten times the distance, about ten to fifteen kilometers, I saw the brick walls standing from an elementary school and there were a few badly burned survivors; all died within fifteen years of some form of cancer."[3]

Notwithstanding the comments of Dr. Rinehart, the Department of Defense never officially commented on what was deemed classified information. The Jesuits themselves may have been asked to maintain silence as well.

While science cannot explain why the priests survived, this event is not unparalleled in history. The Bible's Book of Daniel (3:19-51) records the incident of three young men who refused to worship the golden statue set up by King Nebuchadnezzar: "Nebuchadnezzar's face became livid with utter rage against Shadrach, Meshach, and Abednego. He ordered the furnace to be heated seven times more than usual and had some of the strongest men in his army bind Shadrach, Meshach, and Abednego and cast them into the white-hot furnace with their trousers, shirts, hats, and other garments, for the king's order was urgent. So huge a fire was kindled in the furnace that the flames devoured the men who threw Shadrach, Meshach, and Abednego into it. But these three fell, bound, into the midst of the white-hot furnace. They walked about in the flames, singing to God and blessing the Lord…The angel of the Lord went down into the furnace, drove the fiery flames out of the furnace, and made the inside of the furnace as though a dew-laden breeze were blowing through it. The fire in no way touched them or caused them pain or harm."[4]

The story of the eight Jesuits would be an amazing testament to the power and glory of God even if it ended here, but it

---

[3] Ibid.

[4] The New American Bible, Oxford University Press, New York, 2011. pp. 1,462-1,463.

does not end there. Sixteen hours after the Hiroshima bomb detonated, President Truman called on Japan to surrender unconditionally, warning that Japan could expect *"a rain of ruin from the air, the like of which has never been seen on this earth,"* but Japan's Emperor Hirohito again refused. True to his word, Truman prepared his troops.

A second atomic bomb, this one aptly named "Fat Man," was loaded onto Bockscar, a B-29 named for Captain Frederick C. Bock, the aircraft's commander. Co-piloted by Major Charles Sweeney, Bockscar took flight from Tinian airbase just after four o'clock in the morning. Its destination was Nagasaki, Japan. At two minutes past eleven on the morning of August 9, 1945, Fat Man exploded over Nagasaki, instantly destroying over forty percent of the city. Hospitals were leveled and the thousands of injured people had no place to go for help. Schools, homes, and churches vanished. Between thirty-nine thousand and eighty thousand people were killed, about half of those instantly.

The death and destruction of Hiroshima were mirrored, albeit on a smaller scale, in the atomic bombing of Nagasaki - right down to the miracle of the surviving priests. On August 9, as tens of thousands died and tens of thousands more barely clung to life, the Franciscan Friary established by Saint Maximilian Kolbe withstood the bomb blast. Kolbe, himself a victim of the Nazi death camps of World War II and a well-known devotee of the Blessed Virgin, established his friary in a certain location despite receiving professional advice to locate it elsewhere. As a result, the building was protected from the force of the bomb by an interposing mountain.

None of the Catholic clergy surviving the Hiroshima and Nagasaki destruction ever doubted that they had been protected by God and the Blessed Virgin Mary. Since August of 1945, and until the time of their deaths, the priests had been examined over 200 times by doctors and scientists. None of the men suffered any effects of radiation poisoning. None produced lesions or illness, and none suffered a premature death.[5] Each time the priests repeated the same explanation for their survival, "We believe that we survived because we were living the message of Fatima."[6]

So just what is the message of Fatima to which the Jesuits and Franciscans attribute their survival? Thirty years earlier, as World War I raged throughout Europe and the world, the village of Fatima was a relatively unknown and unremarkable place situated in the hills of Portugal between Lisbon and Porto. In the spring of 1917, Fatima was suddenly plucked from obscurity and became the setting for an extraordinary story when three shepherd children, ten-year-old Lucia dos Santos and her cousins, nine-year-old Francisco Marto and seven-year-old Jacinta Marto, made the startling claim that they had been visited by a lady that later identified herself as Our Lady of the Rosary. The series of events that followed would resonate around the world and culminate with what has been described by many as the greatest miracle of the twentieth century, one that was observed by more than seventy thousand people. Today, the four million pilgrims that descend upon Fatima each year are testament to the global impact of the events that took place in 1917.

The Virgin Mary appeared to the three children on six different occasions between May and October of 1917. During those visits, the Virgin conveyed prophetic messages to them. The secular government, however, didn't believe the children's claims and threatened them with torturous deaths if they did not disclose all that was allegedly imparted to them. It is no wonder that on October 13, 1917, the day that the Mother of God promised a miracle that all could see, some seventy thousand people turned out in the fields of Cova da Iria in the pouring rain to witness the event

---

[5]Fr. Hubert Schiffer was 30 at the time of the explosion and lived in good health to the age of 63.

[6] CAN/EWTN News, The Miracle of Hiroshima – Jesuits Survived the Atomic Bomb Thanks to the Rosary. 2015. p. 2.

for themselves. Even avowed atheists from *O'Seculo*, *O Dia*, and other newspapers of the day attended with full confidence that no miracle would occur, enabling them to once and for all debunk the children's story as the lie that they believed it was. No one expected what was about to happen.

A crowd of 70,000 people turned out to witness the miracle promised to the children by Our Lady of the Rosary on October 13, 1917.

The Miracle of the Sun occurred at the exact hour and on the exact day that was predicted by Our Lady some three months earlier.

This image shows some of the crowd gazing up at the sun as it "danced in the sky."

"As She [Our Lady] ascended, the reflection of her own light continued to be projected on the sun itself. Lucia sensed this to be the promised sign and cried out to the crowd in a loud voice, 'Look at the sun!' Suddenly the rain stopped, the clouds that previously covered the sun dissipated, and the sun appeared in the sky. Though exceptionally bright, the sun was not dazzling. Without warning, it began to turn in the sky as if projecting in each direction bands of light of each color that lit and colored the remaining clouds, the sky, the trees, and the crowd. It stayed for some moments then it went back to its normal position where it remained still for another short while.

As the seventy thousand gazed upon the sky and, in particular, the sun, the children remained focused on the Lady of the Rosary, whose vision, though ascended, was now instantly replaced with a vision of St. Joseph holding the Child Jesus. Next to St. Joseph and standing beside the sun was Our Lady, this time wearing a white robe with a blue mantle. St. Joseph appeared to have blessed the world tracing the sign of the cross with his hand three times. As he did this Lucia said, 'St. Joseph is going to bless us!'

The Child Jesus did the same. In the second vision Our Lady of Sorrows stood in the somber garb assigned to her by tradition, the Mater Dolorosa of Good Friday, but without the sword in her breast, and beside her stood her divine Son, grieving as when he met her on the way to Calvary. Lucia saw only the upper part of His figure. He looked pityingly on the crowd for whom He had died and raised His hand to make the sign of the cross over them.

In the third vision, Our Lady appeared as Our Lady of Mount Carmel. The Queen of heaven and earth held the baby Jesus upon Her knee. A few in the crowd claimed to have seen the visions as well, yet this claim remains unverified. No one else was privileged with such visions.

The entire assemblage, however, all seventy thousand people, became aware that their clothes, as well as the ground beneath them, were completely dry. In amazement and confusion, they prayed, but just as suddenly as before, the sun looked as if it stood out from the sky, appearing to fall on the now terrified crowd below. Most of the assembled fell to their knees and begged for mercy. Though still intensely bright, people could look directly at the sun without hurting their eyes. As the crowd gazed at the burning orb, it seemed to 'dance,' then whirled like a giant wheel of fire. It did this for some time before stopping; then it quickly rotated again. Then brilliant colors began to reach down to the earth, making all that could be seen tinted by the spectrum of colors. No one knew what to make of this and many continued to stare in utter amazement when, in an instant, the fiery orb seemed to tremble, to shudder, and then to plunge precipitately, in a mighty zigzag, toward the crowd."[7]

In addition to the seventy thousand, many others, some as far away as twenty-five miles, also witnessed the events of

[7] Caranci, Paul F. The Promise of Fatima: One Hundred Years of History, Mystery and Faith: Stillwater River Publications, 2017. pp. 213-214.

October 13, 1917. Even the atheistic reporters from the secular newspapers were forced to report the miracle exactly as they had witnessed it.

But there is more to the story of Fatima than miracles and apparitions, for the three children had also claimed that they had been entrusted with a secret and a promise later revealed to be a prophetic vision and a warning for all of mankind. The secret told of a new war, utter destruction, and a vicious attack on the Catholic Church itself. The promise provided a way to prevent such events from ever occurring.

Throughout her six visits with the children, the Virgin Mary told them to *"pray the Rosary every day in order to obtain peace for the world and the end of the war."*[8] In July, she promised that in October she would perform a miracle for all to see. She also showed them a vision of hell saying, *"The war is going to end, but if people do not cease offending God, a worse one will break out during the pontificate of Pius XI. When you see the night illumined by an unknown light, know that this is the great sign given you by God that he is about to punish the world for its crimes, by means of war, famine, and persecution of the Church and of the Holy Father. To prevent this, I shall come to ask for the consecration of Russia to my Immaculate Heart, and the Communion of Reparation on the First Saturdays. If my requests are heeded, Russia will be converted and there will be peace. If not, she will spread her errors throughout the world, causing wars and persecution of the Church..."*[9]

Though the October Miracle of the Sun marked the last of Mary's appearances to all three children simultaneously, she continued to appear to each of them individually and the events she prophesied continued to materialize. On the night of January 25, 1938, Sister Lucia dos Santos, who by now had joined the Sisters

---

[8] Ibid. p. 6.

[9] Ibid. pp. 75-76.

of Saint Dorothy in Tuy, Spain, stood by the window of her room in the convent. *"She noticed a red glow, an ominous glow, that seemed to light the entire sky. Lucia was not the only one to see this light, however, as it was visible throughout Europe and Africa and in parts of America and Asia. The lights persisted and continued to light the sky the following night as well. It was explained scientifically as the lights of the aurora borealis, despite the northern lights being a most unusual occurrence in [or near] Portugal. Lucia knew better, however, sensing immediately that she had just witnessed the fulfillment of Our Lady's prophesy of July 1917."*[10]

It was the reign of Pope Pius XI and just two months later Adolf Hitler overtook Austria. Although World War II didn't officially start until September 1, 1939, much of Europe was already at war.

Mary's message at Fatima is quite clear - **Pray the Rosary every day, sacrifice for the conversion of sinners, consecrate Russia to Her Immaculate Heart** *(something to be accomplished by all the Bishops of the world)* **and make the Communion of Reparation on the five first Saturdays.** *(This reparation requires that on the first Saturday of five consecutive months, we receive the sacrament of reconciliation, attend Holy Mass, and receive the Eucharist in a state of grace, recite five decades of one of the Mysteries of the Rosary, meditate on the decades of the Rosary just recited for fifteen minutes, and do all this with the intent of making reparation.)*[11]

The Russian Bolshevik Revolution took place in March 1917, just prior to the first Apparition of Mary to the three children. Communism, and its destructive ways, however, did not take hold in Russia until November 1917. It is the spread of Communism of which Mary warned when she noted to the children

[10] Ibid. pp. 156-157

[11] Ibid. p. 76.

that, "*If my requests are heeded, Russia will be converted and there will be peace. If not, she will spread her errors throughout the world, causing wars and persecution of the Church...*"[12]

Fr. Hubert Schiffer, one of the eight Jesuit priests that survived the atomic blast in Hiroshima, said that *"he received a protective shield from the Blessed Virgin, which protected him from all radiation and ill effects. He attributes this to his devotion to Our Lady, and his daily Fatima Rosary.*"[13] While Fr. Schiffer, and the other priests who *"prayed the Rosary daily in their house,"* understood the message of Fatima, much of the rest of the world failed to heed that message, causing the spread of Communism throughout the world and triggering wars and persecution of the Church. Even in the United States of America, where constitutional protections are guaranteed to all, the infiltration of Communism with its pronouncements against God and family is evident. We see it in the proliferation of atheism; in the destruction caused by abortion under the guise of choice; in the removal of God from our schools under the guise of separation of church and state; in the disrespect to the Blessed Mother and the Church under the guise of freedom of expression; in the proliferation of pornography under the guise of protected speech; and in the required funding of contraception, abortion, and euthanasia under the guise of health care for all.

In the United States of America, as in most of the civilized nations of the world, people have fallen prey to the "errors spread by Russia" because the call of Fatima has gone unanswered. Only by turning to the remedy provided by Our Lady of the Rosary in her message to the three children of Fatima will good triumph over the evil currently perpetrated on our people through the spread of Communism. Mary, the Mother of God and of the world, calls for

---

[12] Ibid.

[13] TFP.org, The Amazing Story of the Hiroshima Eight. 2008. p. 3.

all people to take shelter under her protective mantle. When will we heed her call?

A Bed of Daffodils

By Jill Fague

I made the mistake of glancing over at the sign as I drove past the animal hospital. Like a stealth attack, distress crept up from my stomach, slowly clotting in my throat. Then the tingling started, like it always did, in the tip of my nose, alerting me that tears of regret were not far behind. I did not have the time for this today. Impatient with myself, I grabbed the ever-present packet of tissues lodged in my driver's side door. Quickly, before my mascara ran, I dabbed the inside corner of my eyes. It would not inspire the confidence of my seventh-grade students if I showed up to homeroom with a tear-streaked, blotchy face.

Somehow, a month had passed since we euthanized our beloved family cat, Jesse. And I simply could not "un-see" the last moments of his life slipping away in the back room of the animal clinic. A first world problem, I guess, but he was a member of our family for nearly seventeen years. The memories did not just disappear overnight. We had been through some horrifying days together, Jesse and I, and the realization that my furry pal would never again curl up in my lap sliced fresh cuts into my already wounded soul.

I was supposed to love him, to care for him, to protect him. He trusted me. And how did I repay him? I lured him into a cage and drove him to his death. A traitor of the worst sort. My husband Matt will tell me that we had no choice, that it was time. Then he will articulate some of the gut-wrenching scenes we witnessed, documenting the demise of our whiskered first-born over the previous month. He will tell me Jesse was suffering. But his words will not help. Not today. Whenever I let my mind wander over the last few moments of Jesse's life, vine-like tendrils of grief bloom in my gut, twist themselves around my stomach, and tighten their grip until I want to scream. I want him back.

I only wish Stephen King's fictional *Pet Sematary* really existed. Like the local children of Ludlow, Maine, I did not even care about the consequences. If Jesse reanimated vicious and destructive, it would serve me right. My loyal companion, and I double-crossed him in the most noxious way possible. Maybe I should have given him more time. I mean, nobody euthanized me when I was diagnosed with cancer.

Jesse loved me through my battle with cancer. During my year-long treatment plan, Jesse never left my side. If I went upstairs, he followed. If I curled up on the couch, he did too. If I napped, he napped. Many times, his soft, striped fur soaked up my tears as I mourned for the life I used to have. Somehow, he knew when to stick his sweet face in mine and rub his furry head against my bald one, easing my grief. When I was forced into germ lockdown, with virtually no immunity, Jesse kept me company and kept me sane. But when Jesse got sick, I could not return the favor.

I can mark the passage of time and document our family's history with images of Jesse. The first night we took our adorable kitten home, he sat upright, well into the night. Matt and I watched his little head tipping, as he began to nod off. Then suddenly, Jesse caught himself and jerked back to vertical, as if he were afraid to sleep in his new surroundings. The bedroom, a foreign setting compared to the barnyard he was raised in for the first few weeks of his life. During the day, Jesse curled up inside my favorite Red Sox baseball hat and napped like a tiny, one-pound champ. A couple years later, when we brought our newborn daughter Riley home from the hospital, Jesse climbed into her crib, a treasured companion better than any teddy bear. Our Jesse Bear.

Once, when Riley was about two years old, I was running a bath for her. Jesse came sauntering into the bathroom, probably jealous of his first human sibling, and he jumped up onto the edge of the tub. At which point, Riley pushed him right into the water with both hands. Jesse scrambled to get out, of course, but not with the degree of frenzy one might suspect of a shocked, submerged feline. He liked water but didn't see that one coming.

Another time, we were in Riley's bedroom getting ready for bed. As usual, Jesse wandered into the routine. I had the side door to Riley's dresser open on its hinges, and before I could pick out some pajamas, Riley pushed Jesse headfirst into the dresser, slammed the door behind him, and turned to me with her tiny, mischievous palms facing upward. "Where did Jesse go?" she asked in her little, high-pitched, cartoon character voice. But she did not always push Jesse around. Sometimes she dragged him. She would corral him under his front paws, heft him upward, and basically sweep the floor with him as she crossed the room. Jesse just took it all in stride. But Riley was still fortunate that Jesse did not have front claws.

And then along came our son Conner, a new playmate. Jesse tolerated being dragged around by yet another toddler. Jesse wandered into countless pictures, photobombing the kids, before photobombing became a national pastime. My favorite incident occurred one Christmas when I took a picture of Conner on his new, big-boy Spider-Man bike. He looked so cute in his fluffy Santa hat, the chubby cheeks of his baby days not quite gone. To celebrate the yuletide season, Riley had painted Conner's toenails fire engine red, and his bare feet proudly displayed his big sister's clever handiwork. As Conner struggled to balance and reach the bike pedals, Jesse photobombed the shot, right next to Conner's painted piggies. I love that picture, that memory. Much to my teenage son's present-day humiliation, that snapshot now permanently resides in a Christmas ornament.

Unlike a shy or fickle cat, Jesse was always in the middle of everything. A gift bag or wrapped present never went unchecked, not on Jesse's watch. He would dive into any bag, any box, and attack it like it was his job. Christmas mornings with the kids always brought unlimited fun for Jesse. Any empty box provided him the perfect opportunity to entertain himself (and us) with hilarious Jesse-in-the-box antics. Matt often closed the flaps over Jesse, scratch the box, and wait until Jesse popped out, ready to rumble. As kids everywhere can attest, the box was always better than any gift it housed.

Last December, we knew it would be Jesse's final Christmas, but we still conducted holiday business as usual. The kids and I dressed Jesse in a new festive outfit, this time a miniature Santa suit. Jesse paraded crookedly across the throw rug in the family room as if he had been day drinking. I'm not sure why the outfit impaired his equilibrium, but his unsteady walk of shame entertained plenty of Facebook friends. Jesse always did earn more "likes" than anything else I posted.

Later that week, as Christmas festivities ramped up, Matt thoughtfully brought home an ornament-making kit. We pressed Jesse's front paws into the ceramic molds, forever etching his prints into our decorations. The poor cat probably wondered why the holidays always brought new ways to torture him, as if he were the youngest sibling instead of the oldest. But he was always a good sport. He never hid or disappeared. He always came back for more.

I'm dreading the yearly unwrapping of ornaments this coming Christmas. I know it will sting when we find those replicas of his paws. We have a stocking for Jesse, too. Santa always gave him a little bag of treats or a cat ornament of his very own. I want to shield the kids from feeling fresh wounds come December. But this much I know: the wounds are worth having loved our precious Jesse.

Matt never really wanted a cat, but he loved Jesse as much as anyone. I still watch the videos of Matt vacuuming fur off Jesse and giving him a shower or bath. He was not a stereotypical cat.

When Matt came home from the police station after his second shift, Jesse would hear the garage door open, hop off my bed, and run downstairs to greet his pal. Sometimes I think Jesse was more dog than cat. If Matt indulged in a midnight snack after work, Jesse dutifully lapped up the milk at the bottom of his cereal bowl. Some police officers have formidable K-9 German shepherds. Officer Matt had a ten-pound, furry tabby cat as his trusty sidekick.

Late last fall, we feared that Jesse would die over the impending winter, leaving us unable to properly bury him in our frozen yard, so Matt dug a hole in the spot I picked out by our shed. Just in case. It was a difficult, morbid chore. Traitorous, really. But we knew we wanted Jesse near us always. While Matt shoveled, I dug up daffodil bulbs from my late grandfather's flower garden. I transplanted them near Jesse's anticipated final resting place. Heartsick tears rolled down my cheeks as I completed my mission, knowing for certain that when I witnessed the daffodils bloom in their new location, the following spring, Jesse would surely be gone.

And that day has come. I still roll over in bed, careful not to nudge Jesse or disturb him from his slumber. But the comforter no longer pulls taut when my legs stretch to his unoccupied spot. The loose covers, another reminder that Jesse really is gone. When I finish showering, out of habit, I still leave the water trickling. But then I realize no little white paws will curl around the door or stick themselves under the shower curtain. Jesse's daily showers, nevermore.

Sometimes, out of the corner of my eye, I swear I see Jesse lounging on the couch. As my brain processes the piece of wayward laundry or tossed blanket, a fresh pang reminds me that my sweet cat will never again occupy that spot. A trick of the mind, another reminder that this road only goes forward. We must forge ahead and assimilate the emptiness that greets us when we push open the house door at the end of a long day. I even miss Jesse's assassination attempts whenever I'm carrying my school tote, shopping bags, or groceries into the house. Vigilant, I still guard myself, expecting him to weave between my feet at the most inopportune moments. Sometimes, before I leave the house, I find myself glancing down to make sure my little Houdini-cat isn't making another great escape.

Each never-again moment creates a fresh wound.

At bedtime, as I close the window blinds, I gaze out at the spot by the shed. Jesse now rests under a bed of daffodils, recently bloomed. His bed in my room, empty and forlorn. Just like the corner of my heart reserved especially for him. My Jesse Bear.

Tomato Pie's Tale

By Cheryl Voisinet

Josie lay on the bare floor by the heat of the wood stove, his leather jacket balled up, serving as a pillow. The sweet little black-and-tan girl goat named Tomato Pie lay alongside, entwining her neck with his. She was gravely ill. Time trickled as an array of emotions tugged at our heartstrings while waiting for a sign that she would recover.

Josie's dad Steve, caretaker of the farm in rural Exeter, Rhode Island, lived in a small, bare-bones dwelling on the property, while steps away from his door surroundings were vibrant and teeming with life in stonewalled fields, open meadows, and vegetable and flower gardens. A row of colorful birdhouses lined the yard and the farthest edges of the farm were bordered by woodlands from each direction. There, one would find him tending the gardens or the flocks of sheep, goats, and wild birds. On any given day while sitting outside it was not uncommon to have a rabbit hop underneath or a squawking chicken peck at the ground by your feet. That one particular day began as any other, filled with chores. When setting about to tend to the goats, Steve's call was sent to Josie and then passed on to me. Sadly, our little goat Tomato Pie, daughter of Mojo and Mama and twin to her brother Sunny, was in poor condition. The usually playful and mischievous one was now unable to stand, and could only manage painful cries. When we hurriedly arrived, she was lying in her shelter in obvious distress. Poisonous plants or shrubs are often suspected, as goats continuously graze on whatever is in sight, it seems. We needed to get a vet to the farm as soon as possible. The task proved daunting, as it was New Year's Eve day. Folks were on vacation and offices were closed. After many attempts we got an affirmative from a vet and her tech partner. It would be a while, though, as other critters had to be attended to in several counties.

We exhaled deep sighs of relief when we heard the truck make its way along the winding dirt road onto the farm. After exchanging smiles and hugs, we beckoned the two women to the shed in the back field. Stooping and creeping into the small enclosure, we nestled on piles of hay surrounding her: me, Josie, the vet, her tech, and Sunny. With stethoscope in hand, the vet listened to Tomato Pie's weakening heart and her four-sectioned belly. No time to waste, she gave a shot of pain meds for the distress. An IV drip bottle with vitamin B and other fluids was hung from a rusty nail on the shed's roof and a line was started. A syringe full of gooey black charcoal was sent down her throat to soak up the toxins. Her heart was becoming weaker and weaker. Efforts were failing and comfort measures were offered as an unlikely recovery loomed. Tears streamed from Josie's swollen eyes and he was not able to agree to stop treatment. We both cried. The vet tech then asked us, as a last attempt, if we would allow her to give Tomato Pie a Reiki treatment. I had heard Reiki was an ancient Japanese healing technique using only one's hands as energy work. With a resounding yes from Josie and me, she bowed her head to begin. With eyes closed, she laid her hands gently above the stricken goat. Open hearts with highest intentions for the well-being of Tomato Pie transformed the energy in our huddled space. A shift had occurred, and the tech was crying along with us. Rechecking her, the vet noted that Tomato Pie's heartbeat was growng stronger.

Tomato Pie was carried gently into Steve's dwelling where we could keep close eyes on her. Her brother Sunny cried out to his sister while pacing the perimeter of his enclosure. She managed a mournful bleat back to him, sounding like a crying infant child. Pain meds, IV fluids, and charcoal continued. Over the course of two hours, more Reiki treatments were given. As the vet needed to attend to more critters elsewhere, I was handed detailed written instructions, along with the necessary equipment and blessings. Hours dragged on endlessly, closing in on midnight, when the first movement came from the little goat. As she lay with Josie by the wood stove she lifted her head, opened her eyes, turned to look about and in one swift jump was standing upright. A bit wobbly, she began munching hay and drinking sips of water. Stunned, we made a call to the vet's home where shouts of joy were heard along with cautionary words that she was not fully out of the woods yet. Being more optimistic than not, I left to make use of a welcoming bed and needful sleep.

On New Year's Day morning I was awakened with an urgent text -HURRY-SICK AGAIN. Half-awake without my morning coffee, I hastily dressed. Feeling an odd tickling beneath my right pants leg, I found an extra undergarment peeking out. I quickly jammed it in my coat pocket, relieved that no one else had seen. When I arrived at Steve's place, Tomato Pie was listless once again. It was my job to poke her tiny body with needles, which became harder and harder for me to do. She would cry out in pain and my hands would shake. I needed to pause and gain my composure before attempting to continue. Nurses and vet techs have my highest regard. More wait and see lay ahead. As evening approached, the little goat regained strength. Suddenly her friskiness resumed, to our delight. Curiosity returned with attempts to nibble the kitchen curtains, a car trader mag, and then Pall Mall cigarette butts in the ashtray. She leapt on the couch where lovable mutt Marty lay, and cozied up next to him. We decided to keep her inside for one more night. Steve's generosity would never be forgotten. Steve didn't blink an eye or think twice about allowing this little unhousetrained goat guest to recover in his home. With many involved in her healing, this truly was a village effort.

The third morning of the third day we brought Tomato Pie outside to be with her brother Sunny. The twins greeted each other with jumps and head butts up on two hooves, the crack of their tiny horns connecting with conviction. It was a good day witnessing all that love had provided. I sat with my morning coffee, smiling at the little goat's antics, tears tumbling to the field below.

Climate Sense: A Practical Guide to Finding Solutions and Keeping Your Cool

By Pat Hinkley

Here are snippets from chapters in *Climate Sense: A Practical Guide to Finding Solutions and Keeping Your Cool.* This is an unusual book about the topic, for it is optimistic. Its steadfast focus on climate science and events allow readers the opportunity to move beyond the immobilizing effects which existential fears put upon human minds. The intention is to inspire readers to lower their carbon impacts and then to feel good about becoming part of a positive movement.

Something out of the ordinary is truly happening everywhere and in the events stretching beyond many of our historical memories. Yes, storms are worse in some years than others, temperatures fluctuate lower and higher; however, the scope and frequency of these events have changed. There appears to be no standard anymore.

Look around you. What do you see? Has normal recently taken on another form in your area? What does your sound judgement tell you beyond the sensationalist, political, or denialist news?

Holding misgivings about the changing climate is part of helping you come to a conclusion. It's good to question. Perhaps though, as you broadly cast your net of inquiry, you may want to weigh the doubts with observations. Your very own common sense will guide you—and there is much to do once acceptance takes hold about the very real reordering taking place all over the world.

Last summer was intensely hot in the Southwest and the western parts of the United States. San Francisco saw one hundred and six degrees in those always chilly hills. Immense, fierce, and far-flung scenes of entire mountains on fire portrayed apocalyptic scenarios across the west. Thousands of residents fled or lost their homes. Hurricane Harvey flooded out people in Houston, and some residents of Puerto Rico lived without electricity for at least seven months after Hurricane Irma passed through.

Good sense says no, these are not ordinary events. Even if you live in a peaceful, delightfully unaffected region, lucky you; nonetheless, it does not feel commonplace for hosts of others. Normal has shifted.

A big overview of climate-related events happening all around you may help you to make sense of the changes, both near to you and in faraway places. These alterations will affect us all eventually. No one is immune.

The scale of the changing planet is daunting indeed. Take a look at the words in this second warning, published in an open letter on November 13, 2017 from 15,364 scientists in 184 countries: "They warned humanity against catastrophic biodiversity loss and widespread misery for humans. Their cautionary message implored people to make major changes—to cut greenhouse gas emissions, phase out fossil fuels, reduce deforestation, and to reverse the trend of collapsing biodiversity. Soon, science says, it will be too late to shift the course away from our failing trajectory, and time is running out. We must recognize, in our day-to-day lives and in our governing institutions, that Earth, with all its life, is our only home." Sydney Pereira, Newsweek Magazine

Climate Sense: A Practical Guide to Finding Solutions and Keeping Your Cool argues for stepping off the curb of by-standing while you wait for a leader to take charge. The book calls each of us to open our eyes and ears and hearts to fully comprehend and to make commonsensical responses. All of us must learn to respect the shared truth of what nature is carrying out. Then we can do what is possible to limit worsening conditions, to protect ourselves, and to plan for the consequences. A positive approach to overwhelming scenarios can be found by taking actions, which keep each of us from simply waiting for the inevitable to come our way. We become actors rather than victims of climate vicissitudes.

The task, as I see it, is for each person to challenge herself to take personal and collective steps to rearrange a lot of what he or she does, as habits of which we aren't even aware. Our actions have consequences. The overriding charge from nature asks each person to become conscious of the results of his actions over time. This is a learning process where we, who live in relative freedom, have great opportunity to examine the repercussions we make on this earth. Residents in the U.S. do not have to duck bombs, and plenty of us have food on our tables and roofs over our heads. This degree of security gives us pause to become more aware of how we are living our lives. Again, this is a learning process.

We can change our habits and behaviors. What do I mean? It's easy to begin. Turn the lights off in a room when you leave it. Dress according to the seasons, and use less heat or air conditioning. Hold onto your clothes long enough to wear them out; then give them away and replace them. Bring a coffee cup to your coffee shop. Ask waiters not to give you a straw or a lid if you use their cups. Explain why. Use bags other than plastic or paper. Many styles of bags are available for carrying your goods. Chose how you get around. Walk more. Ride bikes. More conscious vacation time activities and less carbon intensive automobiles benefit us all. Even eating slightly less meat means less carbon particles filter into the air.

There are so many ways to make a difference and to help us all. Many of us can get along just fine with less stuff. Imagine the combined results of millions of people making unthoughtful choices and harming the life support systems on which our lives depend. My point is to look at and then to think about what you do and what you use.

The way to stop this CC Lines ocean liner of climate change coming directly at us is for many, many, many people all over the world to get busy. Learn what you can, talk to everyone and let your conversations about your discoveries be optimistic with what you are doing. Together we are many. Together we are enormously influential. Do what you can to allow your life to harm to the planet less. Think through ways to afford to do more. Each of us can participate somehow. Have a free energy audit, insulate more, buy those solar panels, lease that electric car, buy that big battery to charge your car and home. Stretch beyond your comfort zones and do what you are able to do. Put on your thinking caps and solve problems. Spread the word with enthusiasm and feel yourself become fired up with your positive actions and the possibilities created by working toward a common goal of keeping our planet livable.

The topic of climate change may sound overwhelming and impossible, but turning the ship around is not out of the question. Author and entrepreneur James Altucher advises, "Begin with small steps-1% per day, which encourage us and motivate others to do the same." We stand up and be counted. We stand up for government, for corporations and for the wealthy to do more. For more is crucially needed.

This is our best way forward. We don't need foot-dragging leaders. We need our wholehearted selves!

Now is a good time to sit down with your family, or yourself, to survey your present actions and what you can do differently to become part of this movement toward living sustainably.

There you have it.
The world is in your hands.
Simply begin.
Use your common sense and take just one small step.
And the world will thank you.

Health Related Information of Interest

By Deb Katz

The purpose of my sharing this information is to boost up the health knowledge bank of the reader. It is not to be used as a substitute for your physician.

I have been accumulating health-related information since the 1970s, using the following means: books, medical newsletters, internet sources of doctors' websites which include discussions of medical studies, scientific trials, etc., my personal discussions with medical practitioners, and my own medical experiences and those of others.

The information can basically be broken down into those things that are potentially beneficial, those potentially detrimental, and those dependent/independent variables determined by one's individuality. There are many factors involved. A discussion of foods, supplements, and life choices is multifactorial. It is very dependent on individual differences. Therefore, when I mention that something might be beneficial, the reader needs to relate this to his or her self-knowledge.

There are certain statements that could be made with more certainty and could apply to most people and situations. Generally speaking, the following could be said.

1. Smoking is not beneficial.
2. Consuming large amounts of refined sugar is not beneficial.

   Idea: Replace refined sugar with chopped fruit such as strawberries or pineapple, applesauce (steamed apples plus cinnamon), raisins, maple syrup, honey, date sugar, stevia, ground figs, or dates.

3. Artificial sweeteners, in many instances, can be detrimental to one's health.
4. Being extremely overweight is not beneficial to one's health.
5. Having a cell phone next to one's head for long periods of time may be detrimental.
6. Staring at a computer for long periods of time, without blinking or looking away often enough, could be detrimental.
7. Using hard core recreational drugs is detrimental.
8. Binge drinking could be detrimental.
9. Certain prescription drugs can be life-saving.
10. Certain prescription drugs can be detrimental, especially to the liver.
11. Particular foods can be helpful to the body against illnesses and/or can lessen symptoms.

Some foods have characteristics which make them beneficial to the liver. The humble apple, with its polyphenols, has an anti-inflammatory effect on the liver.

Olive oil, with its many other known benefits, also helps to increase insulin sensitivity and lipid oxidation, while lowering triglycerides and cholesterol.

Asparagus, with its many minerals and vitamins, helps to lessen toxins in the liver.

The lemon, high in citric acid, is an antioxidant and is helpful in reducing oxidative damage to the liver. Garlic has allicin and can help protect the liver from oxidative damage.

Broccoli, which has isothiocyanates, sulfur-containing compounds which are anti-inflammatory, among other ways protective for the liver. Turmeric, curcumin bioactive compound, with powers such as being anti-fungal, anti-bacterial, anti-viral, anti-inflammatory, and is an antioxidant!

There are many others. The more you know about the benefits of healthy grown foods (not loaded with pesticides) and what these foods can do for your body's health and functioning, the better.

FOOD REALLY CAN BE MEDICINE.

12. Vitamins and other supplements can help the body against illnesses and/or lessen symptoms. Enlightened current researchers point to levels of homocysteine becoming elevated when a vitamin deficiency occurs in the body, related to vitamin B6, B12, and folic acid. The elevated homocysteine level and inflammation are seen as contributing causes of arteriosclerosis. Note has also been made of other factors contributing to heart disease such as low magnesium levels, low antioxidant levels, omega 6 to omega 3 ratios, low levels of coenzyme Q10 (a protector against free radical damage, this antioxidant COQ10 is naturally found in our mitochondria, but is unfortunately depleted by certain medications). Also mentioned as another heart disease factor is the presence of trans fats in the diet.

What is pleasant about this knowledge is that the possibility of a positive result in health could be achieved by improved diet and correct supplementation for nutritional deficiencies as compared to choices presented as limited only to prescription drugs (often with a myriad of side effects), and based on the patient's cholesterol numbers (and sometimes regardless of recognition of high HDL—a good number—as factors in prescribing choice making). Unfortunately, this latter scenario, so limited, is frequently presented in doctors' offices currently.

However, when one comes across a physician's office that includes a nutritionist or dietitian on the staff, one realizes that doctor is sincere when he (she) states that diet and exercise are major factors for your health improvement, when discussing heart health. Such an enlightened practice does exist.

There are so many ways to learn about how to improve one's health and well-being. And there are many approaches offered by naturopaths, chiropractors, and very talented "see the big picture" internists, pediatricians, cardiologists, allergists, etc.

What may be good for one person may not be good for another. That is why it is a good idea for a person to keep a record of personal experiences with responses to foods, prescription drugs, and supplements of any kind when they occur. Self-knowledge is very important. And you really need to be your own best friend when it comes to your health. However, I know that sometimes you cannot help being in an unhealthy situation due to having to make a living etc.: been there, done that. With that having been said, it is most important to have some knowledge of potential remedies and preventive health-friendly steps one can take, even in these kinds of unavoidable situations that life sometimes presents.

A beneficial experience one can provide for oneself, almost anywhere, almost anytime:

A Simple Factor—Breath—a slow deep breath can sometimes help the body.

The miracle of breath—if you think about it and treasure it. It is a sign that you are alive—the gift of life. If you start low down in the breath's beginning and follow it up to the middle and then to the chest and to the throat with your inhale. Then you exhale through your nose or mouth, back down the same route, without rushing. Eyes open or closed. Maybe even thinking a grateful "thank you" for this moment of life-giving breath.

About the Authors

Regina Andrews has been writing for nearly twelve years and has been published for ten years. She is the published author of six inspirational novels with four more completed novels in her publisher's queue to be released.

Currently, she lives on the East Side of Providence. She will be featured in the Fall 2018 issue of *Esprit de Coeur*, a publication of the Associated Alumnae and Alumni of the Sacred Heart.

She is very active in choral singing in Providence, and loves to travel. She continues to find inspiration for her books every day, especially when the unexpected happens.

My themes are double-sided: first, they are inspired by real practical matters of everyday life, especially when good people face tough circumstances. The second side, which works with the first and makes the theme complete and whole, incorporates the major role God has in our lives, and explores how are choices are made based on the character's level of faith. Some characters have an awakening of their faith, others walk away from God.

Inspirational fiction is my genre because it blends spirituality and higher purpose with very real, practical matters of everyday life, always addressing the question: how do we conduct ourselves as good, respectable individuals?

This is a question everyone can relate to. It involves responsibility, challenges, faith, generosity and love--and the happy endings in my work are never achieved without many ups and downs...all centered in some way with the character's relationship with God.

I enjoy writing about this very much and I find that, unlike traditional romances, my romances actually have three main characters: hero, heroine and God.

W. Gauvin Barber is a polymath personality writer of books, essays, short stories, entrepreneur, blogs, and radio scripts. He is a board member of ARIA, the Association of Rhode Island Authors.

Writing theme is about history and new historical sports records, and essays on animal species and their phenology nature calendar. I have been writing for over forty years and created a book by the name of *New England's Golden Years of Racing: Their History and a Glimpse into their Future.*

My genre is memoirs, outdoor essays, and short stories. Historical/Sports automobile racing books and records.

David Boiani is a dedicated father to a wonderful seventeen-year-old daughter, member of the Association of Rhode Island Authors, and guitarist in an alternative rock band called *The Whole Façade*. David's love of reading as a young boy ignited his desire to write fiction.

I have been writing for approximately five years. I draw inspiration from novels, poetry, or short stories I have read through the years. Good art should create emotion, whatever the form. I strive to affect my readers emotionally, to make the reader ponder my writing for days after he/she has finished. The thought of playing God in a universe that I create, without limits or boundaries, with endless possibilities, is intoxicating to me. If I were to place my work into one genre it would be the psychological thriller genre, but I tend to venture into other genres often. My books include *A Thin Line*, *Dark Musings,* and *The Redemption*, which is the sequel to *A Thin Line*. I am currently working on my second collection which will be titled *Darker Musings*.

Adele M. Bourne grew up in a huge family with poetry one of its bad habits. She earned a B.A. from Bryn Mawr, an M.A. from Columbia Teachers College, worked for a U.S. Representative, in educational television, as an editor for the World Law Fund, and taught school for thirty years. She moved to Providence five years ago, and enjoys it mightily.

Adele has published two books of poetry, *A Grocery List and Other Poems* (Finishing Line Press, 2010) and *Tide Roaring In* (Kelsay Books, 2016). She has edited a collection of her late husband's poems, *To Make a Thing of Air* by John Setliffe Bourne (Stillwater Press, 2014). She has been writing, on and off, since the age of six.

Adele has written plays, but found poetry more compatible with a busy work and family life, a notebook stuck in the back of a pocket, a slim book of poetry to read surreptitiously during a boring meeting… She tries to find a form for haunting formless thoughts and sometimes is successful.

Heather A. Caranci attended Roger Williams University. She is a member of the Association of Rhode Island Authors (ARIA), where she serves as secretary and a member of the group's board of directors. She also serves in the capacity of sponsorship coordinator of ARIA's Expo Committee. Heather serves on the board of directors of the Municipal Heritage Group, a non-profit organization dedicated to the preservation of municipal history through the written word. *Monumental Providence: Legends of History in Sculpture, Statuary, Monuments, and Memorials* is her first book.

Paul F. Caranci is a historian and the award-winning author of eight books. The former RI Deputy Secretary of State also served on his local town council for over sixteen years. His experiences working undercover with the FBI for seventeen months to gather video and audio taped evidence of a widespread corruption scheme is the subject of *Wired: A Shocking True Story of Political Corruption and the FBI Informant Who Risked Everything to Expose it* (2017). His undercover work earned him the Margaret Chase Smith American Democracy Award for Political Courage, the highest honor awarded by the

National Association of Secretaries of State. In addition, two of Paul's books, *The Hanging & Redemption of John Gordon* (2012) and *Scoundrels* (2016) were each named non-fiction book of the year. His most recent book, *The Promise of Fatima: One Hundred Years of History, Mystery and Faith,* is the inspiring story of the Marian apparitions to three shepherd children in Fatima, Portugal in 1917.

Paul is a former member of the Board of Directors of both the RI Heritage Hall of Fame and the Heritage Harbor Museum. He currently serves on the board of directors of the Association of Rhode Island Authors and the RI Publication Society. Visit Paul's website at www.paulcaranci.com.

A. Keith Carreiro earned his master's and doctoral degrees from Harvard Graduate School of Education, with the sequential help and guidance of three advisors, Dr. Vernon A. Howard, Dr. Donald W. Oliver, and Professor Emeritus, Dr. Israel Scheffler. Keith's academic focus, including his ongoing research agenda, centers upon philosophically examining how creativity and critical thinking are acquired, learned, utilized, and practiced in the performing arts. He has taken his findings and applied them to the professional development of educational practitioners and other creative artists.

Earlier in his teaching career he was a professor of educational foundations, teaching graduate students of education at universities in Vermont, Florida, Arizona, and Pennsylvania. He currently teaches as an adjunct professor of English at Bridgewater State University, as well as teaching English, philosophy, humanities, and public speaking courses at Bristol Community College.

Keith and his wife Carolyn Ann Carreiro live in Swansea, Massachusetts and have six children and 13 grandchildren. They belong to an eighty-five-pound golden retriever and an impish Calico cat.

Due to his love of family, he has seen his fervor for history, as well as his passion for wondering about the future, deepen dramatically.

Starting on May 23 until October 9 of 2014, he sat down at his computer on a daily basis and began writing the first book of a science fiction/fantasy thriller in a beginning series about the quest for human immortality. http://immortalitywars.com/

R.N. Chevalier completed and published his first novel in 2015, three years after he was diagnosed with ALS. He's published one novel a year. In 2017, along with his novel, he published a book co-authored with his wife, Donna.

I have, from my earliest memories, been drawn, inexplicitly, to science fiction and the bizarre. From the books of H.G. Wells to Stephen King and films from the Star Trek franchise to The Night Gallery and The Twilight Zone, it was only logical that my own writing would reflect those interests.

My current works are, *Are We the Klingons, Advances of the Ancients,* and *Full Circle.* The project with my wife is *Rhode Island Civil War Monuments: A Pictorial Guide.*

I'm planning a 2018 release of a yet-to-be-named novel for younger readers about time travel. It will be illustrated by my daughter, Jasmine, as well as another book co-authored with my wife tentatively titled *The 20 Most Unique Civil War Monuments of Massachusetts:A Pictorial Guide.*

Kathy Clark is a retired Firefighter/EMT-C and a lifelong resident of Rhode Island. Because she was also a former pet-assisted therapy facilitator and her audiences were dog and Christmas-motivated, she created and combined six stories in two books, *One Christmas Eve in St. Bernardsville* and *Beyond the Moonlit Path*, both under her pen name, Estelle Spode.

Her stories have appeared in the New England St. Bernard Club Sentinel, the Pawtucket *Times*, and the Association of Rhode Island Authors anthologies, *Shoreline* and *Under the Thirteenth Star*.

While Clark most often writes about animals, "Take it to Her Grave" was written in 2014 for a writing class that specified writing a dramatic piece. She holds a bachelor's degree in creative writing.

Jess M. Collette has always called New England home. She has lived in Massachusetts, Vermont, and Rhode Island. The beauty and ever-changing seasons in this region inspire her writing. In addition to nature, Jess also writes about love and loss, drawing from her own experience of losing her only child, Joshua. In his honor, she has published two books. In addition to writing, she dabbles in graphic design. Jessica lives in Rhode Island with her husband and their adorable new rescue dog from Texas. Visit www.jessicamcollette.com for updates and to view current poetry.

I have always loved to write. Whether for an assignment, something special for a family member or just for fun, I've filled many a page. It wasn't until the loss of my son, Joshua, that I was inspired to write and publish the children's book on grieving, *Your Special Star*. Shortly after, I published my debut novel, *Naming the Bits Between*, an uplifting adventure about the cycle of life: loss, discovery, and finding renewed purpose.

The tagline on my website is *Fictional Sentiments Inspired by Life.* That really does sum it all up… I write works of fiction and poetry based on what I've experienced and the nuggets of truth I've found along the journey. I love to meld the physical and spiritual worlds together, so always look for hidden meanings in my writing. Currently, my focus is poetry. I love to pair a photo I've taken with a poem or poetic short story I've written. There's always something new to write about when you aim to see the extraordinary in the ordinary. After all, isn't life more fun that way? I think so. I try to live and write from a positive perspective. My hope is to see and learn something new every day!

K. Eric Crook was born in New York, lived out west where he was fortunate to work as a forester, and has now settled in Rhode Island.

When I stop to think about it I am at heart a storyteller. I am inspired by works of great authors, American and otherwise, beginning with Mark Twain and ending with whatever I read this morning. I ask only to humbly tread lightly in their footsteps.

Hawkeye and the Boxcar is a non-fiction essay. But it could easily have been fiction. I write comfortably in either genre. In fact, I can't honestly say I have a specific style. Years ago I worked as a planner in a public agency where I spent much of my time doing technical writing. But I still wrote poetry, hoping it would cleanse my soul. These days I am working on a three-part fictional series that might just as well be true. At the end of the day, what I appreciate most is simply reading or writing a well-turned phrase.

Kevin Duarte says his biography consists of numerous stories written in high school and college as a fine arts minor at Roger Williams University. I had a poem published in the college anthology when I was a senior.

In my late twenties, a local company produced a comic book called "P.R.I.M.E.," which I wrote with a friend. I came up with the main idea, and he, as the illustrator, helped fine-tune the concept and illustrated the comic. The comic was produced and sold quite well in the local area, garnering local TV coverage at one of the book signings in a local comic book store. I am currently working on a novel called *Manifest Destiny* and have completed the first draft.

Ray Bradbury, H. G. Wells, J.R.R. Tolkien, Chris Claremont. Rod Serling and the Twilight Zone have been a major source of inspiration. Other sources of inspiration were the many classic and authors that were part of the creative writing curriculum at Roger Williams University. If not for this course of study, I would not have read and become engaged by many of the classic works of literature such as *The Great Gatsby*, *War of the Worlds*, and *Heart of Darkness*, to name a few.

I love writing speculative science fiction, as well as fantasy. I am inspired by the possibilities of the human collective, both good and bad, and love to create characters as much as I love to create and modify the world around them.

Hank Ellis is a retired environmental scientist with Bachelor and Master of Science degrees in natural resources and wildlife management. He is the author of the recently published fictional adventure *The Promise: a perilous journey,* and is in the process of writing a sequel to his first book.

From grade school through high school and even into my first year at the University of Rhode Island, I didn't think much about writing. Not until I joined the US Coast Guard for four years and spent 10 months in Vietnam did I have a desire to write well. I guess it started with journaling about Vietnam and letters to home, but then moved on to my time in college. It was when I returned to URI, especially under the guidance of a very special professor, that my writing skills began to improve. I have a long way to go (thank goodness for editors) but I have come to love writing. My recent book took twenty years to finish. I especially like the action and adventure genre, but the literary non-fiction genre in this short story was fun. The short story was based on a true story that occurred in 1998.

Jill Fague is a mother and teacher from Smithfield. After beginning her career at the high school level, Jill earned her master's degree in Education and currently teaches middle school English Language Arts. Recently, Jill has teamed up with the American Cancer Society to spread her story of hope and survival. She has also donated proceeds from her memoir, *This Unfamiliar Road*, to the ACS, supporting the fight against cancer. Married for eighteen years, Jill lives with her husband and two teenage children.

With the recent publication of my memoir, I added 'author' to my resume. Six years ago, after being diagnosed with breast cancer, I found myself depressed, home from school, and balder than my husband. So, what does an out-of-work, bald English teacher do? Write a book, of course. In *Harry Potter*, the wand chooses the wizard. In my case, the book chose its author.

I am as surprised as anyone that I wrote a book. As a child who despised and avoided reading, I never developed the ability to visualize the words on the page. It never even occurred to me to try. Today, I encourage my reluctant middle-school readers to use their powers of visualization. Although I love to read now, I still lack the capacity to "see" a story as it unfolds. I envy that ability. Sadly, certain genres are lost on me, such as fantasy and science fiction. I simply cannot conjure up characters, settings, or events imagined and brought to life by their creators. Memoir writing appeals to me because the moments I describe exist in my memory. I can bring them back to life with words. And I am a self-confessed word nerd.

Leo C. Frisk, Jr. was born in Woonsocket in 1950. When he was seven years old, his family moved to a small country town in Massachusetts. It was there, living in a house with a backyard filled with woods and ponds, that he grew up learning about and playing with all kinds of animals and insects. Catching snakes and turtles during the day and lightning bugs at night were just a few of his regular childhood adventures.

But then as all boys do, he grew up, was soon married, and was blessed with a boy of his own. When his son was just two, Leo learned he was going blind. Unable to read any longer, he began to make up stories while pretending to read to his son. He soon discovered that his son liked his stories better than the ones that were in the book.

Today, Leo is totally blind and writes his stories from the many childhood memories he has stored in his imagination. Because of this, he considers himself to be a 68-year-old boy. His wife Gail helps him with his stories, adding a bit of her young heart personality to them.

The story "Stuffy" was written for her while they were dating and of all the stories he has written, it is still her favorite.

Leo now resides in Harrisville, Rhode Island, in a small house in a rural area surrounded by neighbors who he considers friends. He spends his days caning chairs, working in his yard, and writing children's stories, using his talking computer, stories he hopes children of all ages will enjoy.

Hannah R. Goodman wrote her first short story when she was ten and has been writing novels, essays, and short fiction ever since. Currently, she lives in Bristol, though she spent most of her growing up years in Middletown. Her inspiration comes from her own experiences in high school and also working with teenagers for the last two decades. Though she's spent most of her years as an author writing young adult novels and short stories, she has recently had personal essays published on MindBodyGreen, OC87 Recovery Diaries, Zencare.com, and The Mighty. This summer Black Rose Writing published my newest novel, *Till It Stops Beating.*

Patricia Hinkley received a Bachelor of Science from the University of Massachusetts; was licensed as an RN; received a Master of Arts degree in Holistic Studies and Psychology from Lesley University. Comprehensive counseling trainings followed in Hakomi, Internal Family Systems and The Journey. www.patriciahinkley.com

Non-fiction is my naturally best way to get across practical thoughts from professional experience and from what I care deeply about. Hopefully this is an accessible way for readers to benefit.

Claiming Space is a collection of ways I have learned to take moments to get quiet and restful. It's a primer on how to use minutes, not days, a few breaths at a time to still yourself so that peaceful actions fill the spaces in your mind and heart. The book essentially holds a workshop within for discovering the value of quiet times.

One night after years of sleepless nights I woke to the realization that I must write about this dilemma. *Chasing Sleep* came into being as a way to speak about how I and others navigate the lack of reliable sleep. It's a book about the science and history of sleep, and also about trusting your unique sense of what is right for you, especially when many others tell us what to do.

Calm is particularly essential to thinking about climate change. Because nature has been precious to me throughout my life, it felt urgent to speak about the collective misadventure we are all sliding into. *How Not to Freak Out and Shutdown About Climate Change* is my third book, and an optimistic approach to what many consider the most vital issue of our day.

L.A. Jacob has been writing for over 35 years, starting with fan fiction before it was cool. She moved on to writing historical fiction, including an immortal blessed by an American Indian goddess, a gay magician, and the usual "Hero's Journey" story that every epic fantasy writer does at some point in their career.

This is my fourth story in the *Grimaulkin* universe. It is about bullying, and how one person fights back. Just like Mike, I was bullied by the same person in school from kindergarten through sixth grade. Then another person stepped up from seventh through twelfth. So this story, in a sense, is my revenge.

I write magical realism, mostly because I want to believe that magic could really work. I consider myself a sorcerer/magician, so I'm familiar with theory and practice of both spiritual and practical ways of working with energy or "magic." I write what I know and believe, and wish could be.

Sam Kafrissen is a former resident of West Warwick and Cranston. He currently lives in Arlington, Massachusetts. Over the past five years he has published three Doherty mystery novels, *The Mill Town*, *The Lost Survivor*, and *The Missing Films*. They are all part of a series featuring a private detective named Hugh Doherty and which take place in Rhode Island in the late 1950s—early 1960s. In addition, he has had short stories published in two anthologies, *Mosaic* and *Mosaic 2014*. Along with writing mystery books and short stories, he has also written sports and feature stories for his hometown newspaper, *The Arlington Advocate*. Sam is presently completing a fourth Doherty mystery with a working title of *The Girl on the Rocks*.

As a former history teacher, Sam has combined his knowledge of American history and popular culture to provide background for much of his writing. The story submitted for this anthology is a remembrance piece from his early teen years growing up in Rhode Island. In much of his writing he tries to weave a sense of the nostalgic into his work. This is true of the Doherty mysteries mentioned above as well as in a number of the unpublished short stories he has created for various writing groups over the years. With much of his historical research, he has been assisted by members of historical societies in Rhode Island wherever his stories have been set.

Sam is extremely interested in trying to remember and recreate the past with as much authenticity as he can without losing a sense of the imaginative. As a result a lot of his writing is imbued with reminiscences from his own past or that of family members, close friends, and acquaintances. Thus, many of his stories have a nostalgic appeal as well as to plots.

Deborah Katz, a Rhode Islander, holds a B.S. from Boston University and two Master's degrees from URI, in Education and Counseling. She has always enjoyed writing, especially poetry, since a child.

Deborah's love of music (singing and composing) and appreciation of nature (its beauty and its creatures) comes, at least partly, from her birth family. Her brother played piano (standing up), bass, ukulele, guitar, and harmonica - all by ear from an early age, and had small bands often playing in the small music room of their home. Frequently, Deborah and her mother sang together at the piano, which her mother easily played, while they harmonized peacefully in their own little world, with dad joyfully looking on.

To this day, singing with others gives Deborah a natural "high" in life. And in the tradition of her mother's love of nature's creatures, Deborah does not even kill a fly, but tries to catch it and let it out the door.

Since the 1970s, Deborah has researched nutrition and health issues to prepare a book that will help give people a better chance of longevity - something her mother and brother did not get to have.

Donna Lomastro is a wife, mother, and friend to many. By the grace of God, she longs to spread hope, joy, and love. Donna has dedicated her life to working with children, whether it is nursery school, day care, or her current middle/high school position. Donna devotes most of her adult life helping children in different capacities. She enjoys spending time with her family and friends, loves knitting, making fleece blankets, and being creative, especially with writing. Donna has published one book, *Puppup Puppy Barks Real Loud!* which she prays will inspire many children.

My writing is inspired by my love of God and His Word. I love to use rhyme and biblical principles to change negative situations into positive solutions.

My genre is poetry and children's fiction. I aspire to deliver hope and encouragement in everyday life situations by using rhyme. I try to find hope in every situation. My interest in rhyming began when my dad showed me a poem that my grandma Evangeline (whom I never had the chance to know) wrote in rhyme. This inspired me to write in rhyme and use the rhyme in a teaching or healing way to convey a message of joy, love, and hope.

Paul Magnan has been writing stories that veer from the straight and narrow for many years. He has had several short stories published, along with two novels.

It seems to me the act of creation is both objective and subjective, especially with writing. My themes, including the theme of this piece, tend to dark surrealism, especially in my shorter works. I am inspired by Lovecraft, Bradbury, Poe, Shirley Jackson, Neil Gaiman, and so many other giants. My two novels are *Kyu, The Unknown, Book 1: The Coming of Dis*, and *Kyu, The Unknown, Book 2: The Oracle of Xisroc Isle.*

My genre is dark fantasy for my novels, but, essentially, anything goes for my shorter work. I can be surreal, absurdist, humorous, speculative... the only common thread is darkness.

Peter Mandel is a longtime adventure travel journalist for *The Washington Post, National Geographic Kids, The Los Angeles Times, The Wall Street Journal* and *The Providence Journal.* Mandel is an author of picture books for children published by Macmillan, Simon & Schuster, Scholastic, Henry Holt, and HarperCollins. Stories of his have been anthologized in several collections including *Chicken Soup for the Cat and Dog Lover's Soul* and *Adventures of a Lifetime: Travel Tales from Around the World.* One of Mandel's *Boston Globe* articles won the 2005 Lowell Thomas gold award from the Society of American Travel Writers for adventure travel article of the year. Originally from Manhattan's Chelsea neighborhood, Mandel has a B.A. from Middlebury College and an M.F.A. from Brown University. He lives in Providence with his wife, Kathy, and rescue cats, Betty, Emily, and Cecil.

Much of my writing is inspired by my late father, Paul Mandel, who died when I was eight. A reporter and editor for LIFE magazine during the 1960s, Dad covered the Mercury and Gemini space shots for LIFE, including when John Glenn became the first American in orbit—something that has given me a lifelong fascination with writing about adventure. His hardest assignment was reporting on Kennedy's assassination in Dallas, writing the story in LIFE that would accompany the motorcade images from the Zapruder film. (That was Dad's last story for LIFE, since he died in his 30s soon afterward of cancer.) A travel journalist and children's book author since the early 1990s, my books include *Jackhammer Sam* (Macmillan), *Bun, Onion, Burger* (Simon & Schuster), *Zoo Ah-Choooo* (Holiday House), and *Planes at the Airport* and *Boats on the River* (both Scholastic). Over the years, titles of mine have been included in an exhibit at the National Baseball Hall of Fame and The Smithsonian, and have been translated into Japanese, German, Chinese, Italian, Dutch, Swedish, and Danish.

My primary 'genre' in writing about travel is to bring out the humor in extreme (and sometimes 'upside-down') adventure travel. The submitted piece, "Hiking the Great American Strip Mall," is very much along these lines, and is one of the candidates for inclusion in an eventual book collection of these adventures that I'm currently at work on. For *The Washington Post, The Boston Globe, The Los Angeles Times*, and *The Providence Journal,* among other outlets, I've written adventure features on training and suiting up as a theme park character, seeing America by metered cab, visiting a 'city' of penguins at the South Pole, fishing for piranha on Brazil's Rio Negro, experiencing a coup in Ecuador, floating in the Goodyear Blimp, sailing on an Arctic icebreaker, camping in the African bush, and kayaking from Manhattan to the Statue of Liberty.

Author **Richard Maule** is a retired minister, motivational speaker, and all-around trouble-maker. (His friends insist he is yet to retire from the latter.) He presently lives with his beautiful wife and unruly dog in Uncasville, Connecticut.

Richard Maule specializes in historical fiction that brings to life true but untold stories of courage. His upcoming novel, *The Witch's Advocate*, tells the story of his own ancestor, Thomas Maule, a Quaker minister who stood up for the civil rights of the accused witches in Salem, Massachusetts. Thomas Maule's writings, and subsequent court case, became the precedent for our First Amendment freedoms of speech, press, and religion.

Rick's first novel, *Moonlight Helmsman*, told the true story of Robert Smalls, who rose from slavery to steal the Confederate flagship in 1862. Recipient of seven national awards for historical fiction, *Moonlight Helmsman* was praised by Kirkus Reviews, who called it "a riveting story… a seamless weave of historical investigation and fictional drama starring an African-American hero."

Rick has always been fascinated with history, especially the amazing untold stories about quirky or marginalized heroes. His books always involve a lot of research and make special efforts to take the reader back to interesting places and times. As a side note, all profits from Rick's books have been donated to charitable causes. His debut novel made over $20,000 the first year.

Joann Mead is a writer, educator, and researcher and has lived in four countries ranging from A to Z: America (USA), London, England (UK), Moscow, Russia (back in the USSR), and Zimbabwe (Africa). Her written works include speculative fiction, bio-thriller and crime novels, screenplays, short stories, magazine articles, and publications in medical journals on disasters and weapons of mass destruction.

My bio-crime series resides under the broad umbrella of *Underlying Crimes*, the title of my first novel. It is a crime story and medical mystery set in Rhode Island. My second novel, *Tiger Tiger,* is an international bioterror thriller that ratchets up the heat and action. Although my stories span the globe, my novels all feature two recurring protagonists who live in Rhode Island. My upcoming novel, *A More Perfect You,* highlights an international cast of characters and their nefarious crimes in Scandinavia.

As a writer of speculative fiction, my books are not entirely figments of my imagination. I often mix real happenings into my genres of crime, medical mystery, and bioterror thrillers. My "what if?" scenarios often blur the lines between fact and fiction. I truly believe what is real can be imagined. And what is imagined can be real.

Don J. Metivier is a highly decorated United States Air Force Master Sergeant (Retired) and a graduate of the Senior Non-Commissioned Officer Academy, Maxwell Air Force Base in Alabama. He holds an Associate of Arts degree and is the author of *Poems from the Mind of a Madman: Passionate Works of Poetry for Modern Times*, and *O Circo: Collective Poetry*.

Don is inspired to write poetry, by people, places, and emotions that he experiences in his day-to-day living. A strong passion for nature and the unusual add spice to his writings and are at times evident in his works.

G.A. Miller is a new voice in the chorus of horror authors, drawing his ideas from everyday, commonplace events that take unforeseen turns down dark corridors, often with horrific consequences. Find him on the web at http://gamiller.info/ and
http://gamillerdotblog.wordpress.com/

A lifelong reader, I've often thought about trying my hand at writing but never took the time to try. That changed in January of 2017, when I decided to test the waters. The test has been enjoyable, and has resulted in stories being published in many different works.

I don't know if I chose to write horror or if horror chose me. I've been a fan of the genre since I was very young, watching the old Universal classics on television. Reading soon followed, and when I discovered Stephen King in 1976, I never looked back. The story I'm including here might have been a good fit for the original Twilight Zone, when Rod Serling was still at the helm.

Yvette Nachmias-Baeu has led an eclectic life, following her wide range of interests to where they led. She has, for example, been a psychiatric nurse, a working actress, an advertising producer at a major New York agency, a farmer in Rhode Island, and a creative entrepreneur, and the founder of the South County Montessori School, She administered the Master's program in Teaching at Brown University for nine years. Her first book, *A Reluctant Life*, about the death of her husband and process of grief won an honorable mention at the New England Book Festival. Her second book, *Clara at Sixty* is the fictionalized sequel. Her third book, *Best Friends*, has just been released. It is a book of letters spanning a period of 27 years about the life of two aspiring women growing up in the sixties and ending in the eighties when their lives spun off in different directions, one of them tragically. She lives and writes at the edge of a waterfall in rural Rhode Island.

She writes non-fiction and fiction and is inspired by stories that paint a larger universal picture of life and its enduring complexities. Her narratives tend to bend towards prose as she sees the poetry words transforming the honest currency of feelings and situations.

Jack Nolan is a Providence-based writer whose 2017 novel, *Vietnam Remix*, is available online in print and as an ebook and in local book stores. He has lived in Indiana, Illinois, New York City, Tucson, Denver, and Providence, and has been turning out short stories that examine the culture of each of these places. "Castaway" is one of his efforts to capture the feel of the desert Southwest. Twenty other short stories complete this series. He lives with his wife,

Pat, and is currently at work on a sequel to *Vietnam Remix*, based on his experiences with Army Intelligence from 1967-70.

Frances O'Donnell has been President of the Historic Rhode Island Short Story Club for nine years until present. A published author, she has received numerous awards for her poetry and short stories and is working on her upcoming publications. Fran is a dedicated mother of five children. She is a widow and resides in Rhode Island close to her family. Fran enjoyed years of nursing and teaching and has a great love for piano and cello. Her passion for writing began early on. The love of her family and nature continues to inspire her interest.

Dusty Pembroke was born on the island of Bermuda. She now resides in a small New England town. Reading and writing have always been her passions. She has one published novel and has written numerous short stories. She has spent most of her adult life working with children in a local school, helping them to develop their writing skills.

My goal is to write a mystery that can draw the reader in, so that for a bit, they can escape the realities of life. As a young woman, I was drawn to Gothic romance and mysteries. I loved the way I could totally escape into these novels. I have been writing for over thirty years, but only decided to publish *The Family Plot* three years ago.

Marty Pena first realized she had a talent for writing fiction in high school when she wrote an "A" book report on a book she had not actually read. She thrived on the bonus essay questions at the end of exams. She always wrote from some moral high ground theme and teachers seemed to like that. In her senior citizen years she began taking writing more seriously. She retired from teaching horsemanship to focus on her artwork and creative writing.

I enjoy injecting humor into stories and I prefer to write children's and animal stories. I have over forty years' experience in training horses and teaching horsemanship. Along my way I took up the study of martial arts and have over twenty years in that pursuit as well. All this has provided rich inspiration along my creative path.

My muse for my first book was *Little Joe*, a former Amish plow horse, and I swear I could read his thoughts. Martial arts is the inspiration for *Charles vs. Toad Boy*, a story about bullying and is to be followed by a sequel, *The Return of Toad Boy*.

Joanne Perella was born in south Boston and moved to Providence with her family at an early age. She recently retired from a career in the public sector. Now she works as a real estate agent, antique appraiser, and author. She enjoys traveling and photography. Her goal in life is to remain forever young. This is her second piece included in the ARIA anthology series.

I like to write about those aspects of daily living that are inspiring, heartfelt, or incongruous. I have been writing for as long as I can remember and am currently working on more of this type of essay. I do write fiction from time to time, but even then my stories are built out of the theme of coping with life's changes.

The Hat on the Bed is a coming of age essay.

D.R. Perry has been writing for as long as she can remember. Currently, she resides in Coventry, Rhode Island, though she's lived in several other states. Each year, she attends Dragon Con in Atlanta, GA and one of her novels was a finalist in their 2017 contest, The Dragon Awards.

Once a month, you'll find her hosting a featured reading and open mic night at the Bean Barn in Coventry.

I'm inspired by families of all sorts. How do they form? What keeps them together, drives them apart, makes them expand or contract? Characters tend to speak first in my heart and mind until I can't help but get them on a page.

Along with poetry, I write the occasional short story and piece of flash fiction, some of which have been in other anthologies. My main body of work is made up of locally-based speculative fiction, including Urban Fantasy, Alternate History, and Science Fantasy. http://www.drperryauthor.com/, https://www.patreon.com/drperryauthor

Joni Pfeiffer-Moser's love of writing began in her high school years when she was co-feature editor of the school newspaper. College years heavily highlighted English composition, journalism, and children's literature. For many years beginning in 1974, she was a female pioneer in radio, broadcasting at many stations in the Providence market in many roles—an on-air personality, program director, operations manager, consultant, and from early 1990s until 2007, as the voice of Rhode Island PBS. All of these roles required much creative writing.

In recent years, her interests evolved to essay, poetry, a children's book, and memoir. Her work has been featured in several anthologies, the *Providence Journal*, the South County *Independent*, and the Wickford Art Association's Poetry and Art Exhibit three years in a row. Her picture storybook, *Annie the Story of an Apple*, published in 2016, is available online and at several book stores.

While keeping her options open, her present focus is writing memoir and poetry. She juggles her writing life with family time, poetry, and memoir events, a book club, theater, classical music venues, fitness activities and watching tennis.

Over a quarter-century writing about sports, particularly motor racing, for a variety of newspapers and magazines refined my instincts as a chronic observer, says **Thom Ring.** I often see among interacting strangers little scenes played out that hint at bigger stories, even though the stories might only be real in my mind. I try to turn those scenes into short stories that do the same for readers.

Most of my work these days focuses on writing my *Red Racecar* novels for kids, trying to capture the excitement of the sport so well that reluctant readers become reluctant to put the book down. www.theredracecar.com

Victor C. Rudowski is a retired computer programmer who has enjoyed reading fiction and non-fiction since the early 1960's. After serving four years in the U.S. Air Force he attended evening school classes at Providence College and received a Bachelor of Arts Degree in English in 1977. He will have his second fiction short story published in the 2018 Anthology. He has written articles for the Rhode Island Saltwater Anglers Association (RISAA), of which he is a long-time member, and plans to have his first fiction novel published within the next year. He can be reached at rovic57812@gmail.com

Bob Sherman lives in North Smithfield. He holds a master's degree in education from West Virginia University and spent 34 years as a public and private school administrator, developed programs for gifted students, and managed clinical teams that diagnosed and treated educational and psychological school related issues. Following retirement, he developed and licensed software for school departments (administrators and teachers) to track and report student progress using state and federal forms for use in the states of Rhode Island, Connecticut, and Massachusetts. During his time, he also owned a real estate company that invested in rental properties. For the last seven years he has been writing fiction and non-fiction short stories, books, and educational and financial columns. Bob enjoys tennis, running, skiing, sailing, and slipping away for short periods of time on his motorcycle. He is the treasurer for the Smith-Apple House Museum, Historical Society of Smithfield, and coordinates the Woonsocket Library Author events.

My adult and young adult fiction books are about mystery and adventure which is what life is for me today. My stories, inspired by historical events and real people, are character-driven and once created, take me where they want to go. My job is to find the words that do them justice and that's a lot of work that includes waking up in the middle of the night with the word that had escaped me up to that point. *Border Crimes and Other Short Stories,* tales of dark humor and real people, begins in West Virginia and ends in Rhode Island. *The Train Station* is a young adult novel that begins in Woonsocket and transports teens back to the London Blitz. Both books took five years to write and rewrite until I felt I had done justice to the characters' willingness to tell their stories.

Sweet mysteries of life is my genre. I begin with people I have met or read about, add a historical context, look for the mystery, discoveries and twists of fate then begin to fashion a story that I think may be of interest and a surprise to others. After a few weeks, most of these are discarded or overshadowed by an even better idea or some other real-world circumstance. Pairing down my priorities is a never-ending chore.

Alycia Marie Shillan has been writing since the age of eleven, but honestly, there has never been a time when stories and make-believe weren't her favorite way to pass the time.

Fear of rejection has always kept her from the pursuit of publication, and she has 52 unfinished novels to prove it. That was until this past year, when this dream, once deferred, became her sole purpose and passion. Currently, she is seeking a degree in English.

I am inspired to tell stories of heartfelt connection. Tales of reconciliation, redemption, and forgiveness. My writing focuses upon the everyday struggles we all face and those who help us through to the other side. In a time of such cynicism and division, my books offer readers an opportunity for feel-good escape.

With a touch of humor, sincerity, and a little romance too, my characters travel a journey of self-discovery and hope.

I write women's literary fiction, including topics of the Christian faith. Also, I am in the process of producing a series of children's picture books based upon my final project in my Children's Literature class two years ago.

Angelina Singer is a YA author with a YA romantic comedy *Just Like a Pill*, as well as books 1-3 of a YA dystopian science fiction trilogy *The Upperworld Series*, available for purchase on Amazon now. In addition to her writing career, Singer is a college undergrad studying English, Music, and Creative Writing.

In her spare time she enjoys crocheting (with a portfolio of work available for purchase on Instagram @asinger320), as well as mentoring younger music students at a local music store, where she has been studying guitar for nearly a decade. She views her writing as a way to simultaneously escape from and embrace reality. Follow her on Facebook @AngelinaSingerAuthor and Instagram @angelinasingerauthor for exciting updates, exclusive content, and giveaways.

I have been writing my entire life, but only published my first young adult romantic comedy, *Just Like a Pill*, in 2016. Since then I have written books 1-3 of a completed young adult dystopian sci-fi fantasy trilogy - *The Upperworld Series.* Book 1 (*The Sorting Room),* Book 2 (*The Fall of Zephyr),* and Book 3 (*The Rise of Onyx*) are available now. I absolutely love the idea of themes that feature an unexpected twist or a feeling of nostalgia throughout. I also enjoy reading things that feel emotionally real—that's how I know if a piece is the best it can be—if it hits me in the gut and there's no denying that it meant something both to the writer and the reader. I craft my pieces with that goal in mind.

To put it plainly, life inspires my work. There is nothing more interesting or confounding than the emotional and intellectual experiences of day-to-day relationships and thought processes. I draw from my own personal dreams and desires to formulate my own style of young adult romance, fantasy, and drama, especially as seen in *The Pact*. Bestselling authors like John Green, Suzanne Collins, and Tony DiTerlizzi are some of my favorite influences currently, with the amazing F. Scott Fitzgerald at the top of the list for his amazing use of color imagery and deeply emotional content.

J. Michael Squatrito, Jr. has been writing *The Overlords* fantasy book series for over twenty-five years. Currently, he lives in Tiverton with his wife Lea and their Australian Cattle Dog, Zoe. He speaks at middle and high schools, colleges, local libraries, and writers' groups, where his sincere hope is to inspire everyone he meets to be creative and follow their dreams. He's also the vice president of the Association of Rhode Island Authors (ARIA).

When not working on my *Overlords* series, I'm very active in fitness and sports. I continue to play baseball, where I am a knuckleball pitcher for the Rhode Island Brewers, who won the 2008 and 2014 National Championships in Phoenix, Arizona. I also run four to five miles on a regular basis, do interval weight and cardio training, and take Vinyasa yoga classes twice a week. Did I mention that I'm an engineer, too, working on homeland defense projects?

Edward Taylor has been writing ever since his parents bought him a journal and he decided to try his hand at fiction instead. One of the few people to enjoy the politics of the Star Wars prequel trilogy, he graduated with a bachelor's degree in Political Science and Mass Media Communications in 2013, and currently works in government to keep the student loan collectors at bay. He spends much of his free time streaming television and apologizing to his roommate while he learns the violin. The author of two unpublished fiction manuscripts, he is currently seeking an agent while building additional writing credits. Please follow him on Twitter @Edward_Taylor90.

Macchiato stemmed from a writing challenge that required authors to use the words "fisherman, blueprint, and delusion," in a short piece of fiction or poem. The challenge of combining seemingly random words into a narrative inspired me to have a bit of fun with the story and delve into the characters more than I typically do in pieces of short fiction. "Macchiato" explores the tension that comes when siblings grow apart and go on to live separate lives. Forced back together by the death of their father, the two estranged brothers realize they're not as different as they once thought.

I wouldn't say that I write one set genre. Many of my short stories or smaller writing projects can be described as commercial fiction, intended for a wide audience. However, when deciding to tackle a larger project such as a novel I gravitate toward young adult or science fiction. While I do enjoy weaving hidden meaning into my writing, I tend to shy away from literary fiction. My main focus when working on a project is to entertain the reader, and hope enjoying my narrative will help them walk away with whatever theme or metaphor I was intending to convey.

Debbie Kaiman Tillinghast is the author of *The Ferry Home*, a memoir about her childhood on Prudence Island, a tiny island off the coast of Rhode Island. Debbie began writing as she embarked on a quest to reconnect with her island roots, starting with a cookbook for her family. A retired teacher and Nutrition Educator, she now enjoys volunteering as well as writing, gardening, biking, and spending time with her children and grandchildren.

After my first book, *The Ferry Home*, was published in 2015, I continued to write essays and poetry about my life, my family, and nature. I have also been published in *Country* magazine, and two anthologies published by the Association of Rhode Island Authors, *Shoreline* and *Under the Thirteenth Star.*

The Ferry Home is a memoir and whether I'm writing a poem or an essay, my stories focus on the moments in my life that touch me. On Prudence Island, daily existence was guided by the changing seasons and the tides. Perhaps because of my island childhood, my senses are tuned to the world around me, and I still feel bound to island life.

Cheryl A. Voisinet resides in Wakefield, where she began her love for writing in 2012, joining the Neighborhood Guild Creative Writers' Group. She studied at the University of Rhode Island, receiving a B.A. in Early Childhood Education.

Cheryl enjoys multiple genres, mainly short works of non-fiction, with poetry being the focus. Her works have been included in four Guild Anthologies. She has read and had poems on display at art galleries in Tiverton, Westerly, and Wickford.

This past season she was a collaborator with the creator of Poets Speaking Up at Contemporary Theatre, which included a various amount of performances of poetry, dance, and music. She enjoys helping other writers, collaborating in small groups. She appears frequently at poetry readings and is a member of ARIA.

Barbara Ann Whitman has decades of professional experience as an advocate for children and families. She has also been a Sunday School teacher, a youth group leader, a parenting instructor, a Big Sister and a Girl Scout leader.

Barb has been writing since first grade, when she composed a poem about her family's Boston Terrier. Her current writing is inspired by the young people with whom she works. Her young adult novel, *Have Mercy*, was published in May 2018 and tells the story of a young woman trying to make it on her own after growing up in foster care. Her short story "A Changing Sea" was included in the anthology *Shoreline* and her poem, "Galilee," was featured in *Under the Thirteenth Star*.

"A Crown of Diamonds" was written with the hope of empowering young girls. It is her first children's story.

Deb Zannelli was raised in Cumberland, Rhode Island. She married and moved to Connecticut, where she lived for eighteen years. Returning to Rhode Island when her husband's job moved here, she was coming home.

A lonely child, I found myself interested in what made me who I am. I'm inspired by a desire to understand the world and the duality of human nature. I write in the horror genre because it is a safe place to face our fears and the pain in our lives. Here we can examine painful relationships, the cruelty visited on one another more easily. The vampire does not exist. The monster that tortures our souls may live next door or sleep in the other room. Exploring human nature is more easily done outside of our natures, where a hero can display virtues we all wish to claim, and the villains are more obvious in their deeds.

I have written two books: *The Dark Night of the Soul* and *A Darkness Descending*.

www.ingramcontent.com/pod-product-compliance
Lightning Source LLC
Chambersburg PA
CBHW071205250626
47159CB00001B/206
9781946300805